Studies in Biography

Studies in Biography

Edited by
Daniel Aaron

Harvard University Press
Cambridge, Massachusetts
London, England
1978

Library of Congress Cataloging in Publication Data

Main entry under title:

Studies in biography.

   (Harvard English studies; 8)
    1. Biography (as a literary form)—Addresses,
essays, lectures. I. Aaron, Daniel, 1912–
II. Series.
CT21.S85   809   77–18033
ISBN 0–674–84651–6
ISBN 0–674–84652–4 pbk.

Preface

At the close of his life of Thomas Carlyle, James Anthony Froude observed that before very long he would be going to a place where the biographer "will have to answer for the manner in which he has discharged his trust."

Biographers or writers who adopt the biographical mode are not given to such reflections these days, although a fear of heavenly judgment in the offing might make some of them more just and scrupulous. Froude was particularly sensitive on the matter of "trust," for his treatment of the Carlyles' domestic affairs had violated Victorian propriety, and his critics denounced him as an ingrate, betrayer, mutilator, assassin. His reputation survived the assault, but the issues explicitly and implicitly raised in the attacks on Froude the biographer and by Froude himself in his own defense are still with us.

Great biographies like Froude's *Thomas Carlyle* are rare, because such happy conjunctions of writer and subject are rare; great figures more often than not are the victims of their biographers' ineptitudes and biases. Froude undertook the life of Carlyle as a sacred obligation. From 1864 until Carlyle's death in 1881, he saw him two or three times a week, acquiring over the years an intimate knowledge of his thought and character. When he came to write his book, he did not have to "get up" his subject. Nor did he undertake the biography to make money or to win a reputation or to exploit the idiosyncrasies of a splenetic genius. Froude revered his master and, if anything, tended to palliate some of his more outrageous notions; yet, true disciple that he was, he felt it would betray Carlyle's fierce veracity if he were to blot out the disharmonies of his private life. Carlyle had reviled himself, at times but not always unjustifiably: he was insensitive to his wife's moods and frustrations; he could be selfish, thoughtless, unfair, overbearing — a burden to his friends. So in celebrating his mentor, Froude refused to substitute discretion for what he took to be the truth. The responsibilities of the biographer were no less stringent to him than those of the historian. A faithful rendition of facts, the art of bringing "dead things and dead people actually back to life," became his primary consideration: "The facts must be delineated first with the clearness and fulness which we demand in an epic poem or a tragedy. We must have the real thing before we can have a science of a thing."

With a superabundance of written material available to him in the form of letters and journals, and with the words of the celebrated talker echoing in his memory, he enjoyed near ideal advantages. Not only was he Carlyle's authorized biographer; he was also writing a history of his own times as well as a record of his discipleship. This was not a project for an unassured man, and Froude was not overawed by its extensiveness. In four artfully paced volumes, he presented Carlyle in all his brilliance and amplitude, the biographer ever in control of his corruscating subject. The dyspeptic and hypochondriacal sage who behaved at moments like a Jonsonian humor character or like one of Dickens' eccentrics is the same flawed and gifted person many of whose opinions (even some of the less endearing ones) his biographer shared. That he was able to show his very human hero as a man of more than venial faults and yet at the same time to display solicitude and deep affection for him, to reveal as much of the truth about him as possible without wounding the living or discrediting the dead, is no small accomplishment.

Contemporary biography is no longer hedged by the constraints that inhibited Froude and his contemporaries. Save for the threat of libel or the denial of access to private papers, the biographer today is virtually unrestricted. Yet if he can be audacious and even outrageous where Froude had to be circumspect, the old ethical questions (as one of the contributors to this collection of essays makes clear) continue to assert themselves. What is more, the modern biographer's very freedom and the variety of his options create new methodological problems as well as new expectations on the part of his readers.

For all of his bold disclosures, Froude's *Carlyle* did not depart very far from the conventional guidelines of his day. It is the story of a man's life, not a theory about that life, and told without resort to artifice or psychological probing. Read today, it is hard to understand why Froude's account of the Carlyle ménage (conveyed in large measure through quotations from the members' correspondence) should have provoked such a hullabaloo. His *Carlyle* is at once more personal and dispassionate than most multivolumed lives and letters of the Victorian age, but the work as a whole is acceptably reverential and monumental. The Froude who comes through to the modern reader is less the lethal truth-teller than the faithful if sometimes judgmental defender whose attitude toward Carlyle is close to the spirit of Carlyle's apostrophe to his wife on the death of her mother: "Alas! how all the faults and little infirmities of the departed seem now what they really were, mere *virtues imprisoned,* obstructed in the strange, sensitive, tremulous element they were sent to live in!"

Such sentiments are not conspicuous in contemporary biography with its ambitious aims, its exacting professional standards, and its emphasis on accuracy and objectivity. Public opinion no longer makes a pretense of protecting the dead from "malice, obtrusive sentiment, or vain curiosity," to use the words of one of Thackeray's memorialists; nor does it declare the "author's heart . . . a sanctuary into which, except so far as he voluntarily reveals it, the public has no right to enter." The biographer is expected to show all and tell all and to have a more complex conception of the self than Froude had, or at least to be more privy to the protagonist's buried self. He is more likely to dig deeper into such matters as parental influences, stages of growth, historical conditioning — to fix on certain illuminating occasions and to try to penetrate the veil of unconscious or calculated deceptions most people hang between themselves and the world. Froude's observation that all biography is at best "mere delusion and hallucination," that every person is a mystery even to those closest to him, has a measure of validity. But (and this would appear to be the consensus of the essays to follow) biography can still lighten up the subject's interior as well as his public history and at least produce an illusion of Froude's "real thing."

The essays that follow, apart from their other claims to interest, point to some of the new directions biography and biographical criticism have taken since Froude's time. Four of them (I borrow the terminology of their authors) deal with "clio," "ethno," "transcendental," and "symbolic" biography. Several are concerned with biography as a literary art and reappraise two of its celebrated yet still imperfectly comprehended practictioners. Others show what can be learned from even uneventful lives, or by concentrating on a single event or pervasive idea in a person's career, or on the biographical implications of particular pieces of writing. And one, the introductory essay, reverts to the old question of biographical aims and expectations and shows why all good biography, irrespective of subject or intention, is of necessity "literary." (We are back again to Froude, who worked, as he said of Carlyle, in "the fetters of fact" while composing his epic history of a man, yet who thought like a novelist bent upon "the knotting up of incoherences into coherence." When Froude remarked of Jane Carylye, "She had a terrible habit of speaking out the exact truth, cut as clear as with a graving tool, on occasions too, when without harm it might have been left unspoken," he might have been quoting from George Eliot.)

Despite their diversity, the essays in this volume suggest, if only inadvertently, some possible reasons why so many writers and scholars are taking a biographical approach to human experience. At a time when the behavioral sciences are in the ascendant, when the collective and the aggregate gain at the expense of the atypical and idiosyncratic, when criticism and the world of serious fiction seem increasingly remote, perhaps biography fulfills the need once supplied by fiction, poetry, criticism, and history. It is less in danger than these genres, each of which it subsumes, of becoming dehumanized by a surfeit of theory and methodology. Not only is it a useful source of knowledge about individual lives; it also widens the unquantifiable dimensions of human nature and remains one of the most inexhaustible, inclusive, and accessible of literary forms.

D. A.

Contents

Studies in Biography

JUSTIN KAPLAN

The "Real Life"

It is almost a commonplace now to speak of an ongoing "golden age of biography" that had its beginnings in the mid-eighteenth century. Since then the strategies, understandings, and supporting disciplines of biography have become more complex. Contemporary writers and critics occasionally acknowledge its speculative and crypto-fictive nature along with the existence of an old question: whether biography is a branch of history or a branch of literature, a work of record or an imaginative exercise. Some believe, as I do, that the biographer is essentially a storyteller and dramatist — Henri Troyat's superb *Tolstoy* is much to the point here — and that a strong case should be made for enlarging the term "literary biography" to include books that have literary qualities and not necessarily literary subjects.

But the stated aims of biography have remained remarkably consistent during two centuries and also consistently touched with a degree of presumption. "The business of a biographer," Samuel Johnson said, "is . . . to lead the thoughts into domestic privacies and display the minute details of daily life." Boswell's purpose was to enable mankind to see the subject "live, and to 'live o'er each scene' with him, as he actually advanced through the several stages of his life." Another familiar declaration, this one by Henry James, is more congenial to us in its terminology but not different in its fundamental emphasis on the flow of experience. "To live over people's lives is nothing unless we live over their perceptions, live over the growth, the change, the varying intensity of the same — since it was *by* these things they themselves lived."

We contine to expect biography to render not only the public and private events of a life but its intimate existential and perceptual textures, all adding up to the whole sense of a person. Freud and Jung on the one hand, Proust and Joyce on the other are among those who have provided models for the intricate and nuanced notation of interior states of being. And in the faith of a long "golden age" we tend to believe implicitly that biography *can* deliver the essential person and that there is a core personality, the "real Me," which we will find if only we dig deep and long enough. This belief, for the most part unexamined, is echoed in the well-meaning cant found in reviews — "the living and breathing presence," "larger than life," "the definitive account," and so on, evidences, incidentally, that the critical vocabulary of the golden age is still remarkably poverty-stricken.

This extravagant faith in what biography can do has not been universal, of course, and there are distinct currents of reaction and skepticism about just how much biography can deliver even under the loose heading of "history," the documented existence of a real person. Reaction and skepticism have the effect of keeping biographers honest by making them write scared, conscious of what they may not be able to do and of what they do with the greatest difficulty. It appears that at best biography is only a plausible, inevitably idiosyncratic surmise and reconstruction, severely limited by historical materials that are loaded with duplicities and evasions. Even the great instrument of depth psychology, which once promised so much, turns out to be less essential than tact, empathy, empirical experience, and narrative flair.

We say of a successful biography that it is dramatically and psychologically coherent — it makes sense, it is believable, it is a good story. The writer starts off with a number of givens — birth and death, education, ambition, conflict, milieu, work, relationship, accident. He shapes them into a book that has the autonomous vitality of any work of the imagination and at the same time is "true to life" and true to history. In many respects biography is a feat of illusionism, sleight-of-hand, levitation; basic decisions and interpretations that appear to be the results of cautious deliberation are often made instantaneously in, and as part of, the act of writing; and for at least one moment each day the writer may feel like Mark Twain's titled charlatans putting on a performance of "The Royal Nonesuch." At other moments, proud as Ahab, his fixed purpose "laid with iron rails," the biographer may "strike through the mask" only to find, without nudging from Erving Goffman, that the pasteboard mask was what it was all about in the first place and that the work and the career — the public manifestation — may be more significant than the hidden self or selves. Isn't that, after all, one way we distinguish major lives from lesser lives, especially among writers? There may even be a principle in operation which determines that the size of a biography should be in inverse proportion to the size of the subject, as exemplified by Michael Holroyd's *Lytton Strachey* and Sybille Bedford's *Aldous Huxley*. (A notable exception is Geoffrey Scott's spare, elegant, and luminous *The Portrait of Zélide*.)

For all his dedication to interior states of being, Proust claimed that in the long run it was impossible, because of the nature of love, for one person to give an objective or even moderately reliable account of another, much less a "true" one. The nineteenth century was a time of burning archives, for the rise of intimate biographical inquiry and an avid reading public had added a new terror to death. This was the terror not only of having secrets unlocked and privacies violated but also of being misrepresented and misunderstood in a dull, bad book, in "those two fat volumes with which it is our custom to commemorate the dead," Strachey wrote. "Who does not know them with their ill-digested masses of material, their slipshod style, their tone of tedious panegyric, their lamentable lack of selection, of detachment, of design?" Recognizing the risks and adversary relationship inherent even in the best-disposed biographies, some writers turned to autobiography in self-defense. "The volume is a mere shield of protection in the grave," Henry

Adams said when he presented a privately printed copy of his
Education to Henry James. "I advise you to take your own life
in the same way, in order to prevent biographers from taking
it in theirs." Biographers had become murderers, and their subjects, fugitives.

Adams was a burner of papers; so was Henry James. Mark
Twain claimed to be one but in fact kept a personal archive,
parts of it still surfacing, that was nothing less than a monument to papyrophilia, an unreasonable attachment to anything
made of paper. Together with a series of spellbinding but frequently unreliable oral reminiscences that had the effect of a
smoke screen or the ink cloud of a squid, he made this archival
material available to his appointed biographer, Albert Bigelow
Paine, but he imposed severe restrictions. Mark Twain was
skeptical about what biography could accomplish and he resented Paine's venture, even though he himself had encouraged it.

The little prefatory note Mark Twain wrote for his autobiography rationalizes this skepticism and resentment and also
displays a somewhat uncharacteristic, nearly Proustian, concern
with psychological continua:

> What a wee little part of a person's life are his acts and his words!
> His real life is led in his head, and is known to none but himself.
> All day long, and ever day, the mill of his brain is grinding, and
> his *thoughts,* not those other things, are his history. His acts and
> his words are merely the visible, thin crust of his world, with its
> scattered snow summits and its vacant wastes of water — and
> they are so trifling a part of his bulk! a mere skin enveloping it.
> The mass of him is hidden — it and its volcanic fires that toss and
> boil, and never rest, night nor day. These are his life, and they
> are not written, and cannot be written. Every day would make
> a whole book of eighty thousand words — three hundred and
> sixty-five books a year. Biographies are but the clothes and
> buttons of the man — the biography of the man himself cannot
> be written.

Mark Twain was thinking about precisely the kind of life behind life that by and large remains inaccessible to the biographer
except through speculation, and he is derisive on the subject

of speculative approaches even to evident matters like "the clothes and buttons of the man." He describes Shakespeare biography, for example, as "an Eiffel tower of artificialities rising sky-high from a very flat and very thin foundation of inconsequential facts," a fifty-seven foot high brontosaur that looks convincing enough in the natural history museum but is made of six hundred barrels of plaster of paris and maybe only "nine old bones."

Wilfred Sheed once divided American writers into two classes, the hiders and the strippers, and in the popular understanding of their work and personality Mark Twain seems to belong with the hiders and Walt Whitman with the strippers. Like his friend and mighty contemporary Thomas Eakins, Whitman adored the naked truth in all its forms. But if Whitman, one of the fathers of confessional poetry, is indeed a stripper, he manages to make nakedness an ultimate disguise, and so he becomes an extraordinarily problematic subject for biography. This passage from "Song of Myself" may be the Whitman counterpart of Mark Twain's prefatory note:

Trippers and askers surround me,
People I meet, the effect upon me of my early life or the ward
    and city I live in, or the nation,
The latest dates, discoveries, inventions, societies, authors old
    and new,
My dinner, dress, associates, looks, compliments, dues,
The real or fancied indifference of some man or woman I love,
The sickness of one of my folks or of myself, or ill-doing or loss
    or lack of money, or depressions or exaltations,
Battles, the horrors of fratricidal war, the fever of doubtful news,
    the fitful events;
These come to me days and nights and go from me again,
But they are not the Me myself.

He goes on to describe the "Me myself" standing "apart from the pulling and hauling," "both in and out of the game, and watching and wondering at it." What makes this passage especially suggestive is the probability that this "Me myself" is not the biographical Walt Whitman at all but a dramatic persona created for poetic purposes and also for the liberation of the

biographical Whitman from some covert stage of development.
He was both a stripper and a hider. Even when he says,

> Camerado! This is no book;
> Who touches this, touches a man,

he may mean that his book was all that he chose to show of
himself.

The house on Mickle Street in Camden that Whitman occupied as an old man reminded at least one visitor, because of
its disorder, of a field after a cornhusking, piled with shucks and
stalks. From boxes and bundles in the store room, from a big
iron-banded double-hasped trunk standing against the bedroom
wall, Whitman released drifts and billows of paper, almost every
imaginable variety of record — manuscripts, yellowed scraps of
paper, notebooks and diaries, scrapbooks, letters received and
drafts of letters sent, printers' proofs, photographs, clippings.
This paper tide, which he stirred with the crook of his invalid's
cane, covered the floor, churned around his feet, seeped into the
corners of the room and under the furniture and was tracked
out into the hallway.

Horace Traubel, a Camden neighbor who became, as he
liked to think, Whitman's Boswell, found on the floor, among
other things, the celebrated letter Emerson wrote in 1855 greeting the author of *Leaves of Grass* "at the beginning of a great
career" and speculating that there must have been "a long foreground somewhere, for such a start." The floor also yielded up
manuscript fragments and beginnings hinting that in this long
foreground a great transformation had taken place along with
the birth of an overriding purpose, to write his country's poems,
to become, as Whitman said, "a master after my own kind."

Yet there were evidences that a less robust spirit had also
been at work in the foreground, a spirit covert, hesitant,
ashamed, and perturbed. "There is something in my nature *fur-
tive,* like an old hen," Whitman said, adding that as a description of myself he was willing to accept the word "artful." He
said that there were "truths which it is necessary to envelop
or wrap up," that there was an "inexplicable element of every
highest poetic nature which causes it to cover up and involve its

real purpose and meaning in folded removes and far recesses," to create personal myths and suppress personal history. He was hardly even conscious of having consistently reshaped his past to make it conform to an image of himself — ample, serene, and masterful — which he arrived at long after the events concerned. Whitman biography, like practically all biography, has to begin with legend.

"Some day when you are ready and I am ready," he said to Traubel, "I will tell you about one period in my life of which my friends know nothing: not now — not tomorrow — but some day before long. I want to tell you the whole story with figures and all the data so that you will make no mistake about it." A week later he said, "You'll hear that in due time—not tonight. That cat has too long a tail to start to unravel at the end of an evening." He hated to be questioned, and when pressed, no longer volunteering, he closed down into obstinate silence, just as he locked his bedroom door each night. Traubel, as hard as he tried, never managed to get him to tell the "whole story" or even any fragment of it and began to suspect that perhaps there was no story to tell. "There is a secret," Whitman insisted quietly. "You will sometime see that there is a secret." The subject came up again. "I want you to keep on asking till I answer," he said, "only not tonight — not tonight." Biographers have kept on asking.

Despite his unique role as confidant and daily companion, Traubel knew there were papers he could never be permitted to see as well as stories he would never be permitted to hear. From time to time, as he had been doing since he had his first paralytic stroke and thought he was about to die, Whitman systematically sorted out and destroyed parts of his archive. He explained to Traubel that there were certain things "too sacred — too surely and only mine — to be perpetuated." There were documents that he did not destroy but instead carefully altered, disguising identities or transposing genders. By the time he died there was scarcely a period in his life that had not been "revised" in one way or another; there were even years that had practically ceased to exist so far as intimate documentary evidence was concerned.

Whitman's overflowing records, so accessible and careless,

were ultimately guarded and recalcitrant, like their owner. They
are the materials of biography and also the materials of a fable
of biography. "This is not so much of a mess as it looks," Whitman said, pointing to the papers on his floor and table. "You
notice that I find most of the things I look for, and without
much trouble. The disorder is more suspected than real."

EDWARD MENDELSON

Authorized Biography and Its Discontents

Public discussion of the problems of writing an authorized or "official" literary biography occurs only when a biographer decides not to write one. A few years ago there was a brief to-do in the *Times Literary Supplement* following Denis Donoghue's request to be released from his contract to write the authorized biography of W. B. Yeats on the ground that Michael Yeats, the poet's son and literary executor, had failed to give him exclusive rights to read and publish Yeats' manuscripts. Much heat was generated in the resulting debate, but light was shed only on the peripheral question of whether the authorized or "official" biographer should have the sole right of access and publication, and whether he should continue his work if, in Donoghue's words, "too many plums had been given away" before he began.

As everyone who was drawn into the argument agreed, these are matters that should have been resolved at the start, when the contracts were drawn up. Other, and far more troubling, problems are involved in authorized biography, and some of these arose when I began work on a biography of W. H. Auden about a year ago. Like Donoghue, I asked to be released from my contract with the publishers; and this essay, like Donoghue's (*TLS,* February 16, 1973), is concerned with the reasons be-

hind the decision not to proceed with the work. In both the long
run and the short, of course, it does not especially matter what
the reasoning was that led one person not to write a book, but
the issues that came to light during the brief history of Auden's
unwritten biography affect almost all recent literary biographies.

Denis Donoghue's problems arose from a disagreement between the authorized biographer and the man who authorized
him. No such dispute stood in the way of the Auden biography,
as the roles of literary executor and authorized biographer were
combined in one person. The difficulties I faced were not the
legal problems of contracts or conditions. Instead, I found I had
to consider the ethical problems raised by the effect that publication would have on others, and therefore found myself confronted by the problem of finding a form for literary biography
that might resolve the ethical issues. Before even facing these
ethical and literary questions, however, I first had to face the
question of whether to write a biography of Auden at all.
Auden was one of three major English writers of this century
who insisted that they did not want their biographies written.
George Orwell expressed this wish in the final sentence of his
will. T. S. Eliot, in a memorandum accompanying his will,
wrote, "I do not wish my executors to facilitate or countenance
the writing of a biography of me." And Auden, in frequent
essays and interviews, reiterated his disapproval of literary biography under any circumstances — or *some* circumstances.
Auden's will says nothing about biography, but it does ask his
executors to publish his wish that his letters be destroyed by
their recipients; this, he explained in conversation, was to "make
a biography impossible."

Yet Auden's disapproval of literary biography proved to be
far less simple and unqualified than it looked, especially when
one paid attention to his published statements on the matter.
Consider, for example, this passage from a review of a life of
Trollope, published the year before Auden's death:

> As a rule, I am opposed to biographies of writers, but in Trollope's
> case, for a number of reasons, I approve. To begin with, Trol-
> lope wrote an autobiography, published posthumously, which,
> though probably accurate so far as it goes, leaves out a great deal.

... Then, he was not simply a novelist. As an employee of the Post Office, he was also a man of action, and a most successful one. Then, he was an addicted traveler, forever "banging about" the world. More important, he happened to be what one would never suspect from his writings — a very eccentric character who might well, though he would have hated to admit it, have come straight out of a novel by Dickens.

This sentiment is echoed in quite a few of Auden's late reviews of literary or artistic biographies. On Wagner: "On principle, I object to biographies of artists, since I do not believe that knowledge of their private lives sheds any significant light on their works . . . However, the story of Wagner's life is absolutely fascinating, and it would be so if he had never written a note." On Scott (after calling a new biography "magnificent"): "Few writers have led lives interesting enough to deserve a biography, but Scott is one of the exceptions." On Pope: "It is not often that knowledge of an artist's life sheds any significant light upon his work, but in the case of Pope I think it does." There are similar exceptions to an otherwise general rule, similar exceptions to an ethical rule for aesthetic reasons, at the start of all his reviews of collections of letters. Auden's "rule" was evidently flexible enough to be bent backwards.

Besides, the argument about Trollope is very odd. Auden's claim that a biography is justified because Trollope left out a great deal from his autobiography flies in the face of Auden's usual defense of privacy. If this argument applies to Trollope, then what is one to conclude from the comparably selective but extensive autobiographical fragments that Auden inserted in his own poems and essays (they seem to cover all the crises and formative incidents of his life), whose importance he emphasized by setting the most autobiographical of all, "How It Seemed to Us," at the end of his final collection of prose? No postmaster, I hope, will be offended if one raises an eyebrow at Auden's description of Trollope as "a man of action" because he worked at the post office. One sees Auden's point — Trollope did more than sit in his study and write novels — but this, like his reference to Trollope's travels, applies equally to Auden's own experience in the Spanish and Chinese wars and to his military research in postwar Germany, as well as to his theatrical collaborations throughout his career. And what Auden says of the interest attaching to Trollope's eccentricity of character applies surely to the force and complexity of his own.

In short, Auden's justification for a biography of Trollope, against his own "rule," comes very close to justifying a biography of Auden. And in the year he died, Auden published a foreword to E. M. Forster's biography of Goldsworthy Lowes Dickinson, in which he set out some general guides to biographical method. Among them is this comment on the use of letters: "Normally, the chief source material for a biographer is his subject's letters. Forster quotes from a number of Goldie's, and I find them most interesting, but he warns us that they are of small value compared with his conversation." When one reads this in light of the fact that Auden constantly gave permission for individual letters of his own to be printed during his lifetime, the spirit of his objections to literary biography becomes clear. Literary biography, Auden suggests, must be of a certain kind, and a kind more frequently found among biographies of nineteenth-century writers than of more recent ones: a biography not intensely psychological, not directed towards explaining away a writer's work by his neuroses; not, probably, overmuch concerned with what he did in bed. What a biography should do, for Auden to approve of it, is to attend to its subject's conscious choices and free acts — those acts that distinguished him from every other person, as opposed to those physical and psychological necessities that, in all essentials, he shared with everyone else. One recalls in this context Auden's short poem on human limitation, published in 1941, which ends: "Never will his prick belong / To his world of right and wrong, / Nor its values comprehend / Who is foe and who is friend."

I recognized that, acting as Auden's literary executor, I would someday authorize the writing of his biography. Recently both Eliot's and Orwell's heirs had decided to name authorized biographers, and Sonia Orwell has already named Bernard Crick to the task. In each case unauthorized biographies had already appeared, variously flawed or unbalanced, whose errors and omissions both heirs felt obliged to put right. So when Auden's

British publisher, Faber and Faber, proposed that Stephen Spender and I collaborate on a biography of Auden, I agreed. I knew that I must someday authorize such a book, and there seemed no reason to delay, now that the opportunity to write it had arrived. I had in mind also that many sources now available in the memory of the living would not remain accessible for long. Each year some important information would be lost, some letters or papers scattered.

But almost immediately after Spender and I began working, we both found it impossible to continue. In fact we found it almost impossible even to begin. We arrived independently at our decision not to write the book, but our reasons were similar.

One problem we faced — as any biographer must, authorized or not — was our attitude towards our subject. The more we learned of Auden's private life, the more evident it became that there were no shameful secrets hidden there. On the contrary: his private generosity and affection, his attention to the needs and cares of others, were matters he had no wish to display in public, and their unobtrusiveness only added to their excellence. There would be little in a comprehensive biography that could have embarrassed Auden had it been published in the last years of his life. We found an unquestionable amorality in Auden's early youth, but no instance of malice or of deliberate harm done to others; and in Auden's adulthood we found abundant evidence of active and persistent goodness.

We were therefore spared a problem which, because it faces many authorized biographers, deserves brief consideration here. In the case of the unwritten Auden biography, there was no likelihood of a dispute betwen the authorizing executor and the authorized biographer. Normally this is not so, and Donoghue and Michael Yeats provide a painful example of what can happen. So the first practical problem a biographer confronts is that of getting and keeping his authorization in the first place — and, with his authorization, access to the letters and papers he will need if he hopes to be comprehensive. (Some biographers have tried to work without authorization, but the effort has generally failed.) There are other advantages to authorization besides access to private papers. Friends, members of the subject's family, government officials, anyone who might otherwise keep silent, will often give help to a biographer who has the imprimatur of his subject's estate.

Authorization is an advantage that any biographer will want to retain. But heirs and executors are often sensitive and protective and may not wish to aid the publication of anything that, in their opinion, will damage the reputation or the dignity of the dead author. However determined a biographer may be to tell the truth as he sees it, he must surely hesitate, at least for a moment, before probing deeply into matters that will give offense to those who authorized him. Naturally he will have insisted on guarantees of independence before he begins, but even with such guarantees, he may not wish to face the anger of an offended son or daughter, widow or widower. Emotional considerations are here often stronger than legal ones. On one recent occasion, a biographer published a section of his work that gave great (and unexpected) offense to one of his late subject's wives, although not to the widow who had legal authority over the biography as a whole. That anger now appears to have led the biographer to give up his work almost at the point of completing it.

Perhaps more fortunately placed is the biographer whose subject, while still among the living, chose him for the work; he need not fear the consequences of saying unwelcome truths later. (Thus Lawrance Thompson went ahead and portrayed Robert Frost as a monster.) Yet in practice it is common for an authorized biographer to try to respect the dignity of a subject who no longer has much use for it in the grave. Joseph Blotner's massively documented biography of William Faulkner omits all but the most cursory mention of Faulkner's mistress Meta Carpenter. This omission was made not out of respect for Miss Carpenter's sensitivities — she published a memoir complete with physiological details — but out of respect for Faulkner's. Such a gesture seems not only futile, as Miss Carpenter was pleased to publish the story, but self-defeating, as it casts doubt on the rest of Blotner's enormous book. One wonders in reading it whether this or that mass of detail serves as a screen for some other and more important episode that Blotner has deliberately, if chivalrously, passed over in silence.

Blotner was at least motivated by reticence and by respect for a man's privacy. These are admirable motives, but other instances of biographical omission and distortion have a completely different sort of origin. One recent literary biography — an authorized one — implies that its subject had a series of affairs during a period of his life when he was generally too drunk or sick to do much more than shake hands. In one episode the biography places its subject alone with a woman — who is named, and still very much alive — on a long country drive late at night, when the biographer seems to have known perfectly well that a third person had been present in the car throughout. Possibly the biographer felt that the omission made a more interesting story; possibly he wanted to please those who authorized him, by presenting his subject as more capable, more manly than he was. The effect in either case was to embarrass someone still alive by printing a story that implicates her in a sexual relationship that never in fact occurred.

Here the ethics of the case are simple. The basic facts of the matter are not in dispute, and the only person who might be embarrassed by their full publication (as opposed to the actual partial publication) would be the subject of the biography, and he is dead. The biographer not only violated his implicit contract with his readers by implying events that never took place, but he also gave pain to someone who had done neither him nor his subject any harm. This is straightforward enough. But would the issue be any different if the subject had actually had a sexual relation with a person still alive who now wishes to avoid publicity? This is the opposite of the case of Meta Carpenter; in this not-so-hypothetical instance the surviving partner wants nothing to be told. The biographer had a number of choices, none of them without its difficulties. He can omit the whole story, in the certainty that the facts will be known sooner or later and will tend to discredit his work; or he can change the name and circumstances, telling his readers he is doing just that, in order to preserve the outline of his story while blurring or omitting certain details (this would be roughly comparable to the convention of leaving the restored sections of paintings slightly discolored or coarse-textured, to make plain the distinction between the restoration and the original); or he can tell the whole story, insisting that scholarship is more important than one person's feelings.

The problem raised here, and the three basic possibilities for resolving it, are not, of course, unique to authorized biography, but in practice it is generally the authorized biographer who, thanks to his special access to private diaries and letters, must confront it. There is a history of attempted solutions to the problem dating back at least as far as the literary biographies of the nineteenth century. Mrs. Gaskell omitted Charlotte Brontë's passion for M. Heger; John Forster said nothing of Dickens' affair with Ellen Ternan. Total omissions like these are not simply the consequences of prudery — Mrs. Gaskell, who steps silently over Charlotte Brontë's infatuation with her school-master, hesitates for little more than a deep breath before diving into the deeper peripheral waters of Branwell Brontë's affair with Mrs. Robinson — but of an attempt to save the dignity of their subjects. This attempt forced nineteenth-century biogra-phers into some painful contradictions. (I do not of course mean to imply that twentieth-century biographers have not painted themselves into similar corners.) Two conflicting conventions are involved here. The first is the convention by which the sub-ject of a biography is offered as exemplary and admirable, in-capable of indignity. This convention has a long ancestry. Bos-well accepts it almost entirely, but Boswell's notions of what is biographically significant and what is not are entirely consistent with it and never lead him into the contradiction faced by later biographers. Later writers, like Mrs. Gaskell or Forster, try to combine the convention of dignity with another and entirely in-compatible convention — the romantic convention, or set of conventions, by which individual personality is described and notated. This romantic convention is concerned not with dignity but with origins and crises, specifically with those literally shame-ful private secrets of the sort confessed by Rousseau: those unforgettable moments of psychological crisis which, so the romantics and their successors up to the present believe, give personality its individual shape and force.

The romantic and modern biographer takes as his task "to decipher" (in Carlyle's words) "the whole heart of his [sub-ject's] mystery," to decode his secret internal darkness. Thus

Forster revealed the (to Dickens) shameful secret of the black-ing factory — a secret Dickens himself could never bear to reveal in his lifetime — while keeping silent about Ellen Ternan. But the convention Forster observed by reporting the blacking factory he violated in suppressing Ellen Ternan. And the convention he observed by keeping Ellen Ternan in silence he violated by telling of the blacking factory. Because of this sort of contradic-tion, one senses a gap in the texture of biographies like those by Forster and Mrs. Gaskell, a gap one never senses in the much less private world of Boswell's Johnson. And that gap, in one form or another, persists even into the most revealing of modern biographies, which generally work against their own premises at some point in their telling.

If omission is impossible, the choice of publishing the facts without regard for the feelings of the living is intolerable. The ethics of the matter are quite simple. If the person in ques-tion values his or her privacy, then his or her wishes must be respected. The biographer is obliged to practice a thought-experiment comparable to that proposed by John Rawls in *A Theory of Justice:* he should imagine how he would feel if he woke tomorrow morning to find himself the person about whom he had written. He will almost certainly not be happy with the thought that his youthful sex-life is now the public topic of dis-cussion among his friends or his children or his students; he may not care to have old emotional wounds reopened, espe-cially in public; he may not want to have a latent or quiescent source of tension in his marriage erupt into an immediate and present danger; he may, like everyone, simply not want to re-member an incident that would seem harmless enough to others but which he has special reasons for keeping below the surface of memory.

But, the biographer might argue to himself, the demands of scholarship must be fulfilled: knowledge must not be kept under restraint. If a biographer believes this, he must (provided he is not the sort of moral idiot who believes all knowledge to be necessarily a good) be able to say what purpose his scholarship serves. It is no secret that, for all the literary biographies written in the past two centuries, we still lack an adequate theory of the relation of private experience to publicly available works of

art: we still lack the missing link between the continuing life
and the completed work. All psychological theories of artistic
creation founder on the difficulty that they are based on neuroses
and artists. (Surely every man would like to have what Freud
said artists worked for: fame, money, and the love of women.)
said artists worked for: fame, money, and the love of women).
So a speculative psychoanalysis of an artist, while it may account for certain features of his art, can never explain how his
works found their medium (why paint canvases rather than
houses?) or form or genre or tone; it can never say why he
became an artist and not a surgeon, or why he chose to write
poems and not music. And even if the exposure of a writer's
private life could ever tell us these things, we should still need
a moral calculus that confirmed that the understanding of a
poem or novel or play was more important to the world than
the personal unhappiness of even one man or woman. Such a
calculus, fortunately enough, is unlikely ever to exist.

The same objections apply even when the story is told with
all the names changed and the circumstances altered, for the
pain and embarrassment that may result from publication are
not limited to public aspect of the lives of those involved. Memory is painful even in private. The man or woman whose story is
told in disguise, against his or her wish, in the biography of
someone else, knows perfectly well whose identity has been hidden; and the story will excite difficult or problematic memories,
fears of exposure, the discomfort of seeing oneself in a distorted
mirror — feelings that no literary biographer has the right to
make anyone endure. (Political biography may be a different
issue, but peripheral figures even there would deserve the same
consideration.)

If a biographer has any ethics at all, he must decide to omit
a painful story of the sort to which I have been alluding; but
omission inevitably contradicts the premises by which modern
biography is made. A biographer can try to slide over the problem by writing a deliberately vague paragraph to the effect that
his subject enjoyed a sexual relation with someone unnamed and
unspecified in the year X and that the poem Y or the novel Z
was written in this period, although nothing more can be said at

present. Yet to give so little space to a possibly crucial sequence of events is to throw the whole book out of balance. Faced with such a problem, the biographer may (as did Spender and I) decide not to publish at all while those who might suffer from publication are still alive. Literary scholarship is not so urgent as to render delays of twenty or thirty years intolerable. But the whole problem raises the question whether our present manner of writing literary biography is adequate to its task. In fact, any mode of literary study potentially harmful to the innocent, though unchallenged and unexamined for decades, surely requires reexamination.

I have referred already to the problems faced by biographers who try to maintain incompatible conventions. The psychological conventions of personality-description, with its roots in romantic confession and autobiography, conflict inevitably with the more Augustan convention that hopes to demonstrate the dignity of a biography's subject through the excellence of his work. The matter is complicated by the apparent consistency of both these conventions with the purposes and methods of biography. The romantic convention provides (or at least seems to provide) the means of accounting for the uniqueness of a personality, while the Augustan convention follows logically from the choice of a major artist as the subject of a book. Although the romantic convention seems to be primary — it offers a basic notation for personal experience — for literary biography it is the Augustan convention that provides the initial impulse, as the biography of any artist is an exemplary account of accomplishment. (It is hard to imagine a literary biography that is not in some way offered as exemplary; such a book could be written only by a biographer who regards it as contemptible to write well.) Auden wrote of this conflict as early in his career as 1940:

> Great masters who have shown mankind
> An order it has yet to find,
> What if all pedants say of you
> As personalities be true?
> All the more honor to you then
> If, weaker than some other men,

>You had the courage that survives
>Soiled, shabby, egotistic lives . . .
>   ["New Year Letter"]

As Auden recognized, modern literary biographers have increasingly paid the Augustan convention of honor little more than lip-service while they have served the romantic conventions with enthusiastic *Schadenfreude*. This is the case in biographies as different in quality as, on one hand, Ellmann's Joyce or Bell's Woolf and, on the other, Thompson's Frost or Blotner's Faulkner. Literary biographers have found encouragement in this tendency not only from the general run of modern biographies (and not least from the politically potent psychological profiles put together by Allied intelligence services during the Second World War), but also from the analogy between modern psychological theory and the modern literary theory (by this I mean supposedly "pure" literary theory without explicit psychological terminology) in which most literary biographers gained their education. The tendency of modern biography, like the tendency of modern literary study, has been a progressive narrowing of focus, an ever-increasing concern with the interior organization of its subject, and a lessening of attention to its subject's relations with the world outside. Recent literary biographers perceive their subjects as complex sets of internal psychological relations, which cast up signs of themselves in the form of literary works. (The idea of public occasions or purposes for literature has in this way tended to disappear.) In this narrowing of focus into the inner workings of the self, modern biography has taken a course exactly parallel to that taken by the main currents of literary theory, first in the New Criticism and now in its European philosophical successors, who understand literature primarily as a complex of internal and self-referential relations, concerned almost exclusively with (for the New Critics) irony or (for their successors) self-contradiction and deconstruction. In short, the basic *structure* of modern literary theory is identical to the theory of psychoanalysis, even when literary theory explicitly repudiates psychoanalytic methods, because both theories descend from the set of ideas that may be localized in the term Romanticism.

From both the psychoanalytic and the modern literary theories specific acts of interpretation may be derived. But when theory is transformed into interpretative practice, a crucial difficulty arises: if a person or poem is a structure of internal relations, as these theories hold, cut off in all essentials from the outer world, then how is the interpreter to make his way inside that structure in order to describe it? The observer is necessarily a part of the world that the theory excludes from the model derived from it. By what door does he enter the closed system of psyche or language? Recent literary theory, to its credit, has devoted much energy to this question and now sometimes tries to resolve it by analyzing a reader's active engagement in the production of meaning from a text. But this solution simply replaces one closed system with another: instead of the closed New Critical poem, either a reader–text dyad or an autonomous system of language that generates both the poem and the criticism of it.

Recent theorists of literary biography have evaded their comparable dilemma by choosing to devote most of their attention to a form in which the dilemma appears not to exist at all — *auto*biography, which is of course a special case. A glance at recent MLA and similar bibliographies shows that critical studies of autobiography far outnumber studies of biography written by others. What the numbers suggest is confirmed by the studies themselves: far more theoretical energy is being expended on the problem of self-presentation than on the problem of presenting another self. So literary biography has been left to make do with a more or less undefined and unconscious theory — one too confused to withstand much scrutiny — based loosely on the analogy between the internal workings of interpreted self and the internal workings of an interpreted poem.

The consequence of this loose analogy is seen in the way the most distinguished recent literary biographies of modern authors have been written: as if they were psychological novels, historically grounded equivalents of books written by, say, John Updike or Iris Murdoch. Often the lives of their subjects have encouraged precisely this approach to biography: most modern writers have made themselves exiles in one way or another, and so their biographers can suppress — as recent novelists suppress

— their subjects' position in their economy, their history, their reading public, and so forth. The triumph of this kind of biography is of course Richard Ellmann's monumental *James Joyce*. Ellmann chose the ideal subject for his conventions. After Joyce began writing he had no relations whatever with the Ireland that was his ostensible subject; in his exile Joyce's politics, in both the narrow and broad sense of the word, were virtually vestigial; and the economics of his career amounted to a primitive system of begging letters and postal orders. To understand Joyce the man in a way that he himself wanted to be understood, one need focus only on the tiny circle of his family and friends; Joyce was in exile from everything else. The form of *Ulysses* is in effect a paradigm of the form of Joyce's life: just as the later chapters of *Ulysses* are concerned most of all with transforming the earlier chapters of the book itself, so the later years of Joyce's own life were devoted to writing about the recollections of his earlier years. Joyce's life — like the kind of poem admired by modern criticism — turned in on itself. And so Ellmann was able to apply the techniques of the New Criticism to Joyce's life with enormously effective results.

There are nonetheless some disturbing consequences of this method. For example, in order to describe the patterns of Joyce's life through methods appropriate to literary criticism, Ellmann had first to transform Joyce's life into a literary artifact. This transformation he performed by writing a novel at the same time, and on the same pages, that he wrote his biography. Any attentive reader may find this novel in the interstices of the book's archival reportage. Its presence announces itself whenever Ellmann (like all recent biographers) tells us what Joyce was thinking in such-and-such a city or what he felt when such-and-such happened. We have learned to take this technique for granted, but its defenders have not been entirely convincing.

Ellmann is possibly the most prominent defender. He celebrates his technique, and offers some predictions for its future development, in an essay entitled "Literary Biography" in his book *Golden Codgers*. He writes that "more than anything else we want in modern biography to see the character forming, its peculiarities taking shape." Comparing ourselves (or himself) to Boswell, Ellmann writes: "Primarily Boswell wants to reveal

Johnson's force of character, while today we should ask him to disclose for us the inner compulsions, the schizoid elements — such is our modern vocabulary — which lay behind that force." A few sentences later Ellmann dismisses part of Boswell's account of Johnson's early life with the remark that "this is the panoply of the mind, not its basic workings." Then, recalling that Boswell was not entirely a slouch at his trade, Ellmann offers him some backhanded praise: "The greatness of Boswell's biography, the sense it imparts of a man utterly recognizable and distinct, demonstrates that other methods of biography [our own] are not necessarily better; but none the less we feel compelled today to explore carefully aspects of the mind and of behavior that he would have regarded as not worthy to record and not suitable to publish." To give Ellmann his due, he does occasionally sound a bit desperate about what he must defend in this essay — apologizing for "our modern" vocabulary at one point, as if it were something forced on him, and at another point saying we are "compelled" to write the way we do — but he never acknowledges the possibility of a way out of "our" compulsions and vocabulary. Indeed, he predicts that future biographies will be just like recent ones, only more so: "The form of biography, then, is *countenancing experiments comparable to those of the novel and poem* . . . Biographies will continue to be archival, but the best ones will offer speculations, conjectures, hypotheses. The attempt to connect disparate elements, *to describe the movements within the mind as if they were movements within the atom,* to label the most elusive particles, will become more venturesome" [emphasis added]. Like almost all critics who were trained in the decorum of the modernist movement, Ellmann predicts a future that will be even more modernist than the recent past, not different from it. If our biographies now focus on the inside of the mind, then in the future they will do so to an ever greater degree.

One wishes one could be as confident as Ellmann seems to be that current biographical methods need only become bigger and better; and one wishes even more that one could be as confident as he claims to be that we know more about the art of biography than Boswell did. In many ways we seem to know a lot less, and we are forced — as he was not — into increasingly unsatisfying "speculations, conjectures, hypotheses." We have focused our gaze on the inaccessible inner reaches of the authorial psyche without quite facing the fact that we have no way of making the inaccessible accessible. So we invent what we cannot know and call the result "biography." More of the same is unlikely to improve matters.

Probably we need to do precisely the opposite of what Ellmann recommends. That is, we need to reexamine the possibility that Boswell's methods can serve as models for our own, as well as the possibility that we need to turn away from the recent styles of internalized biography and attempt instead to write biographies that focus on the *effect* of literary works on their author and the world around him, not the internal *affects* that may or may not have shaped those works. Literary biography may be able to resolve some of its dilemmas by learning to pay attention to the relation between a writer and his audience — that is, to external and social matters ranging from the economics of publication to the larger question of a modern writer's social role. In thinking about the latter, it will be important to separate the facts of the matter from the mythical language in which they are commonly discussed; there should be no more faith in the self-appointed artist–hero. Recent literary theory has attended to the relation of a writer's work to the literary tradition that preceded him, but this must be supplemented by a social–historical understanding of the changing tradition of the styles and roles of authorship itself (as, for example, in the relatively recent idea that it is the artist's task to *create* an audience for his art, rather than serve an audience already in place).

There are few recent models for such biography, although Sonia Orwell may have made one possible by naming a literate political scientist instead of a literary critic as her husband's biographer. Also encouraging, if slightly peripheral to the matter at hand, is a 1975 biography of Henry Cockburn, Karl Miller's *Cockburn's Millennium,* of which the author writes in the preface: "Considered as a biography, the result is a little peculiar, and it is as well to say straight away that it is perhaps less of a biography than a series of arguments and reflections on the subject of his life and works, and on the process of social and cultural change by which they were affected." Other biographers are making similar efforts, necessarily with a comparably tentative air to them. Recent work in the use of artistic style in social history (most accessibly Michael Baxandall's *Painting and Experience in Fifteenth Century Italy*) can provide models for a biographical account of a writer's changing relation with his audience; and social history, in many of its forms, can provide models for interpreting individual lives that may prove, in the long run, more useful than the familiar psychological models. Recent biography has taken its theory of human nature essentially from Freud; the results suggest that biographers ought to start looking elsewhere. The logical place to turn is not Marx as much as Weber, if the complex and changing role of an author is at last to be recognized (or recognized again) as a matter of equal or greater interest to a biographer than his subject's childhood neuroses.

Whatever happens, Ellmann's prescription of more of the same in literary biography should at least be treated with caution. But if biographers want to try something different, they come up against the barrier that prompted this essay in the first place: the system and conventions of authorized biography. This system inevitably encourages the writing of psychological biographies of the type Ellmann welcomes. Heirs and executors have the right to permit access to unpublished manuscripts and personal papers, and the biographer who has the more-or-less exclusive privilege to use these papers will certainly want to use them as his prime exhibits. The effect once again is to focus attention on the internal and private aspects of personality at the expense of the public ones.

There may be an argument for jettisoning the whole system of authorized biography (although this would probably do even more damage to personal rights of privacy than the system itself even at its worst), but such a course is entirely impractical. Heirs and families cannot be expected to open their memories and their files of letters to anyone who wants to write a book about their famous ancestor. Even if private papers are deposited in libraries, accessible to all, biographers can receive only limited access to personal memories: heirs cannot spend their time telling their life story to anyone who comes along. Although the recent revision of the copyright law limits the rights of heirs

and executors to a term of fifty years after the death of an author
(in Britain this has long been the case already), biographies will
certainly be written before this term expires. All these circumstances combine to encourage internalized, authorized biographies — and it is precisely this sort of biography that gives pain
to the living and fictionalizes the dead.

When, then, should a biographer do if he concludes, on one
hand, that publication of his subject's private affairs will hurt
the living, and, on the other hand, that the biographical tradition
in which he works offers no other way of writing a biography
except to concentrate on the private affairs of his subject? The
simple solution to the first part of the problem may perhaps provide an opportunity to find the more difficult solution to the second. A biographer must accept a delay in publication: he has no
ethically tolerable choice other than to postpone his biography
until after the death of those who would be injured by its appearance. During this delay he might usefully spend his time on
a critical study of his author, or an account of his background
and milieu; and in doing this he might work towards alternative
methods of biography, methods that make use of typical or exemplary models of personal experience rather than novelistic
ones. He may find the most significant aspects of his author's
life were not what he expected them to be, on the basis of his experience of life as filtered through his experience of fiction.

I began this essay with the circumstances of an unwritten
biography of W. H. Auden. It was Auden who stated perhaps
the best and most difficult standard for any interpretation of an
author's work, including the interpretation that goes into biography. He wrote: "What every author hopes to receive from
posterity — a hope usually disappointed — is justice." If a literary biographer keeps this hope in mind, the ethical resonances
of the word "justice" will remind him that the value-free assumptions of internal psychology and internalized criticism are
inadequate to the task he has set for himself. Justice is never
easy, but in the case of biography, a biographer who does justice
to an author serves that author's readers — his posterity — as
well.

JOHN CLIVE

English "Cliographers": A Preliminary Inquiry

The number of outstanding biographies — whether in the form of books or essays — of modern English historians may not be large enough to merit "official" consideration as a separate genre of the art. But it is certainly varied, ranging as it does from monumental classics like Trevelyan's *Macaulay* and Froude's *Carlyle* to the delicate filigree of Lytton Strachey's *Portraits in Miniature*. Varied enough, perhaps, to serve as a sounding board for the question: what can one expect to find in the biography of a historian that will best illuminate the relation of his life to his work as well as instruct current practitioners of the art of history?

One obvious component of any answer to that question comes readily to mind: formative influences. We want to know why the great historians chose to write history in the first place, and what it was that led them to write the kind of history they eventually produced. Native talents and childhood influences (nowhere better depicted than in Sir George Otto Trevelyan's *Life and Letters* of his uncle, Thomas Babington Macaulay) can be highly revealing. The extraordinary little boy who, at the age of four, replied to Lady Waldegrave's question as to whether he was still feeling pain from some hot coffee a servant had accidentally spilled over his legs, "Thank you, Madam, the agony

is abated," and who, before he had reached the age of ten, was
already working on a compendium of universal history, composing hymns and epics, and displaying awesome powers of
memory, emerges graphically from Trevelyan's early chapters.
And so does the atmosphere of political activism and moral endeavor that characterized the Clapham Sect and helped to shape
young Macaulay's mind and character. Just as the stern presence
of that leading Evangelical reformer, Zachary Macaulay, the
historian's father, dominates the son's early life, so does the
far more jovial presence of Thomas Babington Macaulay domi-
nate the entire life of his nephew and future biographer, G. O.
Trevelyan.

Indeed, in reading G. M. Trevelyan's memoir of his father,
George Otto, one cannot help but be struck by the extent to
which the Trevelyan family had fallen under the magic spell of
the author of the *History of England.* Macaulay, who must
surely rank at or near the top in any enumeration of devoted
Victorian uncles, lived long enough to take intense interest and
pride in his nephew's attainments at Harrow and Cambridge.
And the younger man amply repaid his debt, not only with the
masterly *Life and Letters* of his uncle but also with his *Early
Life of Charles James Fox* and his *American Revolution,* both
of which bear unmistakable traces of consanguinity with Lord
Macaulay's work. When, in addition, we remember that George
Otto's own son (and memorialist) George Macaulay Trevelyan
not only bore his great-uncle's name but himself wrote a series
of books that carried on the family tradition of combining Liberal sentiments with a special interest in social history, we cannot help but reflect that there exist historiographical as well as
royal dynasties, and that, at least in the case of the House of
Macaulay, they seem to supply their own best biographers.[1]

Lord Acton was distantly related to Edward Gibbon. But that
particular family tie was hardly decisive in molding the younger
historian's spiritual outlook or approach to history. As Gertrude
Himmelfarb demonstrates in her study of Acton, the drama of

1. G. M. Trevelyan left instructions that no biography be written of
him. But see Joseph M. Hernon, Jr., "The Last Whig Historian and Consensus History: George Macaulay Trevelyan, 1876–1962," *American
Historical Review,* 81 (1976), 66–97.

his life was the drama of his ideas; and the forces that shaped those ideas derived as much from teachers and guides, living and dead, as they did from the historian's Catholic family background.[2] Among the living guides, the chief was Ignaz von Döllinger, who purged his pupil of those Whiggish and Macaulayite sympathies he had brought with him to Munich in 1850. Another was Ranke, whose lectures and writings instilled both Döllinger and Acton with the necessity of writing history, whenever possible, from original manuscripts and documents. Among the dead, perhaps the principal influence was Edmund Burke. As Miss Himmelfarb points out, it was partly to reinstate Burke and to expel Macaulay as the sage of politics that Acton undertook his first major task, the editorship of the *Rambler.*

If Acton's life, then, illustrates the influence that powerful minds, past and present, may exert over a historian's intellectual development, so does the biography of John Richard Green, author of *A Short History of England,* as set forth in his *Letters* (edited by Leslie Stephen). There we learn not only that the sixteen-year-old Green was, like Gibbon at the same age, tempted to become a Roman Catholic — a temptation to which, unlike the historian of the Roman Empire, he did not yield — but also that his reading of Gibbon at about the same time had an enormous effect on him: "What a new world that was!" he later recalled. Along with Addison and Steele, Gibbon remained one of his favorites at Oxford. Another was Macaulay, whose *History* apparently suggested to Green his own first historical work, a description of eighteenth-century Oxford (1859). Three years later it was a reading of Sismondi that finally persuaded Green to abandon the more limited theme of a history of the English Church and to write his own history of England. Stephen's edition of Green's *Letters* shows that a historian does not merely benefit from actual discourse with his contemporaries (in Green's case, Stubbs and Freeman) but also that the influence of the great historians through their writings may do much to determine the direction his own work takes.

Much, but not everything. We need only recall how Gibbon acknowledged the usefulness of his service in the Hampshire

---

2. *Lord Acton: A Study in Conscience and Politics* (Chicago: University of Chicago Press, 1952).

Militia in writing the history of the Roman Empire to remind us
that practical experience as well as books helps to shape both
the work and the life of the historian. Green himself is a good
example. For some years he was the incumbent of an Anglican
parish in the East End of London. This experience strengthened
his sympathies with different types of human beings. Indeed, as
Leslie Stephen remarks, "The history might have been written
in a very different tone had the writer passed his days in aca-
demical seclusion."[3] Green himself, by the way, carried the en-
vironmental interpretation of English historiography to the point
where he saw something in the English atmosphere of freedom
that made it impossible for any historian living there to sink
into a "paper-chaser" on the German model. Even those historians of his own day who consciously strove to be merely external and pragmatic failed in their aim: witness, Green pointed
out, the contrast between Freeman and Pauli, and between
Gardiner and Ranke.[4]

Macaulay, of whom it cannot be said that he ever attempted
to be a "paper-chaser," gained practical experience in public
life. Trevelyan's *Life and Letters* shows how, first as a Member
of Parliament during the Reform Bill debates and subsequently
as Legal Member of the Indian Council, Macaulay acquired the
knowledge that enabled him to deal more effectively with the
public transactions of the past in the *History of England*. And
from Lady Namier's biography of her late husband, Sir Lewis,
the reader learns that that great prober into the practical affairs
of politicians and statesmen in eighteenth-century England had
himself garnered ample practical experience in both business
and diplomacy. That experience must be kept in mind in any
appraisal of the empirical and anti-ideological nature of Namier's method. One should also be aware, from Namier's own
account, of his rejection in turn of what he came to consider
two delusive ideologies: his parents' belief that the principal difference between Jews and Gentiles was religious, and the formu-
laries of socialist doctrine. Finally, one should recognize the
intellectual context of what Sir Isaiah Berlin has called Namier's

3. Leslie Stephen, ed., *The Letters of John Richard Green* (London:
Macmillan, 1902), p. 59.
4. Green to Freeman, Feb. 26, 1867 (Ibid., p. 427).

"deflationary" approach to history in a Viennese milieu that included Mach, Freud, Loos, and the members of the Vienna Circle.[5]

Childhood and family influences, intellectual and social environment, teachers and guides (living and dead), practical experience in the affairs of the world — all these are shaping forces that we expect to see delineated in any worthwhile biography of a major historian. But those of us who try to write history ourselves want something more: at least a glimpse, preferably a long look, into the master's workshop, which will go some way toward satisfying our curiosity about how the great historians went about the workaday business of actually writing their histories. Macaulay told his young nephew in 1843 that he was going to spend five more years collecting materials to write a history of England. "The little boy thought he meant to spend five years buying the very best pens and plenty of blue and white foolscap paper."[6] But readers of Trevelyan's *Life and Letters* know better! They know that the historian tirelessly visited archives and battlefields in search of documents and local color; that he sometimes read twenty books to write a single sentence; that Macaulay the historian, unlike Macaulay the essayist, did not rely on his famous memory, but filled scores of notebooks before putting pen to paper; and that he wrote only when he felt at his best, first a rapid rough draft, with gaps filled in and revisions and corrections made later. The manuscript of the last volume of the *History* (now at the Morgan Library in New York), with its innumerable crossings out in the search for the perfect word or phrase, amply confirms what Trevelyan tells us.

One thing Macaulay did not have to do, however, was to rewrite a whole volume of his history after it had been inadvertently destroyed. That, as we know, was the heroic task facing Thomas Carlyle after volume I of the *French Revolution* was thrown into the fire by John Stuart Mill's careless maid. Even after he decided to rewrite what had been lost, Carlyle, who had by this time destroyed his notes and could remember nothing of the

5. Isaiah Berlin, "L. B. Namier: A Personal Impression," *Encounter*, 27 (1966), 32–42.
6. George Macaulay Trevelyan, *Sir George Otto Trevelyan: A Memoir* (London: Longmans, Green, 1932), p. 30.

volume, failed for some time to make any progress. As his biographer, James Anthony Froude, remarks: "A man can rewrite what he has known; but he cannot rewrite what he has felt."[7] Finally, he decided to read nothing but novels for two weeks; thereafter he was able to rewrite the volume in a version he judged to be worse, but not much worse, than the original.

In his early days, Froude tells us, Carlyle made no "foul" copy. "The sentences completed themselves in his head before he threw them upon paper."[8] He was no longer able to do this when he wrote *Cromwell* and *Frederick*. At the start of any literary work, he was distracted by every trifle. Noise in particular was anathema to him while he was trying to write, and he complained bitterly about being disturbed by a young lady who practiced the piano at the time he was attempting to begin his *Cromwell*. Froude's comment here (unlike that piano) will strike a sympathetic chord with anyone who has ever been engaged in writing history: "And after all it was not the piano, or very little the piano. It is in ourselves that we are this and that, and the young lady might have played her fingers off, and he would never have heard her, had his work once been set going, and he absorbed in it."[9]

Like many other historians since, Carlyle knew that the British Museum contained the best collection of the materials he needed for *Cromwell*. But he was reluctant to work there since, Froude explains, "he required to have his authorities at hand where his own writing-tackle lay round him, where he could refer to them at any moment."[10] Unlike those other, later historians, he did something about the situation: he founded the London Library, still (because its books circulate) a blessing to those who, like Carlyle, prefer to work at home. It was there, in any event, that J. R. Green had to work after the museum closed and he had finished his daily parish duties — sometimes staying up from midnight until two A.M., at other times from two to five A.M. In 1866 Green got into a fight with the British Museum staff. He had lost his ticket, and they, rather than issuing him

7. James Anthony Froude, *Thomas Carlyle: A History of His Life in London* (New York, 1884), p. 31.
8. Ibid., p. 82.
9. Ibid., p. 281.
10. Ibid., p. 130.

a new one, told him to "search" for the old one. He was furious about the delay this caused in his work. But at least he finished his magnum opus, the *Short History of England,* or, as he liked to call it in his letters, "Shorts."

Acton never did finish his "Madonna of the Future," the *History of Liberty,* that "greatest book that was never written." And if Froude, Trevelyan, and Stephen, in their biographies of great historians, supply some positive hints for aspirants to that class, Miss Himmelfarb's biography contains some implicit warnings about what *not* to do if one intends to complete a major historical work. She shows how Acton was unable to stop himself from prolonging research at the expense of writing. Every week, he complained to Mary Gladstone, brought new publications to throw fresh light on or add fresh difficulties to his subject. He could not make the necessary decision to ignore these new materials and go forward without them. Instead, he threw himself into the *Cambridge Modern History,* which in the end prevented him from doing any major work of his own. What really defeated him, as Miss Himmelfarb perceptively concludes, was his own restless, dissatisfied, ambitious mind.

Thus it is possible to learn from existing biographies of modern English historians not only how to finish but also how not to finish work in hand. Of course, we do not read those biographies primarily as "how to" manuals, or even as "how not to" manuals. Nor should we. What concerns us most is, I suppose, to find an answer to the question: is there such a thing as a special historical imagination or temperament and, if so, how does it work? Richard Ellman, in an essay "Literary Biography," has admitted that "we cannot know completely the intricacies with which any mind negotiates with its surroundings to produce literature. The controlled seething out of which great works come is not likely to yield all its secrets."[11] That applies equally well to the creative process out of which comes great historical writing. But at least we can keep trying to come close to that process, to gain a greater understanding of it. Namier, singling out a "historical sense" as the crowning achievement of historical study, defines it as "an intuitive understanding of how

11. Richard Ellman, "Literary Biography," in *Golden Codgers: Biographical Speculations* (New York: Oxford University Press, 1973), p. 16.

things do not happen (how they did happen is a matter of specific knowledge)." Alan Bullock has drawn an analogy between the historian's preference for the concrete and particular, his distrust of the abstract and the general, and the approach of the painter and novelist. "Probably," he writes, "it is a question of temperament, of the way your mind works."[12] It is worthy of note that these two twentieth-century historians, neither of them noted for lack of realism, stress supra-rational elements in their definition of the ideal historian's cast of mind. Namier, as his widow's biography reveals, always wanted to write a novel — to be entitled *The Torn Out Pages* — whose highlights and turning points he sketched out over the years. Another eighteenth-century historian of note, J. H. Plumb, actually wrote a novel in his twenties that, we are told, came very close to publication.[13]

Few biographers of English historians have dealt in an adequate manner with this difficult subject of the historian's imagination. Some skirt its edges, usually in the process of pointing out some defect in their subject. Thus William Ewart Gladstone, whose brilliant essay about Macaulay still remains one of the best things ever written about the historian, quotes him to the effect that "some books which I would never dream of opening at dinner, please me at breakfast, and vice versa." Gladstone's comment on this remark (largely, but perhaps not wholly unjust) is: "There is more subtlety in this distinction, than could easily be found in any passage of his writings."[14] Lytton Strachey, equating the virtues of the metaphysician with the vices of the historian, criticizes Hume's historical style in these terms: "A generalized, colorless, unimaginative view of things is admirable when one is considering the law of causality, but one

12. L. B. Namier, "History," in *Avenues of History* (London: Hamilton, 1952), p. 4; Alan Bullock, "The Historian's Purpose: History and Metahistory," in Hans Meyerhoff, ed., *The Philosophy of History in our Time* (New York: Doubleday, 1959), p. 298.

13. Julia Namier, *Lewis Namier: A Biography* (London: Oxford University Press, 1971), p. 264; Neil McKendrick, "J. H. Plumb: A Valedictory Tribute," in McKendrick, ed., *Historical Perspectives: Studies in English Thought and Society in Honour of J. H. Plumb* (London: Europa Publications, 1974), p. 5.

14. W. E. Gladstone, *Gleanings of Past Years: 1845–1876* (London, 1879), II, 274.

needs something else if one has to describe Queen Elizabeth."[15]
Neither Gladstone nor Strachey gets us very far. Nor, for that
matter, does Lady Namier, even though she makes us privy to
the result of her late husband's Rorschach Test: "Intelligence
superior and concrete. Approach often intuitive. There is also
evidence of imagination."[16] The most interesting attempt to
analyze the historical temperament of a famous English historian was made a hundred and twenty years ago by Walter
Bagehot in his essay on Macaulay. He spoke there of "the temperament which inclines men to take an interest in actions as
contrasted with objects."[17] Some people, Bagehot remarks, are
(and, truth to tell, he precedes the next two words with the
adverb "unfortunately") "born scientific." They are curious
about shells, snails, horses, and butterflies. As the result of the
absence of an intense and vivid nature, their minds are directed
to scenery rather than to man's actions. In their intellectual
make-up, "the abstract reason, and the inductive scrutiny which
can be applied equally to trees and to men, to stones and to
women, predominates over the more special qualities solely
applicable to our own race, — the keen love, the eager admiration, the lasting hatred, the lust of rule which fastens men's
interests on people and to people."[18]

Scientific men, Bagehot continues, are calm men. Euclid may
be compared to fine ice, Newton to a peak of Teneriffe. The historian's mind differs from that of the naturalist, because he has
more interest in human affairs. But it is also characterized by
a certain quality of passivity. "It can bear not to take part."
That is why Gibbon, as a Member of Parliament, could watch
Fox and Burke debate without ever intervening himself. That
is why Macaulay, who *did* speak memorably in Parliament,
was not a debater, but rather a man for great occasions: "Some-
body had to fetch him."[19] Why, Bagehot asks (tongue partially

15. Lytton Strachey, "David Hume," in *Portraits in Miniature and
Other Essays* (New York: Chatto and Windus, 1931), p. 145.
16. Julia Namier, *Namier,* p. 280.
17. Walter Bagehot, "Mr. Macaulay," in *Collected Works* (Cambridge:
Harvard University Press, 1965), I, 397.
18. Ibid., p. 399.
19. Ibid., p. 402.

in cheek, as usual), is history dull? "The answer is, that it is written by men too dull to take the common interest in life, in whom languor predominates over zeal, and sluggishness over passion."[20] It was Macaulay's "inexperiencing nature" that made his greatest speeches so abstract; that prevented him from absorbing and learning more than he did from his sojourn in India; that explained his ultimate lack of real sympathy with either Cavaliers or Puritans.

But, granted the truth of all of this — and a twentieth-century reader would have to say that that is granting a good deal — why, Bagehot asks, is Macaulay's *History* as readable as it undoubtedly is? The answer is that he was able to unite two apparently discordant qualities: a flowing fancy and a concern for the coarse business of life. He could "throw over matters which are in their nature dry and dull, — transactions — budgets — bills, — the charm of fancy which a poetical mind employs to enhance and set forth the charm of what is beautiful."[21] And he was able to do this because he combined a vivid imagination with an impassive temperament.

Curiously enough, the appearance of Trevelyan's *Life and Letters* twenty years after that of Bagehot's essay confirmed much of what Bagehot had written about Macaulay's cast of mind. It contained a letter from him, written in 1830, in which the historian described individual items of furniture in the Duc de Broglie's salon in such detail that he himself felt obliged to add: "You will think that I have some intention of turning upholsterer."[22] At the same time, it revealed that what Macaulay loved more than anything else was to build castles in the air, to daydream; so that walking the streets of London, he would fancy himself in Greece, in Rome, in the midst of the French Revolution. He himself, so he told his sister Margaret, felt that those two ways of looking at the world — she for her part referred to them as a combination of a romantic disposition and a common-sense way of looking at things — stood in a fruitful relationship to one another. For, he told her, it was precisely

20. Ibid., p. 399.
21. Ibid., p. 415.
22. George Otto Trevelyan, *The Life and Letters of Lord Macaulay* (London: Longmans, Green, 1959), p. 130.

when he built his castles in the air, when he daydreamed about the past, that factual accuracy became absolutely imperative: "Precision in dates, the day or hour in which a man was born or died, becomes absolutely necessary. A slight fact, a sentence, a word, are of importance in my romance."[23]

Is it possible that this seemingly paradoxical union of daydreaming and factual accuracy characterizes more than one historian, past and present? It is difficult to answer that question, since — Bagehot aside — few biographers of historians have hitherto occupied themselves with the nature of the connection between the historian's personality and his imagination. What, if anything, differentiates historians in this regard from other creative artists — or from scientists? One can make a quick list of desirable qualities for historians: love of puzzles and gossip; interest in power and personalities; a vigorous fantasy life; above all, perhaps, the negative capacity for not taking anything for granted, an ingrained skepticism about human motives and human testimony of any sort, as well as a fierce determination to get to the roots of matters. But is it axiomatic that all Western historians, from Herodotus to Toynbee, have needed to possess those qualities in similar proportions? After all, even in the course of just the last two centuries there have been fundamental changes in the sort of history generally praised and accepted as "great" by the society in which it is written. Gibbon's distantly ironical approach to the past went out of fashion after Herder and the historicists made *Einfühlung* the key to historical insight. Subsequently, Ranke and the "scientific" school that derived from him have given way to an awareness that a treatment of the past that is to some degree subjective is at once inevitable and desirable. As these changes in historiographical modes occurred — and England was not immune from them — has the result been to set up new kinds of elective affinity between certain personality traits and the ability to write history?

One might confidently assert, in answering that question, that Clio's many-mansioned house has always contained rooms to accommodate the whole range of human personality. Cer-

23. Ibid., p. 133. On Macaulay's historical imagination, see John Clive, "Macaulay's Historical Imagination," *Review of English Studies,* 1 (1960), 20–27.

tainly, today, one need do no more than look around the table
at the meeting of any history department (or to compare the
Journal of Economic History with the *Journal of the History of
Ideas*) to conclude that it takes all kinds . . . Nevertheless, this
should not deter biographers of historians, whose task it is, after
all, to study character and psyche in relation to achievement,
from at least raising the question as to whether there exists a
"historical" personality type, and whether that has always been
the same.

Other questions suggest themselves: Why do historians write?
J. H. Plumb has given one answer: "to try and understand the
forces which impel mankind along its strange course; to justify
a religion, a nation or a class; to make money; to fulfil ambition;
to assuage obsession; and a few, the true creators, to ease the
ache within."[24] It would be of special interest to hear more
about the last category, those "true creators." How do they
achieve those breakthroughs in historical interpretation that
revolutionize the field when they occur? According to one recent
writer on this subject, the crucial element in the breakthroughs
made by four twentieth-century historians is their capacity to
conceive of not just a single problem or issue or theme, but,
like the great novelists, of an entire self-contained world.[25] The
late Helen Maud Cam called Maitland's brilliant conclusion —
a real breakthrough — that in the thirteenth century the English
parliament was not primarily a national assembly or legislature
but rather a session of the King's Council whose function was
chiefly judicial and administrative "a magnificent attack on
after-mindedness."[26] Is the essence of such a revolutionary insight, then, as one historian has suggested, the ability to see the
past not through the distorting medium of what followed after,
but in its own terms?[27] Yet by no means all historians who are
able to look at the past in that manner achieve greatness or
even distinction. What else is required from the historians who

24. McKendrick, "Plumb," p. 16.
25. Bernard Bailyn, "History and the Literary Imagination," Carl L.
Becker Lectures, Cornell University, 1975.
26. Quoted in Trygve R. Tholfsen, *Historical Thinking: An Introduction* (New York: Harper and Row, 1967), p. 252.
27. Ibid., pp. 249–250.

really made a difference? The biographers have not as yet supplied us with more than approximations to an answer.

Yet another question they might well pose concerns the language and style of historians, in particular their use of imagery and metaphor. Lady Namier tells us, for example, that in the course of his early visit to the United States, Sir Lewis was particularly struck by the New York skyscraper. Thenceforth, he used it as an ideograph for man's creative adaptability, since to him it represented a felicitous example of interplay between independence and interdependence. He even wrote an essay entitled "Skyscrapers."[28] Was Namier's fascination purely accidental, or is it of some significance for his work as a historian? Do historians, especially those dealing with abstract entities like groups and classes and movements, have to possess a special metaphorical capacity, a plastic or tactile imagination that can detect shapes and configurations where others less gifted see only jumble and confusion? In what ways is the sort of imagery any great historian chooses integrally related to his personality and his general outlook on the world? Did these historians, consciously or otherwise, derive inspiration and verve for writing particular passages of their histories not merely from contemplation of their sources but, to some extent, from extraneous experiences? One thinks of Macaulay's noting in his journal after a visit to the Great Exhibition (1851) that the sight had produced in him a "glow of eloquence" that supplied him with just the right touches for his description in the *History of England* of the battle of Steinkirk.[29] Was this experience unique to Macaulay? Surely not. But how often does it occur? And what are its psychological dimensions?

What the ultimate answers to those questions will turn out to be is uncertain. What is certain is that there remains a good deal to be done by that group of writers, present and future, whom (at the risk of perpetual obloquy and derision) I shall here refer to as Cliographers.

28. L. B. Namier, *Skyscrapers and Other Essays* (London: Macmillan, 1931).

29. Trevelyan, *Macaulay*, p. 503.

JAMES CLIFFORD

"Hanging Up Looking Glasses at Odd Corners": Ethnobiographical Prospects

"In more ways than one Zachary had cast a long shadow." So concludes John Clive's narrative of the youth and early adulthood of Thomas Babington Macaulay, Zachary's son.

"Virginia Woolf was a Miss Stephen," begins Quentin Bell. "The Stephens emerge from obscurity in the middle of the eighteenth century. They were farmers, merchants and receivers of contraband goods in Aberdeenshire. Of James Stephen of Ardenbraught practically nothing is known, save that he died about 1750, leaving seven sons and two daughters. Following the tradition of their race most of the sons wandered abroad."

Consider too Dorothy Lee and her Wintu Indian informant: "When I asked Sadie Marsh for her autobiography, she told me a story about her first husband, based on hearsay. When I insisted on her own life history, she told me a story which she called 'my story.' The first three quarters of this, approximately, were occupied with the lives of her grandfather, her uncle and her mother before her birth; finally she reaches the point where she was 'that which was in my mother's womb,' and from then on she speaks of herself, also."

Where, in short, does a person begin? Where does he or she

41

end? These are basic questions to be asked concerning the practice of biography as it intersects with ethnology. The following essay attempts, rather speculatively, to identify a broad area of convergence that may provisionally be called ethnobiography. The term attempts to mark off biography's synchronic aspect, its concern with portraying a person "in his time," as distinguished from attempts to trace the trajectory of an identity "over" or "through" time. The two elements of any biographical synthesis, diachronic and synchronic, may be separated analytically; in practice they are closely interwoven. In distinguishing them I hope to establish the importance of ethnobiography for the writing of any life, and in the process to suggest a possible redefinition of the biographical subject.

The term "ethnology" as I have loosely used it here should bring to mind two separate practices. One is the familiar tactic of using a sharply different cultural experience as a means of shedding light on our own problems and ideas. The other directs our attention to the complex ways in which cultural patterns shape individual behavior and experience. From the latter perspective, following the French tradition, I do not sharply distinguish ethnology from sociology.

In its first, or exotic, use ethnology has developed as a comparative human science concerned with cultures said to be "without writing," "without history," "without industry," and so on. They may also be said to be without the biographical attitude, but it is safer to say simply that the cultures studied by ethnologists often possess positive modes of conceiving the person that differ significantly from our own. Western biography would do well to consider these alternatives, if only as a way of refining and making more explicit its own presuppositions.

In 1810, Coleridge identified a new cultural configuration which he termed "the age of personality."[1] Within this context of "individualism" (a nineteenth-century term) the modern biographical genre took shape, transcending the traditional concerns of spiritual autobiography and political/religious hagiography. But the fascination with individual lives as ends in themselves has never gone unchallenged, and in recent decades

1. S. T. Coleridge, "A Prefatory Observation on Modern Biography," *The Friend,* January 25, 1810, pp. 338–339.

a strand of thought loosely denoted as structuralism has again placed sharply in question the status of the individual subject. The philosophies that take individual experience as their points of departure — existentialism and phenomenology — must justify themselves anew. Even the psychoanalytic unconscious, that most tangled of secret gardens, has been declared open to the public. Its shrubs are now trellised on language, trees pruned into binary branching signs, unruly vines cut away . . .

Formal gardening has never been the biographer's strong point. Nor can it be. Without notions of personal uniqueness in culture, biography is out of a job. But although its point of departure, the individual self, has been questioned, the genre is not about to be sent into early retirement. To be convinced of this, one need only scan the current book reviews, which every week announce the arrival of a new batch of lives — to be read, presumably, by a public avid for such news. Structuralism may be premature to the extent that it proclaims a transcendence of the first person singular. But it is right — and the popularity of biography attests to this also — in maintaining that the experience of individuality in modern industrial culture is increasingly problematic.[2] For its own part, biography, that most Anglo-Saxon of literary forms, has not seemed particularly aware of the debate going on around it.

Yet the composition of a life inevitably involves the writer in delicate problems of portraying the person in his or her trans-individual contexts — linguistic, social, historical, professional, familial, and so forth. A review of Clive's *Macaulay* quoted on the paperback's front cover calls the book "as much a history of Pre-Victorian social and political thought and action as it is of Macaulay himself." And so it should be. But where

2. In his preface to a recent interdisciplinary seminar, *L'Identité, séminaire dirigé par Claude Lévi-Strauss* (Paris: Grasset, 1977), Lévi-Strauss casually writes-off the much-discussed Western "identity crisis" as a passing symptom. Those who experience it, he thinks, are simply learning what archaic cultures have always accepted, and what modern sciences as diverse as mathematics, biology, linguistics and philosophy are rediscovering—that "substantial identity" can never be assumed, but must be constructed from given historical and natural relationships "supremely indifferent to our autism" (p. 11). Lévi-Strauss's contention that personal identity is purely relational is challenged by more than one participant in the seminar (pp. 331–332).

does Thomas Babington Macaulay stop and pre-Victorian society begin? Or where does Zachary cease and his son take over? These are the kinds of problems, issues of personal definition and freedom, which are routinely solved by way of the biographic arts of arrangement; for biography contracts to deliver a self. However riven the personality described, however discontinuous the experience, the final written effect is of wholeness. Whether treating of failure or success, of fulfillment or suicide, the biographer's perspective brings life together for us. And if the life does not take shape, if we do not in reading it encounter a distinct person whose voice, gestures, and moods grow familiar to us, then we judge the biography a failure.

It is something of a mystery that so many biographies do in fact succeed in uniting a coherent personality. And the feat is particularly remarkable in a time and culture whose philosophers, psychologists, sociologists, and poets cannot come to any real agreement as to what structures and practices add up to a "person." Biography, relying on little theoretical sophistication but placing its faith in the storyteller's arts, manages with surprising consistency to make us believe in the existence of a self.

Its success may be partially explained by positing the existence of an underlying mythic pattern in our culture, a myth that finds an important mode of expression in the biographical genre. Let us call this pattern the "myth of personal coherence." It must exist to some degree in all cultures, though in different forms, for there probably cannot be a human culture composed entirely of anonymous functions, and without some concept and experience of the person.[3] But only a Western, humanist, industrialized culture has proclaimed an "age of personality" and has thereby created a personal norm whose version of wholeness emphasizes completion at the expense of plenitude. The narrowness of this new norm has begun to be felt as intolerable: a self that cannot adequately express its numerousness is a prison. The "age of personality" possesses relatively few cul-

3. See on this and other issues in this essay an important collective survey edited by Germaine Dieterlen and Michel Cartry, *La notion de personne en Afrique noire* (Centre National de Recherche Scientifique, 1973).

tural manners or mythic forms that actualize an experience of personality not defined as exclusiveness but rather as openness to others, to situation, to cultural background. We strain for an unlivable identity.

The desired unity can at least be known vicariously, through the reading of biographies. But this very demand placed on the genre, the demand to deliver a self, ensures that its rendering of the person will emphasize closure and progress towards individuality, rather than openness and discontinuity. Biography's perspective is thus doomed to one-sidedness inasmuch as it attempts not to portray a life experience but to shape a life. For the genre is probably less often true to the way life is than to the way we might like it to be. Camus jotted in his *Carnets:* "Nostalgia for other people's lives. This is because, seen from the outside, they form a whole. While our life, seen from inside, is all bits and pieces. Once again, we run after an illusion of unity."[4]

To pose the issue practically and from a slightly different angle: what is the biographer to make of a Charles Baudelaire who writes in his *Intimate Journals:* "Religious intoxication of large cities. Pantheism. I am everything; everything is me."[5] Is the study of Baudelaire properly the study of a modern city, Paris? And would such a study, like Walter Benjamin's, be a disjointed series of illuminations: man and milieu seeming to meet haphazardly on street corners?[6] No biographer of Baudelaire could eliminate Paris from his subject's personality. But most would adopt a more common solution to the problem of portraying a person in context than that chosen by Benjamin. Biographers tend to rely on an approach that, in effect, sets up a relation between foreground and background. In the manner of a Renaissance painting, the principal figure or group appears in the front, while behind, seen perhaps through a window, the

4. A. Camus, *Carnets, 1942–51,* Vol. II, trans. P. Thody (London: Hamilton, 1966), p. 17.

5. C. Baudelaire, *Oeuvres Complètes* (Paris: Gallimard, 1954), p. 1190.

6. W. Benjamin, "On Some Motifs in Baudelaire," in *Illuminations* (New York: Schocken, 1969).

landscape or cityscape is traced as minutely as necessary. Historical background, family background, professional background, and so on are described in distinct sections.

But is this a true rendering of the self's relation to the world?
The various backgrounds, or "patterned occasions of experience,"[7] are actually so densely woven through a life that one
risks real violence to reality in separating them out. The life
outside the window spills into the room. Benjamin's studies of
Baudelaire provide a sense of alternative, though they are not,
strictly speaking, biography. His is a mosaic, or "field," approach
in which a poet's intimate imagery and a Paris arcade or quirk
of *la mode* seem to coexist simply as equal expressivities within
a pattern.[8]

This is not to say that biography should attempt to dissolve
the individual, only that the nearer the background can be
brought to the lived surface, the better. The genre is, as I have
said, embedded in a complex of cultural expectations of individuality. But it may be hoped that in general the myth of
personal coherence which biography expresses — or better, embodies — will be able to make room for a concomitant myth
of personal participation. Of course, practicing biographers will
be aware of the difficulties involved in composing lives not on
the model of the Renaissance painting but rather, shall we say,
in a more cubist style. Nonetheless, it should be possible to
portray a more open, less complete, person, and thus to create
a less centered biography.

My suggestion is prompted, in part, by the work of psychoanalytic revisionists who have recently redefined and extended
the boundaries of the Freudian self. Erik Erikson, in a variety
of well-known books, has emphasized the sociocultural determi-
nants of personality. R. D. Laing expands the concept of individuality into a "political" network of interpersonal relations.
And Jacques Lacan, returning to a linguistic model inherent in

7. Following Whitehead: see *Adventures of Ideas* (New York: Macmillan, 1933), esp. chap. 12.
8. Another suggestive example is William Carlos Williams' experiment in writing the history of a person and a city within a single plane,
and name: *Patterson* (New York: New Direction, 1963).

Freud's rendering of primary psychic drives, has presented us with a person radically decentered in an external symbolic order. Such approaches challenge us to inject sociality into the most individual expressions of an ego conceived as continually "outside" itself.

The biographer tends to be skeptical of abstract theories. He has a practical task at hand; and the notion of a person forever losing and recreating himself in his social contexts, in his "others," and in language, seems to render narration impossible. Without some thread joining a life's occasions of experience it would seem useless to continue to speak of a person. Nevertheless, biography must attempt to transcend in practice any absolute choice between identity and dissolution of the self.

An ethnological example may help us pose the issue with more clarity.

A Melanesian, in the good old days at least, would not have been likely to suffer from Camus' nostalgia for personal unity. He or she would be incapable of seeing another person as a single entity. For example, an unmarried woman would be addressed in a plural form, thus including in her personality the child to which she might one day give birth. Two people seen approaching would be identified with a single term containing no element of twoness, but a specification of relationship, like "twin" in Western parlance. But it would be impossible to say "a twin." A complex repertoire of dual locutions would be employed to express grandfather/grandson, maternal uncle/nephew, husband/wife, homonymic relations, and so on. Nor would both parties need to be physically present for the common name to be applied to one or the other.

It would be better to have said: one *and* the other. For Melanesian relational entities are not, as we tend to see them, composed of two parts. "Two" is not a sum. "One" does not exist except as an experience of otherness, as a fraction of two, which is the basic "unit." An individual who cannot be circumscribed with a locution of plurality (relationship) is *bwiri,* adrift, without consistency, not a "person." This was the structure of experience in archaic New Caledonia, as reconstructed and analyzed by Maurice Leenhardt.[9] I am providing, of course, a highly abstract version of his account — Melanesian experience stripped of its social, linguistic, and geographical specificities. But perhaps the spareness of the example will serve to make it more available to us, not generalizable, but translatable.

Leenhardt, following Marcel Mauss, termed the archaic self a "personage."[10] The term's theatrical resonances are most relevant to the discussion. A personage exists only in his role, and the role has no meaning except within its play. Role implies relationship with an occasion, which in Melanesia is provided by myth. Participation in mythic occasions involves the self in relations of identity with a mythic personality. This figure, whose double the individual becomes, may be a god invoked through specific rituals at an altar; or it may be a totem, less personified, perhaps a lizard encountered along a path; or it may be an ancestor recognized in the eye of a shark; or it may be a maternal uncle who, because he transmits the uterine source of life stemming ultimately from the clan totem, shares mythic vitality with his nephew. Nearly all social relationships are also mythic occasions: society is composed of a patterned synthesis of the paternal lineage of "power" and the maternal lineage of "life," the former flowing from ancestral gods and the latter from the totemic forces of nature. Thus the pairs, brother/sister, mother/child, father/son, man/wife, are more than encounters between individuals. They are structured reciprocities that express convergences in the larger mythic pattern. New Caledonian society, as Leenhardt has portrayed it, is a network composed of dual relationships.

Thus the Caledonian personage is a multiplicity of doubles. This "self" is not to be visualized as a body moving from one dual relationship to another — a set of trajectories that oscillate

9. The principal sources for my summary are: "Le temps et la personnalité chez les Canaques de la Nouvella-Calédonie," *Revue Philosophique*, Sept.–Oct. 1937, pp. 43–58; "La personne mélanésienne," *Annuaire de l'École Pratique des Hautes Etudes*, sec. 5, 1941–42, pp. 5–36; *Do Kamo, la personne et le mythe dans le monde mélanésien* (Paris: Gallimard, 1947, 1971; the University of Chicago Press is now preparing an English translation of *Do Kamo*).

10. See M. Mauss, "Une catégorie de l'esprit humain: La notion de personne, celle du 'moi,'" *Sociologie et Anthropologie* (Paris: Presses Universitaires de France, 1950), pp. 333–362.

out and back through a common center. Rather, the personage exists *only* as a double in an occasion of reciprocity, and sometimes of identity, with another. The personage does not hold some part of him or herself apart from a given relation. The Melanesian enters fully the "time" of the other, which is a myth-time.

The New Caledonian experience of the self as double is, of course, not without its Western resonances. A classic statement is Rimbaud's "je est un autre." And the pervasive fascination with *doppelgänger* in recent literature is well known. The Melanesian personage is, in fact, not very distant from the feeling that "all the world's a stage / And all the men and women merely players; / They have their exits and their entrances; / And one man in his time plays many parts."

But too many parts too fully entered into involve us, we tend to think, in the risk of madness. However, for traditional Melanesians, madness would reside in singleness. The personage as they experience it is without a center. We must not think of this cluster of couples as a crossroads, with a point of intersection located materially in the body and linguistically in a single name. We must attempt to imagine a being who is involved in a variety of names, each of which is indicative of a different occasion. While participating in one, there is no missing of the others. And there is no central space or time which, named, can partake of all. Such an experience is not madness or fragmentation. Rather it is a life of full involvement made possible by the mediational immanence of myth. The Melanesian does not worry about loss of self; he is free to rise to the occasion.

The point here is not to idealize the archaic life. (Leenhardt shows its fragility in the face of growing external pressures. A new world of drastically expanded time and space inevitably undermines any local and encompassing sociomythic landscape. The personage risks moral disintegration for lack of a supporting life raft of individuality.)[11] The point, rather, is to show

11. Leenhardt, *Do Kamo,* chaps. 11 and 12. (One is reminded, in this connection, of Lévi-Strauss's remark that in Western Civilization the individual "has his own personality for a totem." *La Pensée Sauvage,* Paris: Plon, 1962, p. 285.)

that the life of a person without a "center" is conceivable, if not actually livable today. If however, its opposite — the life of a singular identity — is equally impossible, then we must search out a compromise.

In moving away from the biographical strain towards identity, the life writer would become more suspicious of portraying a person as a compromise of influences, negotiated once and for all. Biography could be content to identify the subject's various doubles, that is to say, the people or situations that in some way command the subject to enter their time, to play a role for them. And these participations would not be seen as merely compulsory or determining. If the occasions of a person's life are exterior, patterned realities — familial, cultural, historical, mythical — they should, ideally, be portrayed as such, juxtaposed in the narrative or mosaic as recurring constituents of the personality. I am not suggesting any model or classification, merely an awareness that the person may be quite different in each of a variety of contexts. The Melanesian example encourages us to allow these occasions *not* to amount to an individual.[12]

Another helpful formulation that challenges the biographical self without, however, eliminating it, is to be found in the work of a modern philosopher who was not averse to building on archaic precedents. Whitehead, in accounting for what he termed the "inescapable fact" of personal unity, had recourse to Plato's doctrine of the "Receptacle," an almost completely permeable form.

> [Personal unity] is a perplexed and obscure concept. We must conceive it [as] the receptacle, the foster-mother as I might say, of the becoming of our occasions of experience. This personal identity is the thing which receives all occasions of the man's existence. It is there as a natural matrix for all transitions of life, and is changed and variously figured by the things that enter it; so that it differs in its character at different times. Since it receives all manner of experiences into its own unity, it must

---

12. As, apparently, it encouraged Jacques Lacan in his early critique of the psychoanalytic "subject." For Leenhardt's influence, see Lacan's "Discours de Rome," 1953; trans. in *The Language of the Self* (Baltimore: Johns Hopkins University Press, 1968), p. 35; and the extensive commentaries of Anthony Wilden, pp. 168, 181–182, 188.

itself be bare of all forms. We shall not be far wrong if we describe it as invisible, formless, and all-receptive. It is a locus which persists.[13]

It is common in writing a life to posit, a priori, the contours of this highly problematic receptacle. Almost inevitably, the biographical self is a locus which *insists*.

Turning away from the metaphors of theory to the practical problems of actually composing more open-ended life studies, we can envisage only solutions that are partial and ad hoc. Not merely does the project run counter to deep-seated cultural expectations, but in addition, there is an irreducible separation between the experience of a life's occasions and the writing of a life. The diarist's art is not the biographer's. The latter stance, inevitably, is outside and post facto. And yet if the biographer's viewpoint is that of the historian, it must also be that of the ethnologist. There is a diachronic strand running through any life, the thread of an identity forming and reforming itself. (The importance of its developmental path varies with each particular subject.) But the most difficult task of biography is synchronic, the task of rendering personality as an experiential world. The problem is inescapable. Whether one is reconstructing the key moments in a life or the life as a whole, one is involved in the domain of ethnobiography.

Biography shares this domain with the realist novel. In both genres the central problem is the portrayal of character, its ambiguous participation in elaborate cultural and historical "backgrounds." The novel, enjoying as it does fictional freedom of movement, has sometimes been able to achieve coherent solutions to the basic problems of ethnobiography. Thus, perhaps, novelistic realism can provide stimulating models for the practice of composing a "life and times."

In one form of realism a central character — say, Julien Sorel — is portrayed moving through a series of situations specific to the society of Restoration France. The tensions and ambiguities of his participations in a set of contexts provided by history form one of the book's chief thematic structures.

13. *Adventures of Ideas*, p. 218.

Another example, closer to ethnology because less centered on a single life, is provided by the *Comédie humaine,* a work in which Balzac frequently assumes the stance of a natural scientist vis-á-vis the society that is his subject. To call Balzacian realism "fiction" is not to do justice to its localized ethnographic specificity or to its attempt to construct characters in the form of what Lukacs calls "types."[14] A type is the fusion of the extraordinary and the typical; it is a character that "stands out" not because he is different from his contexts (in the manner of Julien Sorel) but because he embodies them. The characteristic occasions of his historical period are immanent in his life.

The biographer might also consider the handling of character in another novel that is explicitly sociological, *Middlemarch.* As an example of the rendering of a whole culture, Eliot's achievement stands among the classics of ethnology. The cultural situations she analyzes are precisely observed and locally situated, while at the same time moving within broader historical processes. In her world, Durkheimian "social facts" impose on individuals, but without wholly erasing the leeways of personality and initiative. The fashion in which Eliot allows her characters to be invaded by sociality while still retaining specific identity is not simply a novelistic technique; it is the central theme of the book. *Middlemarch* is thus a proper model for both the ethnologist and the biographer.

The novel has tended to move away from realism, leaving the field to biography on the one hand and ethnology on the other. One discipline's point of entry is the individual person, the other's the general culture. A convergence is increasingly desirable and, perhaps, possible. For if, as I have suggested, biography is bound to a still-active myth of personal coherence, its redefinition as a narrative of transindividual occasions can, at least, be envisaged. This development does not require a sharp break with tradition. In the past the most convincing biographies have to a high degree managed to weave the collective through the individual.

Ethnology, on the other hand, has tended until recently to shy away from the study of extraordinary individuals. Although

14. G. Lukacs, *Studies in European Realism* (New York: Grosset and Dunlap, 1964), pp. 6–7, 42, 71.

there exists a minor tradition of American Indian autobiography and of "life histories,"[15] true biography is rare in the general anthropological literature. (It would be interesting to pursue the question of why ethnographers, who rather frequently have paid tribute to outstanding informants, have so seldom written these individuals' lives.) The vast majority of ethnological work has been directed towards the analysis of cultures as wholes. The "Science of Man" has made its greatest advances by means of the supra-individual approaches of funtionalism, social structure analysis, culture–personality wholism, ecological materialism, structuralism, and semiology. The role of the atypical person has been neglected, and with a few exceptions in the work of Paul Radin and Dorothy Lee, the patterns of personal leeway and freedom in culture remain unanalyzed.[16]

But there is reason to hope that this tendency is now being reversed — especially as the individuals who were formerly the objects of ethnographic study become its subjects. It probably requires cultural insiders to recognize adequately the subtle ruses of individuality, where outsiders see only typical behavior. Thomas Babington Macaulay might have been regarded by a Melanesian ethnologist as a typical Englishman, which he certainly was — and just as certainly was not.

In a complex sense, every possible subject for biography is both typical and extraordinary. (Even the most extreme genius or noncomformist is tied to his surroundings, at least by language and opposition. And, as oral history is making clear, the most "ordinary" person will have amassed his portion of special wisdom and eloquence.) A person is not a mere social or linquistic function. But neither is the self to be considered as a figure clearly distinguished from a background. A person, seen from the perspective of ethnobiography, is a sequence of culturally patterned relationships, a forever incomplete complex

15. Two important examples are: P. Radin, ed., *The Autobiography of a Winnebago Indian* (Berkeley: University of California Press, 1920), and Don Talayesva, *Sun Chief: The Autobiography of a Hopi Indian,* ed. L. Simmons (New Haven: Yale University Press, 1947).

16. See P. Radin, *Primitive Man as Philosopher* (New York: Dover, 1957); *The World of Primitive Man* (New York: Schuman, 1953), esp. the Introduction by Stanley Diamond, p. xxxi; and Dorothy Lee, *Freedom and Culture* (Englewood Cliffs, N.J.: Prentice-Hall, 1959).

of occasions to which a name has been affixed, a permeable body composed and decomposed through continual relations of participation and opposition.

How is the humble biographer to seize this protean form? As best he can. There is, of course, no such thing as a definitive biography, and the biographical occasions of a life will vary according to the specifics of the author/subject coupling, the nature of the available evidence, and the culturally determined notions of personhood that are available at any given moment. The biographical genre will probably continue to operate in the vicinity of the realist novel. But I would argue, finally, that a certain belated evolution in the direction of modernism is possible and in order, without going as far as the *nouveau roman*. (The self cannot be dissolved into its perceptions to such an extent that the minimal narrative of identity which remains the essence of biography is lost.) Biography can, however, aspire to something of the openness and immediacy of intermediate forms of the novel. Consider, for example, Virginia Woolf's *Jacob's Room*.

The "room" here is akin to the "Receptacle," the time-space of a self which persists. The final scene begins:

> "He left everything just as it was." Bonamy marvelled. "Nothing arranged. All his letters strewn about for anyone to read. What did he expect? Did he think he would come back?" he mused, standing in the middle of Jacob's room.

Jacob is dead. Arrangement of the room falls ultimately, to the biographer. In this abandoned life, love letters are mixed with bills and invitations to garden parties. The scene, in all its poignant inevitability, renders the biographical occasion. What is to be done with Jacob's old shoes?

However, in the novel as a whole Jacob's life is not haphazard, or not entirely so. It is organized into a lurching sequence of situations which, though not always related to one another causally or temporally, are consistently interwoven with a specific social and historical milieu. Self and culture, in skillful, partial collaboration, proceed together toward the disaster of World War I.

A final and rather different example for biography to consider is Chinua Achebe's extraordinary ethnological novel, *Things Fall Apart*. Here a renewed realism attempts once more to seize in a single dynamic the vicissitudes of culture and protagonist. A typical/untypical hero participates in the disaster of his traditional African community. The culture's flaws and strengths are laid out with ethnographic precision; and they are set in motion through their interaction with the personal strengths and weaknesses of an individual. In Achebe's work, cultural and personal narratives are inseparable. To the extent that ethnology has provided us with tools for grasping cultures as wholes, it has made possible this kind of novel, and also, perhaps, this kind of biography.[17]

Between the social phenomenology of *Jacob's Room* and the ethnological realism of *Things Fall Apart,* biography must improvise its own techniques. If biography shares with the novel the problem of portraying character and milieu, it is not in any simple sense a form of fiction. The genre does not enjoy the relative freedom of the novel to invent a world and characters. For this reason Virginia Woolf, who was experienced in both genres, thought biography a craft and not an art. The work of the life writer cannot be an imperishable fictional invention, she says, but is rather "something betwixt and between."[18] This is indeed biography's fate; but it is also its opportunity. To the extent that it succeeds in showing how a personal life may be pulled together, and to the degree that it is able to render life experiences drawn from the broadest pattern of appropriate occasions, biography surely participates in the projects of art. For we are currently witnessing a rapprochement between art and at least some of the social sciences. In such a climate, the biographical genre's appeal is enhanced by the fact that it makes do with materials "on hand," specific records and relationships having to do with a real person in a given cultural-historical dynamic. Like ethnology, biography works with overlapping

17. An excellent recent example, the history of an individual and an ethnic group intertwined, is Leonard Thompson, *Survival in Two Worlds, Moshoshoe of LeSotho* (Oxford: Oxford University Press, 1975).
18. V. Woolf, "The Art of Biography," in *The Death of the Moth, and Other Essays* (London: Hogarth Press, 1942), p. 196.

patterns that the author can only arrange and not invent. But can invention be distinguished from arrangement?

Biography remains, then, "betwixt and between," clinging to its subject in a culture where a person's beginnings and endings have become uncertain. In the words of Virginia Woolf, the biographer "lives in an age when a thousand cameras are pointed, by newspapers, letters, and diaries, at every character from every angle." The life writer will be increasingly obliged to admit "contradictory versions of the same face." And yet, biography (she sets out its task bravely) "will enlarge its scope by hanging up looking glasses at odd corners. And . . . from all this diversity it will bring out, not a riot of confusion, but a richer unity."[19]

19. Ibid., p. 195.

VIRGINIA SPENCER DAVIDSON

Johnson's *Life of Savage:*
The Transformation of a Genre

Harold Nicolson, attempting to set a definition general enough to subsume the eclecticism of the genre, reverts to the *Oxford English Dictionary*'s signification of biography as "the history of the lives of individual men as a branch of literature."[1] If the terms of the definition are unexceptionable, their relation remains stubbornly ambiguous, for it is precisely in the tension between the fact as history and its rendering as literature that biography has traditionally foundered. By rendering I do not mean to imply the merely rhetorical; Walton's *Lives* exhibit perhaps as much pure eloquence as any writer may hope to attain, although at the same time his work suffers from a propensity toward total hagiography. The difficulty of "rendering" involves, rather, a revealing range of truth and selection along with the transformation of ephemeral and scattered incident into some fixed proportion; otherwise a work is merely reportorial.

Henry James recognized that the very fact of a person's death irrevocably alters one's image of him. Describing his idea of James Russell Lowell, he says: "The hand of death, in passing over it, has smoothed the folds, made it more typical and gen-

1. Harold Nicolson, *The Development of English Biography* (New York: Harcourt, Brace, 1928), p. 7.

eral. The figure retained by memory is compressed and intensi-
fied; accidents have dropped away from it and shades have
ceased to count."[2] Yet James's comment takes us only so far as
the impulse toward elegy and thus toward what Leon Edel calls
the commemoration as opposed to recreation of a man.

Virginia Woolf comes closer to the complex pressures on the
biographer. She asserts, "By telling us the true facts, by sifting
the little from the big, and shaping the whole so that we perceive
the outline the biographer does more to stimulate the imagination than any poet or novelist save the greatest. For few poets
and novelists are capable of that high degree of tension which
gives us reality . . . [the biographer] can give us the creative
fact; the fertile fact; the fact that suggests and engenders."[3] By
means of "the creative fact" Johnson's *Life of Savage* breaks in
upon the classically elegiac (that is, commemorative and panegyric) biography, establishing priorities of verisimilitude and
moral sensibility sweeping enough to represent what Walter
Jackson Bate aptly refers to as a "genetic jump" in its nature.

We do not see the contours of a work like *Savage* emerging
with any clarity in Johnson's own earlier and numerous biographical essays. Even his interesting and congenially chosen
"Life of Boerhaave" (1739), written out of deep admiration
and displaying heroic strength of character in its subject, is still
little more than an extended obituary. Johnson's ardent, if
almost touchingly juvenile, exhortation in his summation to
"Boerhaave" may be instructively compared to his grave peroration in *Savage*. He appeals evangelically to his "Boerhaave"
readers: "May his example extend its influence to his admirers
and followers! May those who study his writings imitate his life!
and those who endeavor after his knowledge, aspire likewise to
his piety!"[4] The *Life of Savage* introduces an earned solemnity:

2. Henry James, quoted by Leon Edel, *Literary Biography: The Alexander Lectures* (Toronto: University of Toronto Press, 1957), p. 11.

3. Virginia Woolf, *The Death of the Moth and Other Essays* (1942;
rpt. New York: Harvest–Harcourt Brace Jovanovich, 1974), pp. 196–
197.

4. Samuel Johnson, "Boerhaave," in *Works of Samuel Johnson*, VII
(Cambridge: Harvard Cooperative Society, New Cambridge Edition, n.d.),
p. 183.

> Those are no proper Judges of his Conduct who have slumber'd away their Time on the Down of Plenty, nor will a wise Man easily presume to say, "Had I been in *Savage's* Condition, I should have lived, or written, better than *Savage*."
>
> This Relation will not be wholly without its Use, if those, who languish under any Part of his Sufferings, shall be enabled to fortify their Patience by reflecting that they feel only those Afflictions from which the Abilities of *Savage* did not exempt him; or if those, who in Confidence of superior Capacities or Attainments disregard the common Maxims of Life, shall be reminded that nothing will supply the Want of Prudence, and that Negligence and Irregularity, long continued, will make Knowledge useless, Wit ridiculous, and Genius contemptible.[5]

In the case of Savage we must first examine the facts of his extraordinary career. Johnson's *Life* is *sui generis* in one important sense precisely because the historical record alone affords Johnson as sensational and even melodramatic a tale as Defoe or Richardson or Fielding might fabricate in an attempt to achieve a dramatically heightened realism. Johnson needs no inflated protestations of literal "truth" for his story beyond those set out in his advertisement in the *Gentleman's Magazine* announcing his intention to publish an account of the "unfortunate and ingenious" Mr. Savage that "may have a tendency to the preservation of [his memory] from insults or calumnies . . . It may be reasonably imagined, that others may have the same design; but as it must be expected they will supply from invention the want of intelligence . . . [and] they will publish only a novel, filled with romantick adventures, and imaginary amours."[6] Johnson's version is to "gratify the lovers of truth." His association with Savage from 1737 to 1739 already argued for his authority; his prolific contributions to the *Gentleman's Magazine* for more than five years argued for his professionalism.

Common gossip as well as early published accounts in the *Plain Dealer* had already apprised the public of the essentials

5. Samuel Johnson, *Life of Savage,* ed. Clarence Tracy (Oxford: The Clarendon Press, 1971), p. 140. Future citations of *Savage* are to this edition.

6. James Boswell, *Life of Johnson,* ed. George Birkbeck Hill, rev. L. F. Powell (Oxford: The Clarendon Press, 1934), p. 165.

of his career:[7] the divorce of his putative mother (the Countess of Macclesfield) on grounds of adultery with his purported father, the Earl Rivers; Savage's relentless pressing of his claims to noble birth, especially in his poem "The Bastard"; his condemnation for murder in a tavern brawl and the Queen's own pardon nearly foiled by his "mother's" false testimony that he had made an attempt on *her* life; his stormy yet long continued friendship with Pope; his patronage and final repudiation by the Countess' nephew Lord Tyrconnel; and, finally, his imprisonment for a tavern debt and his subsequent death in double exile from friends and country in Bristol's Newgate Prison.

The counterpoint to all these experiences is the consistently perverse and intractable pride and incivility beneath Savage's ingratiating manners and irrepressible wit. When he was at last rejected by Tyrconnel for invading his benefactor's wine cellar and pawning the valuable books given him along with an already generous maintenance, Savage's basic defense was that he was resolved "to spurn that Friend who should presume to dictate to him."[8] Johnson might sympathize with Savage's "obstinacy of Spirit" in despising clothes left for him at a Coffee-House "with some Neglect of Ceremonies" by an annonymous donor,[9] though he observes of a similar episode later on, "It is probable . . . he submitted with a good Grace to what he could not avoid, and that he discovered no Resentment where he had no Power."[10]

Yet more often resentment prevailed. Savage's relationship with contributors to his pension in Bristol strains Johnson's judgment to the verge of casuistry: "It may be alleged, and, perhaps, justly, that he was petulant and contemptuous, that he more frequently reproached his Subscribers for not giving him more, than thanked them for what he had received; but it is to be remembered, that his Conduct, and this is the worst Charge that can be drawn up against him, did them no real Injury."[11]

7. For a full account of Savage's relation with the editors of *The Plain Dealer,* see Clarence Tracy, *The Artificial Bastard: A Biography of Richard Savage* (Cambridge: Harvard University Press, 1953), pp. 72ff.

8. *Savage,* p. 60.

9. Ibid., pp. 109–110.

10. Ibid., p. 112.

11. Ibid., p. 117.

The source of Savage's vicissitudes, then, occasionally resembles a kind of inversion of the hero's vision in *The Pilgrim's Progress*. Where Christian keeps his awestruck eye on the Celestial City, marshaling all his efforts toward attaining the divine standard that promises salvation, Savage keeps his bemused gaze riveted on his own romantic delusions, ignoring the overwhelming external evidence that perpetually dissolves his dreams of influence and literary fame. The extent of his self-deceit is more than once ironically announced by the ambitious and exalted sentiments in his poetry:

> Think not light poetry my life's chief care!
> The muse's mansion is, at best, but air;
> Not sounding *Verse* can give great Souls their Aim
> *Action* alone commands substantial Fame.[12]

> Be Posts dispos'd at Will! —— I have for these,
> No Gold to plead, no Impudence to teaze.
> All secret Service from my Soul I hate;
> All dark Intrigues of Pleasure, or of State.
> —— Where these are not what Claim to me belongs;
> Though mine the *Muse* and *Virtue, Birth* and *Wrongs*?[13]

It is central to the significance of Richard Savage that his flamboyant career, while replete with the most perplexed "mistakes and miscarriages, escapes and expedients,"[14] is yet as elemental as a morality play in depicting the divided nature of man. For Savage the polarity is not between Christian sin and redemption but is the secular, humanist, ultimately Greek struggle between reason and passion. The "facts" open out to a large moral (as opposed to moralistic) conception. Truth inheres as a constituent in the very action and event of the tale rather than

12. Richard Savage, "The Picture. To Mr. Dyer, When in the Country" in *The Poetical Works of Richard Savage,* ed. Clarence Tracy (Cambridge: Cambridge University Press, 1962), pp. 56–57.

13. "The Poet's Dependence on a Statesman," in *Savage,* p. 88.

14. Samuel Johnson, "Rambler No. 60," in *Selected Essays from the Rambler, Adventurer, and Idler,* ed. W. J. Bate (New Haven: Yale University Press, 1968), p. 110. Future essay citations are to this edition, except where noted.

as an imaginative ideal projected by the artist in novels like
Roxana or *Amelia*. To clarify this point we may turn to Donald
Stauffer's observation upon one of the innumerable obscure
memoirists of the century: "His life has no neat and happy
ending. He is like Tom Jones in actual life, and there is no
creator to step down like a god from the machine, 'interpose at
the difficult minute' and, at the end, save the creature he has
grown to love."[15] The *Life of Savage* is an enactment of truth
even as *Rasselas* is a fictionalizing of it. But, significantly, in
Savage the moral grows organically out of the data of the life
and does not precede the creation of character as a didactic
position.

Generations of readers have dutifully genuflected before
Johnson's own austere insistence on Truth as a value in composition, but its direct relevance to the "genetic jump" in the
development of biography as evidenced in the *Life of Savage*
has not been pressed far enough. It is not simply that in *Savage*
Johnson abjures panegyric (for there are instances of it throughout). Nor is it, further, that he anticipates Strachey's emphasis
on Voltaire's "je n'impose rien, je ne propose rien, j'expose."[16]
While Johnson allows the truth to reveal its own severe pattern,
and at the same time insists on the implications of the pattern
from his own viewpoint, that viewpoint is not ironic in the
caustic mode of Strachey. Perhaps for the same reason he is
considered a satirist *manqué* by Bate, Johnson's view of even so
dissipated a life as Savage's is essentially great-hearted. Along
with such great-heartedness, and saving it from maudlin senti-
mentality, goes Johnson's appetite for comprehending experience.

The link between that appetite and the consequent innovation
in biography is Johnson's own basically tragic imagination. Animated by neoclassical confidence in the existence of general
truth and with concomitant faith in the possibility of its uniform
apprehension, such an imagination points toward Savage as a

15. Donald A. Stauffer, *The Art of Biography in Eighteenth Century
England* (Princeton: Princeton University Press, 1941), p. 116.
16. Lytton Strachey, *Eminent Victorians* (1918; rpt. New York:
Capricorn Books, 1963), p. vii.

paradigmatic human being and away from him as an eccentric, even pathological human specimen.[17]

Johnson's own words in another context embody the paradox of man's complicity in his own destruction: "Nothing assuredly can be more unworthy of a reasonable nature than to continue in a state so opposite to real happiness."[18] Nothing assuredly is more certain than the fact that men, here specifically Richard Savage, do precisely this. Although Johnson vigorously resists the Augustan idea of a ruling passion, he is easily capable of discerning how a man may be hounded by his own nature more destructively than by the most malign adversary. Johnson's complex pessimism and his Christian belief in sinful nature keep him always cognizant of what Sir Philip Sidney in the *Apology* called "man's erected wit and his infected will."

We are not surprised, therefore, to find Johnson's opening comment in his first essay on biography (postdating the *Life of Savage* by six years) addressing itself to the underlying psychological premise of tragic catharsis, though ostensibly he speaks directly of biography:

> All joy or sorrow for the happiness or calamities of others is produced by an act of the imagination, that realizes the event however fictitious, or approximates it however remote, by placing us, for a time, in the condition of him whose fortune we contemplate; so that we feel, while the deception lasts, whatever motions would be excited by the same good or evil happening to ourselves ... No species of writing seems more worthy of cultivation than biography, since none can more certainly enchain the heart by irresistible interest, or more widely diffuse instruction to every diversity of condition.[19]

17. Edmund Bergler, "Samuel Johnson's 'Life of the Poet Richard Savage': A Paradigm for a Type," *American Imago,* 4 (December, 1947), 42–63. Bergler's article sees Savage's career from a clinical psychiatrist's viewpoint. His reductive conclusions may be summarized by his conviction that Savage displayed every symptom of the classic masochistic parasite.

18. "Rambler No. 197," in *The Rambler, Yale Edition of the Works of Samuel Johnson,* V, ed. W. J. Bate and Albrecht B. Strauss (New Haven: Yale University Press, 1969), p. 262.

19. "Rambler No. 60," *Essays,* p. 109.

This sympathetic identification (catharsis) is, however, but one part of Johnson's strategy in *Savage*. To understand how he transmutes the facts of Savage's career into a genuinely tragic account that diffuses instruction as well as irresistible interest we must also recognize Johnson as a choric voice. Catharsis is complemented by *methexis,* or what may be best translated as Johnson's own dramatic participation in the action. In an intuitive mimetic response to the tragic canon's great end of teaching, Johnson accepts the role of commentator within the action he sets forth. What critics have lavishly appreciated as Johnson's generosity of spirit and even "Godlike and irreplaceable"[20] justice toward Savage takes on a more complicated aspect in such a light. As the biography proceeds, Johnson exhibits the richly various responses available to the chorus in an almost rhythmic regularity, accommodating to himself typical choric patterns of omniscience, severity, compassion, caution, and regret.

Several examples of choric comment are quoted below to demonstrate this variety, as well as the liturgical quality of Johnson's remarks. Taken in context, they are at the farthest possible remove from the merely didactic aside. Rather, they form an intricate antiphonal response to the inexorable unfolding of event and are themselves an enactment of Johnsonian compassion striving with Johnsonian judiciousness.

The very first paragraph of the *Life* raises Savage's history to a plane of inscrutable and generic misfortune apprehended by an all-knowing consciousness:

It has been observed in all Ages, that the Advantages of Nature or of Fortune have contributed very little to the Promotion of Happiness; and that those whom the Splendor of their Rank, or the Extent of their Capacity, have placed upon the Summits of human Life, have not often given any just Occasion to Envy in those who look up to them from a lower Station. Whether it be that apparent Superiority incites great Designs, and great Designs are naturally liable to fatal Miscarriages, or that the general Lot of Mankind is Misery, and the Misfortunes of those whose

20. Bertrand H. Bronson, "A Note on the Life of Savage," in *Samuel Johnson: Rasselas, Poems, and Selected Prose* (New York: Holt, Rinehart and Winston, 1971), p. xxi.

Eminence drew upon them universal Attention, have been more carefully recorded, because they were more generally observed, and have in reality been only more conspicuous than those of others, not more frequent, or more severe.[21]

Soon after, in the account of Savage's early and continuous rejection by his mother, the tone changes from Olympian serenity to one of severe censure and even incredulity as Johnson catalogues Lady Macclesfield's malignity:

> It is natural to enquire upon what Motives his Mother could prosecute him in a Manner so outragious [sic] and implacable; for what Reason she could employ all the Arts of Malice and all the Snares of Calumny, to take away the Life of her own Son, of a Son who never injured her, who was never supported by her Expence, nor obstructed any Prospect of Pleasure or Advantage; why she should endeavour to destroy him by a Lie . . .
>
> This Mother is still alive, and may perhaps even yet, though her Malice was so often defeated, enjoy the Pleasure of reflecting, that the Life which she so often endeavoured to destroy, was at least shortened by her maternal Offices; that though she could not transport her Son to the Plantations, bury him in the Shop of a Mechanick, or hasten the Hand of the publick Executioner, she has yet had the Satisfaction of imbittering all his Hours, and forcing him into Exigencies, that hurried on his Death.[22]

The following examples are distinguished by the even-handed dispensation of the compassion Johnson especially valued:

> It is not indeed unlikely that *Savage* might by his Imprudence expose himself to the Malice of a Talebearer; for his Patron had many Follies . . . there are few who do not sometimes in the Wantonness of thoughtless Mirth, or the Heat of transient Resentment, speak of their Friends and Benefactors with Levity and Contempt . . . The Fault therefore of Mr. *Savage* was rather Negligence than Ingratitude; but Sir Richard must likewise be acquitted of Severity, for who is there that can patiently bear Contempt from one whom he has relieved and supported, whose Establishment he has laboured, and whose Interest he has promoted?[23]

21. *Savage*, p. 3.
22. Ibid., pp. 38–39.
23. Ibid., p. 16.

And, again, following an exposition of the humiliations of dependency, a condition with which Johnson was intimately familiar, he observes:

> To this unhappy State it is just to impute much of the Inconstancy of his Conduct; for though a Readiness to comply with the Inclination of Others was no Part of his natural Character, yet he was sometimes obliged to relax his Obstinacy . . . if his Miseries were sometimes the Consequence of his Faults, he ought not yet to be wholly excluded from Compassion, because his Faults were very often the Effects of his Misfortunes.[24]

Circumspection, another common theme of the tragic chorus, is evoked by a prior description of Savage's massive reserves of self-vindication based on the projection of his personal liabilities outward:

> The Danger of this pleasing Intoxication must not be concealed; nor indeed can any one, after having observed the Life of *Savage*, need to be cautioned against it. By imputing none of his Miseries to himself, he continued upon the same Principles and followed the same Path; was never made wiser by his Sufferings, nor preserved by one Misfortune from falling into another.[25]

Finally, at one of the lowest recessions of Savage's fortunes, Johnson sounds a plangent note of lament that is made all the more poignant by the distance it implies between expectation and fulfillment:

> In this Manner were passed those Days and those Nights, which Nature had enabled him to have employed in elevated Speculations, useful Studies, or pleasing Conversation. On a Bulk, in a Cellar, or in a Glasshouse among Thieves and Beggars, was to be found the Author of *The Wanderer,* the Man of exalted Sentiments, extensive Views and curious Observations, the Man whose Remarks on Life might have assisted the Statesman, whose Ideas of Virtue might have enlightned [sic] the Moralist, whose Eloquence might have influenced Senates, and whose Delicacy might have polished Courts.[26]

24. Ibid., p. 52.
25. Ibid., p. 74.
26. Ibid., p. 97.

Savage's singular history offers Johnson a contemporary objectification of the reality principle before which he had to bow in his own life and upon which Greek tragedy is posited, the Aristotelean insistence that it is by men's actions that they are virtuous or not. So much has been made of Johnson's concern with formal elements such as the unities in the *Poetics* that we are likely to devitalize the regard, not to say reverence, he holds for the broad foundations of Aristotelean and Socratic ethics.

When the Greek epic mentality had looked only at the deed itself, Aristotle questioned the moral implications behind it. To Johnson the great praise of Socrates was that "he drew the wits of Greece, by his instruction and *example* . . . to moral inquiries, and turned their thoughts . . . upon the various modes of virtue, and relations of life."[27] While affording ample instruction toward virtue, neither Aristotle (nor Johnson) is unmindful of the resistance built into human nature. Hence, although Aristotle acknowledges that "it is no easy task to be good," he nevertheless proposes a program aimed at achieving the virtuous life that bears directly on Savage's headlong disregard of its most basic principles.

Particularly apposite is the elaboration in book 2 of the *Nichomachean Ethics* of the dramatic, better still, the experiential nature of virtue. "It makes no small difference, then, whether we form habits of one kind or of another from our very youth; it makes a very great difference or rather *all* the difference."[28] Aristotle goes on to discriminate the modes of virtuous action, all depending on the apprehension of morality as kinetic as distinguished from "potential" or theoretical good. "It is activities exercised on particular objects that makes the corresponding character . . . So, too, to the unjust and to the self-indulgent man it was open at the beginning not to become men of this kind, and so they are unjust and self-indulgent voluntarily; but now that they have become so it is not possible for them not to be so."[29] Johnson discerns at the precise midpoint of his biography just how Savage is responsible for his own

27. "Rambler No. 24," *Essays,* p. 57.
28. *Introduction to Aristotle,* ed. Richard McKeon (New York: Modern Library, 1947), p. 332. Future citations are to this edition.
29. Ibid., p. 359.

defeat in the world: "The reigning Error of his Life was, that
he mistook the Love for the Practice of Virtue, and was indeed
not so much a good Man, as the Friend of Goodness."[30]

We are left in no doubt that the declension of Savage's character is based on his inability to develop beyond the adolescent
demands of his own vanity or the compensations of chimerical
performance. Johnson notes that "he always preserved a steady
Confidence in his own Capacity, and believed nothing above his
Reach which he should at any Time earnestly endeavor to
attain. He formed Schemes of the same Kind with regard to
Knowledge and to Fortune, and flattered himself with Advances
to be made in Science, as with Riches to be enjoyed in some
distant Period of his Life . . . and was remarkably retentive of
his Ideas, which, when once he was in Possession of them, rarely
forsook him; a Quality which could never be communicated to
his Money."[31]

Thus, Johnson's careful observation and intuitive recognition
of the springs of behavior subsume the essential wisdom of the
second and third books of the *Ethics,* and even comprehend
their logical connection with Aristotle's emphasis on action and
tragic blindness in the *Poetics.* For, although it is "activities
exercised on particular objects that make the corresponding
character" for Aristotle,[32] actions and states of character are not
voluntary in the same way. We are masters of our actions "from
the beginning right to the end, if we know the particular facts,
but though we control the beginning of our states of character
the gradual progress is not obvious, any more than it is in an
illness."[33]

Savage, inured to his recurrent lethargy, insensible to legiti-
mate personal and literary obligations, is essentially, and in the
most classic sense of the analogy, blind. Johnson, in another
sure grasp of Savage's tragic flaw, uses metaphorical language
reminiscent of Milton's Samson at the mill to convey this condition accurately: "He proceeded throughout his Life to tread
the same Steps on the same Circle; always applauding his past

---

30. *Savage,* p. 74.
31. Ibid., p. 102.
32. *Aristotle,* p. 359.
33. Ibid., p. 361.

Conduct, or at least forgetting it, to amuse himself with Phantoms of Happiness, which were dancing before him; and willingly turned his Eyes from the Light of Reason, when it would have discovered the Illusion, and shewn him, what he never wished to see, his real State."[34]

It is characteristic of "simple" tragedy and of the *Life of Savage* seen as a tragic action that no *anagnorisis* or recognition by the hero of his own errors occurs. Though Aristotle expresses his preference for recognition in "complex" action, the omission of Savage's progress to self-knowledge is appropriate to the artistic coherence of Savage's particular tale and is an almost eerie example of actual life imitating art. The full irony of Savage's fate is more dreadfully completed as an aesthetic unity if he in fact is never transformed. The static and circular existence carries its own negative stimulus to our pity and fear.

Supporting the dominating irony of distance between expectation and fulfillment in this tragic circularity are individual emanations of irony that reinforce the ironic tone on other levels. Savage's own remarks in the poetry Johnson quotes represent one such level. The favored antithetical device of the Augustans often provides an appropriate form for ironic sentiment and circumstance. In Savage's "The Friend" we find both:

> —— Kind are my Wrongs, I thence thy Friendship own,
> What State could bless, were I to thee unknown?
> —— While shun'd, obscur'd, or thwarted and expos'd,
> By Friends abandon'd, and by Foes enclos'd,
> Thy Guardian Counsel softens ev'ry Care,
> To Ease sooths Anguish, and to Hope, Despair.[35]

Later, in "The Bastard," the whole statement hinges on a reversed conceit positing great advantage in the very liabilities of illegitimacy:

> —— What had I lost, if conjugally kind,
> By nature hating, yet by vows confin'd,
> { Untaught the matrimonial bounds to slight, }
> { And coldly conscious of a husband's right, }

34. *Savage,* p. 74.
35. Ibid., p. 22.

> You had *faint-drawn* me with a form alone,
> A lawful lump of life by force your own!
> ⎧ Then, while your backward will retrench'd desire, ⎫
> ⎩ And unconcurring spirits lent no fire,   ⎭
> I had been born your dull, domestic heir;
> Load of your life, and motive of your care;
> Perhaps been poorly rich, and meanly great;
> The slave of pomp, a cypher in the state.
> Lordly neglectful of a Worth unknown,
> And slumb'ring in a *Seat,* by *Chance* my own.[36]

In his first "Volunteer Laureate" address to the Queen, Savage assumes a birthright which, coming from a foundling, sets new standards for both audacity and incongruity. In these lines he incorporates his mother's repudiation, the Queen's responsibility for once saving his life by royal pardon, and an unprecedented piety:

> Hated by her, from whom my Life I drew,
> Whence should I hope, if not from Heav'n and you?
> Nor dare I groan beneath Affliction's Rod,
> My Queen, my Mother; and my Father, God.[37]

In another direction, the irony of episode argues not only for Savage's profligacy but also for mankind's perfidy. The final scene in which the gregarious Savage dies alone in a Bristol jail, his jailor the very model of benevolence after his friends have all fallen away, points toward the "hypocrite lecteur" accusation of Baudelaire. We are implicated in Savage's declension not simply as Savage but as his deserters. The inability (and perhaps necessary inability) of human charity to extend beyond its own self-interest becomes irrefutable. Johnson's paradoxical view of Savage thus goes far beyond the intricate fabric of Virtue versus Debauchery, Want versus Plenty, Legitimacy versus Bastardry — or even Precept versus Action, which is the nucleus of the ethical statement.

36. *Savage,* p. 71, and Savage, *Poetical Works,* ed. Tracy, p. 90. Following Tracy's edition, I have included the bracketed material to restore the true sense of the lines. Their omission by Johnson shows his sense of duty toward public morality.
37. Ibid., p. 78.

These antagonisms are but refractions of the underlying paradox of existence as Johnson perceived it, the "wearisome condition of humanity . . . created sick, commanded to be sound."
Johnson's tragic and ironic stance is not posited on personal
superiority but rather on common vulnerability. Moving throughout *The Life of Savage* is the Swiftian assessment that lay behind
so much of that unhappy author's agony, "for life is a tragedy,
wherein we sit as spectators awhile, and then act our own part
in it."[38]

If, as Nicolson maintains, "biography is always a collaboration between the author and his subject . . . the reflection of one
temperament in the mirror of another,"[39] the distance between
The Life of Savage and all previous efforts in the genre becomes
clearer. In the career of Savage, Johnson saw the ineluctable
justification for his profound mistrust of self-indulgence and the
demonstration of the necessity for human responsibility even if
it must be in a context of essential inadequacy. But in the very
midst of his disapprobation arises the turbulent, even romantic, imagination that Johnson, through rigid self-discipline, attempted to control. The very gravity of his sense of moral
obligation put him in a paradoxical relation to Savage's profligacy.

Against all the negative implications of Savage's sorry decline
we must set Johnson's regard for good humor, that " 'balm of
being', the quality to which all that adorns or elevates mankind
must owe its power of pleasing."[40] Savage's insouciance was
irresistibly attractive to Johnson, who for so long mistrusted his
own social adequacy and was terrified to the end of what might
result from his constitutional melancholy.

In addition, the spectacle of Savage attempting to publish his
scurrilous attack on Bristol, when the kindness and attention of
a few citizens and his jailor made all the difference between
misery and as much melioration of it as possible, brings Johnson

---

38. Swift, quoted by John Bullitt in *Jonathan Swift and the Anatomy
of Satire: A Study of Satiric Technique* (Cambridge: Harvard University
Press, 1953), p. 11.
39. Harold Nicolson, "The Practice of Biography," in *The English
Sense of Humour and Other Essays* (New York: Funk and Wagnalls,
1968), p. 153.
40. "Rambler No. 72," *Essays,* p. 124.

to a near impasse of ambiguous response. His morality dictates censure but his perception of incongruity argues a nearly comic abeyance of judgment: "Such was his Imprudence and such his obstinate Adherence to his own Resolutions, however absurd. A Prisoner! supported by Charity!"[41] It is the same extremity of situation that gives us at one instant the far ends of both comic and tragic in the human spectrum in remarks like Johnson's "Oh brave we!" or Lear's "Every inch a king."

To the question, then, that seems to plague Boswell — what did Johnson see in Savage — the best answer, as often was the case with Boswell, comes from Johnson. In *Rambler* number 72 he reminds us: "It is remarked by Prince Henry, when he sees Falstaff lying on the ground that 'he could have better spared a better man.' He was well acquainted with the vices and follies of him whom he lamented, but while his conviction compelled him to do justice to superior qualities, his tenderness still broke out at the remembrance of Falstaff, of the chearful [sic] companion . . . who had gladded him with unenvied merriment, and whom he could at once enjoy and despise."[42]

By taking biography beyond the merely commemorative (or defamatory) and demonstrating the complexity of his subject, Johnson established the genre's significant mimetic relationship to actual human nature. In so doing he altered its subsequent course (always allowing for frequent defiant Victorian detours toward encomium), and proved that biography, like poetry, might aspire to be "more philosophical and a higher thing than history."[43]

41. *Savage,* p. 132.
42. "Rambler No. 72," *Essays,* pp. 126–127.
43. *Aristotle,* p. 636.

WILLIAM C. DOWLING

Boswell and the Problem of Biography

Some years ago, during a general discussion of symbolic meaning, Ernst Cassirer referred to the literary work as a "self-contained cosmos with its own center of gravity." The phrase may be seen to express an axiom of modern criticism, that life and literature, whatever else we may find to say about them, are entirely separate realities. At the same time, as a metaphor giving shape to a powerful intuitive conviction, Cassirer's phrase calls to mind a stage in modern theory when the notion of literary autonomy was still a matter of some controversy. Ordinarily one might suppose this controversy long since laid to rest — no critical axiom, perhaps, is without its troubled history — and feel free to turn to the work of the moment. When the work of the moment is literary interpretation of three major biographical narratives written by James Boswell, however, one soon discovers that one has wandered well out of the ordinary course of things.

Any literary consideration of Boswell raises certain questions about biography as a genre, and behind these questions may be glimpsed the larger problem of our usual distinction between fiction and nonfiction. A reader equally interested in biography and literary theory will come to see the debates of the recent past in a curious light: what is usually assumed to have been a straightforward advance in the theory of interpretation now appears as a more complicated maneuver designed to avoid, in the interests of general strategy, the positions so formidably occupied by biography and factual narrative generally. To view *Tom Jones* and *Hamlet* and *Paradise Lost* as self-contained worlds of motive and action is now both comfortable and orthodox. To approach the *Life of Johnson* or *The Decline and Fall of the Roman Empire* in the same way is neither.

The emergence of modern critical theory provides a background against which our normal distinction between factual and imaginative literature appears as something of an anomaly. It is when we attempt to explain the anomaly that Boswell assumes a special importance, for the history of Boswell criticism in the modern period is in one sense the history of a general effort to come to terms with a categoric distinction going back at least as far as Aristotle. In preferring poetry to history in the *Poetics,* and thereby implying that the real and the imaginary present antagonistic claims, Aristotle was taking for granted something which only now begins to appear in the light of a dilemma. The reluctance of a modern critic to approach the *Life of Johnson* as he would approach *King Lear* or *Paradise Lost* may be explained in Aristotelian terms: behind the *Life,* he feels, lurks the presence of a "real" Samuel Johnson who, because he once existed in historical reality, does not belong entirely to the world of the literary imagination.

The question of whether the *Life of Johnson* may be approached as a literary work is in this context a question of whether Johnson as he exists in the pages of the *Life* is a hero in the sense that Hamlet or Lear are heroes, one whom we must dissociate from the historical Johnson in much the way we dissociate Shakespeare's Richard II from Richard II of England. From a purely theoretical viewpoint, the same question may be put in broader terms, not as a question of whether the two Johnsons do not to some degree correspond but whether a certain type of meaning in the *Life,* a meaning we usually consider valuable and worthwhile, becomes accessible only when we make some such distinction. Such questions reveal the sense in which our normal conception of biography stands in an anomalous relation to modern criticism.

At the same time, as the very terms in which we pose them suggest, modern theory has provided answers to questions like these. Even to speak of "two Johnsons," we will be told by the theorist, is to speak of two imaginary beings who exist on precisely the same plane of ideal reality. The argument here is a familiar one: the process through which one comes to know Boswell's Johnson is the process through which any reader comes to know any literary protagonist, from Odysseus to Leopold Bloom. Yet the "real" Johnson, though the process through which one comes to know him is somewhat different, is scarcely more substantial a creature, and when analyzed closely dissolves into the scattered evidence from which he has been constructed — Piozzi or Hawkins or Burney, letters or writings or gleanings, a voice heard in the *Rambler* or *Rasselas,* a visit during some scholarly holiday to the house in Gough Square.

From this perspective, literature and the version of reality we call "history" are equally provisional, and any defense of the distinction between factual and imaginative literature assumes the uncomfortable burden of showing why we should discriminate against one in the name of the other. Again we are dealing with a familiar theoretical argument, that to approach the *Life of Johnson* as literature is simply to regard it as belonging to a special realm of provisional reality, one created solely out of language. At the level of the individual work and at the level of relations among works — for example, among the *Life,* the *Tour to the Hebrides,* and the *Tour to Corsica* — this is a complete and autonomous realm, and if its truth is a provisional truth, so perhaps is any other. To speak of Boswell as narrator and Johnson as hero, to speak of Reynolds and Burke and Goldsmith as characters in a biographical story — all this is only to announce a concern for *literary* truth.

Modern criticism of Boswell, and of biography as a genre, has never really come to terms with this argument, for theory is only an embarrassment when we assume an essential antagonism between the factual and the imaginative. Yet there has been some uneasiness among critics of biography, and a tentative compromise: Aristotle's categories have disappeared, only to reemerge as what criticism now calls correspondence and coherence, correspondence being the relation of a written work to the world of historical fact, coherence the symbolic principle we recognize when we talk about its "meaning." Might not criticism, it has been asked, take the comfortable view that coherence is simply something a good biography manages to achieve even while it is giving us dates and names and places, something that leaves the impress of the artistic imagination on a lifeless mass of factual material? Such a view, if it were reasonable, would seem to avoid most of the problems raised by the old antagonism of art and history by seeing biography as a kind of synthesis of the two.

Unfortunately, this view merely preserves that antagonism in disguise, for under the names of coherence and correspondence we are still dealing with the concepts of the literary and the unliterary. This is why Boswell's role as a reporter of events has continued to trouble modern criticism, for whenever we make claims for Boswell's literary artistry by protesting that he was "more than" a reporter, we reveal a certain hidden assumption: the more "artistic" or "imaginative" Boswell was, the less will he appear as a mere transcriber of facts, a mere reporter. But then the contrary is true also: the more "objective" Boswell was, the more assiduous and accurate in getting down on paper what he actually saw and heard, the less will he appear artistic or imaginative. This, pushed to an extreme, would be to take the *Life of Johnson* as pure record, what we would get if we had been able to set a tape recorder in the corner of the drawing room at Bolt Court or Streatham.

This is in fact the way the nineteenth century looked at the *Life of Johnson,* and at Boswell as its creator. The twentieth-century reaction, and the beginning of the compromise with modern theory, may be dated from the discovery of the Malahide papers, which for the first time provided scholars with the actual materials Boswell used in writing the *Life of Johnson,* among them the notes from which he had recreated Johnson's conversation. Geoffrey Scott, the first editor of the Malahide papers, undertook the final refutation of the Boswell-as-stenographer view, basing his argument on an appeal to these notes: "*They are not written during the conversation, but . . . when he gets home, at the end of the day, or the next day.*"[1] Since the appearance of the Isham edition of the papers, Scott's argument has been repeated in virtually every piece of commentary on Boswell that could accommodate its reiteration, often with a barely-disguised air of triumph.

Scott's discovery was a momentous event in Boswell scholarship, and only the most careful survey of subsequent writing on Boswell will reveal the process through which his argument was gradually made to assume a burden of implication it was never meant to bear. For a time, at least, a way out of the impasse seemed clear: though we do not often let simple information about an author's habits of composition alter our total perception of his works, Boswell, transported by the magic of new evidence from the drawing room to his study, was now taken as the very symbol of the biographer as artist. Boswell in his study, in dressing gown and slippers and working from notes, was selecting and recalling rather than merely reporting: "Boswell generally knows his story something as a novelist does . . . It would be naive to suppose that his knowledge of subsequent events is not affecting his details meaningfully, to create a significant forward-straining tension."[2]

From tape recorder, in other words, to artist *manqué*. This is the approach that has dominated Boswell criticism in recent years, one represented at its most intelligent in W. K. Wimsatt's essay "The Fact Imagined." Wimsatt focuses on Boswell's selection of detail, in which he sees something not so very different from what we normally think of as the creative process: because life as Boswell experienced it was reconstituted in Boswell's imagination before he wrote, and because the imaginative act always lies behind the act of writing, we can trace in his narratives the transforming impulse that makes life into art. If we

1. Scott's argument, which originally appeared in volume 6 of the privately printed Isham edition, now appears more accessibly in "The Making of *The Life of Johnson* as shown in Boswell's First Notes," in *Twentieth Century Interpretations of Boswell's Life of Johnson,* ed. James L. Clifford (Englewood Cliffs, N.J.: Prentice-Hall, 1970). The sentence quoted is on page 33 of this volume.

2. Frederick A. Pottle, introduction to *Boswell's London Journal, 1762–1763,* ed. F. A. Pottle (New York: McGraw-Hill, 1950), p. 12.

are to claim Boswell's works as literature, we will find our justification "in the subtle ranges and conflicts which he manages, in his firmness of detail and purity of verbal style — in his general artistry as a journalist."[3] The solution is not unattractive, and only from the viewpoint of interpretive logic are we likely to notice that it leaves the question of correspondence unresolved: we are still talking about the way Boswell handled "real" experience.

If we take the path of recent Boswell criticism, we thus begin with something like the nineteenth-century notion of the *Life of Johnson* as pure biographical record, but we immediately add that "it is more than a biographical record, that it is a work of art."[4] The dilemma here is unhappily obvious: as long as we are assuming some crucial relationship between the *Life* and "objective" reality, all we can do is keep showing in newer and more ingenious ways that although Boswell was a reporter, he was in some mysterious sense "more than" a reporter. In a recent significant essay on Boswell and the problem of biography, Ralph W. Rader pursues this logic to its end, which is a purely affectivist posture. Rader does not argue for anything quite so simple as a *je ne sais quoi* which allows certain works of history and biography to qualify as literature, but some such view lies behind his observations on Boswell and Gibbon. Both the *Life of Johnson* and the *Decline and Fall* are works which have somehow "transcended" an unliterary category: "Such works become literature by transcending while fulfilling the usual purpose of history and biography, to provide true knowledge of the human past."[5]

In what follows, I should like to explore an alternative way out of this dilemma, one suggested by the theoretical arguments earlier presented in summary form. Art and history, coherence and correspondence, have from the viewpoint of modern theory

3. In *Hateful Contraries* (Lexington: University of Kentucky Press, 1965), p. 12.

4. Frank Brady, introduction to *Boswell's Life of Johnson,* ed. and abridged by Frank Brady (New York: Signet, 1968), p. 11.

5. Ralph W. Rader, "Literary Form in Factual Narrative: The Example of Boswell's *Johnson,*" in *Essays in Eighteenth-Century Biography,* ed. Philip B. Daghlian (Bloomington: Indiana University Press, 1968), p. 4.

been placed in false conflict: they are not qualities of biography but aspects in which biography can be seen, in much the same way as we can look at a Greek vase both as an expression of man's visual imagination and as a thing for carrying water. The consequences are obvious: to read the *Life of Johnson* as literature is only to begin where all criticism must begin, with a controlling awareness of its self-contained nature as a work of art — something that is in no way inconsistent with its being simultaneously a repository of facts about the "real" Samuel Johnson. If one discovers, as Strabo did, that Homer tells us a good deal about the geography of the ancient Mediterranean, that does not make the *Iliad* and the *Odyssey* chiefly valuable as geography texts.

In the context of modern criticism as a whole, a suggestion that one approach the *Life of Johnson* as a self-contained world of motive and action is very nearly orthodox: literary critics are after all no longer much interested in discussing such questions as whether Shakespeare adequately represented the "real" — that is, the historical — Macbeth. Yet the strategic maneuver that carried literary theory around and past the strongly-held position occupied by "factual" narrative also isolated modern readers with a serious interest in biography. It is easy enough to maintain, from a purely theoretical viewpoint, that the problem of biography will not be resolved until scholars and critics have learned to recognize as meaningful a mode of argument about the *Life of Johnson* that makes no reference to any "real" Boswell, any "real" Johnson, but a question remains about the direction in which this leads us.

If one looks backward, the path seems somehow comfortless: a solid world of presumed actuality recedes, and one is left with the *Life of Johnson* and two other biographical narratives written by James Boswell. The theorist's assurance that the *Life* or the *Tour to the Hebrides* represent worlds in themselves seems to offer little enough comfort at such a moment, and one may recover a sense of the dismay that once greeted the concept of autonomy as applied to the genres of imaginative literature. At the same time, one is reminded of how that dismay eventually gave way before the discovery that literature may be

meaningfully viewed as an autonomous realm, that interpretation at the level of relations among works may approach a poem
or play or novel as belonging, if not to the world of everyday
reality, to the universe of literature perceived as a simultaneous
order. Here, perhaps, is the comfort one seeks: if we have left
behind a situation where comparison of Boswellian narrative
with "objective" reality tells us little, we have entered a realm
where comparison with the *Odyssey* or eighteenth-century com-
edy may tell us everything.

Seen in this light, biography in general and Boswellian narrative in particular appear in a new focus: one is aware not only
of possible solutions to old problems, but of new problems —
problems in literary and symbolic meaning — which need solv-
ing. As the present argument is concerned not simply with the
meaning of Boswell's works but with the tradition of Boswell
criticism and criticism of biography, we may perhaps take for
purposes of demonstration the problem, something of a crux
in Boswell scholarship, of Boswell as biographical narrator. It
is not only that the question of Boswell's role as narrator of his
own works is problematic precisely as the status of biography
has remained problematic — indeed, one reads in its successive
formulations the history of Boswell criticism writ small — but
that its resolution along the lines suggested here requires that
we approach biography, and not simply Boswell's contributions
to the genre, in a new way.

In the nineteenth century, of course, the problem was not
perceived as a problem: Boswell as he appeared in his works
was Boswell, and any suggestion that one inquire about the
"meaning" of his role as narrator would have met with polite
incredulity. In this context, Macaulay's picture of Boswell as an
inspired idiot who managed to write a great work precisely
because of his assiduous sycophancy could be taken as con-
clusive. In less vitriolic form, the same reaction can be found
among Boswell's contemporaries. Let us take as our text Thomas
Gray's comment, well-known to Boswellians, on the *Tour to
Corsica:* "Mr. Boswell's book . . . has pleased and moved me
strangely, all (I mean) that relates to Paoli. He is a man born
two thousand years after his time! The pamphlet proves what
I have always maintained, that any fool may write a most valu-

able book by chance, if he will only tell us what he saw and heard with veracity. Of Mr. Boswell's truth I have not the least suspicion, because I am sure he could invent nothing of this kind. The true title of this part of his work is, 'A Dialogue Between a Green-goose and a Hero.' "[6]

Even when we suspend questions about any "real" Boswell, we shall see that certain elements of Gray's description remain surprisingly suggestive, especially his awareness that Boswell's narrative is simultaneously concerned with an impression of complete veracity and with the hero as a figure existing spiritually outside his own age. At the same time, any suspension of the usual questions leads, as we have seen, to a consideration of the *Tour to Corsica* as a self-contained world, and eventually, because the *Tour* belongs to a more general tradition of biographical narrative, to a search for the internal or symbolic principles controlling biography as a literary genre. This is the context, long since explored elsewhere in modern criticism, in which a concern with one or two or three works moves irresistibly towards a perception of literature as composing a simultaneous order.

The problem of Boswell's role as narrator is in this sense a problem in literary conventions, if by conventions we mean the symbolic principles governing literary forms. The nature of the problem thus invites us to consider not the role of the narrator in biography merely, but of a narrator always seen in relation to some biographical hero, for only within the symbolic dimensions of this essential relationship do we discover the conventions that allow us to meaningfully discuss biography as a narrative mode. The dim beginnings of this mode, as Arnaldo Momigliano has pointed out in *The Development of Greek Biography,* are to be found in the *bios* of the hero, a form of "mythical biography" which concerned the lives of such heroes as Heracles, Theseus, and Oedipus.[7] No example of these *bioi* exists today — Momigliano is working by careful and delicate inference from fragmentary materials — but the form adduced

6. Gray made these remarks in a letter to Horace Walpole, February 25, 1768. See *Horace Walpole's Correspondence,* ed. W. S. Lewis and others (New Haven: Yale University Press, 1937–), XIV, 174.
7. (Cambridge: Harvard University Press, 1971), pp. 24–25.

suggests much about the conventions of later biographical narrative.

If we concentrate for the moment on the figure of the hero, we may perceive in the *bios* form (I use this as shorthand for "*bios* of the hero") a symbolic paradigm which was to serve as well for the medieval saint or the great man of the eighteenth and nineteenth centuries as for Heracles or Theseus, and which answers a number of troublesome questions about biographies we are accustomed to regard as classics. For the mode of mythical biography described by Momigliano would in one crucial aspect have resembled epic, positing the existence of an unseen world behind the visible one and giving us the hero as Victor Brombert describes him: "God, demigod, or intimate with the gods, he provided a transcendental link between the contingencies of the finite and the imagined realm of the supernatural. Time and the timeless, man's mortal state and the realm of eternal laws, were brought through him into conflict with each other. Through him also these orders overlapped."[8]

The hero in this situation is a symbolic figure in part because most men, including the narrator and readers of his story, are not heroes — as ordinary beings, they look through the hero to an unseen world whose existence is normally a matter of faith or belief. Though this does not in itself explain the symbolic structure of all biographies, it is at least evident that something like the *bios* principle is at work in widely varying forms of biographical literature. This is why, for instance, when Plato and Xenophon tell us about the *daimon* of Socrates, we are no longer dealing with Socrates merely as a philosopher but as a philosopher-hero divinely possessed. For similar reasons, Plutarch's description of the supernatural happenings following Caesar's death — "the great comet, which shone very bright for seven nights after Caesar's death, and then disappeared, and the dimness of the sun, which remained pale and dull for the whole of that year" — unavoidably reminds us of the events surrounding Christ's death in the Gospels, and both dramatize the hero's participation in an unseen world.

8. Introduction to *The Hero in Literature,* ed. Victor Brombert (Greenwich, Conn.: Fawcett Publications, 1969), p. 11.

Ancient biography, written in an age when the gods still spoke through oracles, drew unself-consciously on the elaborate mythologies that survive in Homer and Virgil. In the Christian era, we discover an obvious version of the *bios* form in the medieval saint's life, where the unseen world always appears as a providential presence interfering miraculously on behalf of a religious hero or heroine. After the Renaissance, as the idea of an unseen external order gradually gave way to an inner order of subjective and intense experience inaccessible to ordinary men, the hero of the *bios* form became the hero as Carlyle would describe him in the nineteenth century, one "who lives in the inward sphere of things, in the True, Divine, and Eternal." Thus Southey's Nelson, standing on his deck in a moment of "prophetic glory" — "from that time, he often said, a radiant orb was suspended in his mind's eye, which urged him onward to renown" — is as much in contact with an unseen world as Theseus or Heracles, and thus Norman Malcolm's recent *Memoir* of Wittgenstein is able to portray a philosopher-hero as much possessed by a *daimon* as Socrates.

When we search for symbolic continuities in the tradition of English biography to which Boswellian narrative belongs, we may trace the beginnings of the long transition from medieval to modern back to Roper's *Life of More,* a sixteenth-century narrative which, even as it portrays More as a complex figure living uneasily in a Machiavellian world of power and intrigue, possesses strong affinities with the saint's life. In the seventeenth century, amid a growing stream of biographical writing, Walton's *Lives* look back over two centuries to both the *bios* form and the hagiographic tradition. Both Roper and Walton, unable to portray their heroes as figures participating directly in an unseen order, shift their emphasis to the almost supernatural piety of the hero; yet strong evidences of the miraculous remain, giving us in Roper such scenes as that in which More's prayers rescue his dying daughter — "God showed, as it seemed, a manifest miraculous token of his special favor towards him" — and in Walton such episodes as Donne's mysterious vision of his absent wife and daughter.

At the same time, the symbolic relation of the hero to an

unseen or divine world had become problematic for biographers in the *bios* tradition. Writing at the dawn of the age of the Royal Society, Walton is compelled to undertake an anxious defense of his own credibility, as when he addresses his audience after giving an account of Donne's miraculous vision: "If the unbelieving will not allow the believing reader of this story a liberty to believe that it may be true, then I wish him to consider, many wise men have believed that the ghost of Julius Caesar did appear to Brutus, and that both St. Austin, and Monica his mother, had visions in order to his conversion." As Walton's anxieties suggest, the *bios* in its traditional form was becoming untenable in a climate of thought soon to come under the influence of Newton's *Principia* and Locke's *Essay on Human Understanding,* for a narrator can scarcely look beyond his hero to an unseen world when the unseen world, at least as a miraculous or mysterious presence, has ceased to exist.

By the time Boswell began writing biographical narrative a century later, in an age increasingly troubled by the powerful scepticism of the Enlightenment, only some compromise with the phenomenon of unbelief would leave the biographer free to continue working in the *bios* tradition. Boswell was not only to achieve this compromise but also to discover within its context a new kind of biographical hero, a figure standing in solitary opposition to the Enlightenment as represented by such *philosophes* as Hume and Voltaire and Holbach, an age of moral chaos and revolutionary tendencies in which men, to borrow Burke's phrase, had shrunk from their natural dimensions. To fully understand the nature of Boswell's compromise, however, one must turn from the role of the hero in the *bios* form to the role of the narrator, and to what might be called the symbolic dimension of the relationship between them.

The narrator and hero of the *bios* tradition are coordinate figures, for as the hero is an extraordinary being participating in a world invisible to ordinary men, the narrator is a spokesman for the ordinary world, and his role is symbolic in a sense well described by Thomas Edwards: the ordinary man, says Edwards, "is, like 'the hero,' a fiction . . . The normal has meaning only in reference to the abnormal, the unexpected phenomenon that creates an opposing sense of mutuality where none was apparent before."[9] In its simplest form, the coordinate relation of narrator and hero demands only the implied notion of ordinariness we find in ancient biography, where the narrator as in Plutarch or Nepos exists outside the story he is telling, or in the medieval saint's life, where the hero is identified with a divine world of grace and miracles and the narrator is identified with unredeemed mankind.

In English biography, we may again turn to Roper's *Life of More* and Walton's *Lives* as reflecting changes in the *bios* form in the two centuries before Boswell. As biographical narrators, both Roper and Walton bear a strong resemblance to the anonymous storytellers of the saints' lives, though in the more personal context of their narratives the narrator's identification with unredeemed mankind is replaced by a sense of unworthiness in relation to their heroes, as when Roper represents himself as "most unworthy" to tell More's story, Walton as "the poorest, the meanest" of Donne's friends. At the same time, the Renaissance saw an important change in the *bios* form, for in Roper we have for the first time in English biography a narrator who has eaten and talked and joked with the hero. And in Roper's recollections of his conversations with More — "so on a time walking with me along the Thames side at Chelsea, in talking of other things he said unto me" — we discover the beginnings of an altered biographical tradition leading to the *Life of Johnson.*

Once more we are dealing with the symbolic dimensions of the narrator–hero relationship central to the *bios* form, and now with the narrator in a new and vulnerable situation. For when intimacy with the hero is introduced as a narrative principle in biography, both narrator and hero exist within the confines of a single dramatic situation, and the moral superiority separating the hero from ordinary mankind appears specifically as superiority to the narrator. The great danger, of course, is that the symbolic or representative dimension of his "ordinariness" will simply collapse, and that he will emerge as a prosaic and credulous speaker whose estimate of the hero's greatness fails to win our assent. The way in which Roper and Walton moved

9. *Imagination and Power* (New York: Oxford University Press, 1971), p. 9.

to circumvent this danger returns us to the problem of veracity raised in Gray's comments on the *Tour to Corsica.*

In one important sense, we may say that Roper, Walton, and Boswell reached identical solutions to the problem of veracity, the illusion of purely factual truth that, along with other things, defines biography as a narrative genre. An awareness of the problem moves Roper in the *Life of More* to assume a posture where a certain artlessness or naiveté becomes a guarantee of fidelity, as is evident even in the way he speaks of his role as narrator of More's story: "I have as far forth as my mean wit, memory, and knowledge would serve me, declared so much thereof as in my poor judgement seemed worthy to be remembered." A century later we encounter Walton's "artless pencil, guided by the hand of truth" — this same artlessness, he assures us, "ought to beget faith in what is spoken: for he that wants skill to deceive may safely be trusted" — and a motif of conscious naiveté that runs throughout the *Lives.*

Our search for symbolic continuities in the *bios* tradition thus brings us not only to the emergence of the naive narrator in such works as the *Life of More* and Walton's *Lives,* but to a point where we may perceive the odd suggestiveness of one of Gray's comments on the *Tour to Corsica:* "Of Mr. Boswell's truth I have not the least suspicion, because I am sure he could invent nothing of this kind." In Boswell's version of the *bios* form the naiveté of the storyteller operates, as in Roper and Walton, as a guarantee of truthfulness, but something essential — moral sympathy for the narrator in relation to the hero — has clearly been lost. The compromise through which Boswell won the freedom to work within the *bios* tradition may thus be seen to underlie the central paradox of Boswell's biographical narratives — that they reveal Pascal Paoli and Samuel Johnson to be genuine moral heroes even as Boswell, in his veneration of them, seems somehow foolish and excessive.

A consideration of the *bios* tradition in English biography, then, allows us not only to isolate this paradox in its formal or conventional aspect, but to attempt to explain its meaning through examination of the symbolic structure of Boswellian narrative. To this we must now turn, with one final observation on the evolution of the *bios* form: though Roper and Walton discovered in the naive or artless narrator an important solution to a difficult formal problem, they did so while remaining within the comparatively safe bounds of the hagiographic tradition, and managed to write a kind of biography still sustained by a notion of the hero's participation in a divine and coherent order. As the artlessness of a biographical narrator appears in this context as an aspect of his unworthiness, and as this unworthiness merely identifies him with unredeemed mankind, his naiveté and simplicity appear attractive and even virtuous qualities. In the secular, low-mimetic world of Boswellian narrative no such universal standard of human unworthiness exists, and naiveté is seen not as virtuous simplicity but as — naiveté. This was Boswell's compromise.

There is a certain poignancy in Boswell's attempts to draw attention, during his own lifetime, to what we should call the modern distinction between author and narrator, as when in the dedication to the *Life of Johnson* he writes in defense of certain scenes in the earlier *Tour to the Hebrides* which had shown him among the victims of Johnson's wit: "I trusted I should be liberally understood, as knowing very well what I was about, and by no means as simply unconscious of the pointed effects of the satire. I own, indeed, that I was arrogant enough to suppose that the tenour of the rest of the book would sufficiently guard me against such a strange imputation." Boswell's protests, overwhelmed by the powerful illusion of actuality we have seen to be associated with the naive narrator of the *bios* tradition, were to have little effect: for Macaulay, describing Boswell as an inspired idiot who had managed to write a great book, and for Gray, describing one Boswellian narrative as "a dialogue between a green-goose and a hero," the naive narrator and the biographer were indistinguishable figures. As they concern the symbolic structure of Boswellian narrative, however, such remarks serve to locate Boswell as a biographical narrator in the formal tradition of the *naif* or *ingénu,* and as belonging to a literary family extending back through Chaucer in the *Canterbury Tales* and Dante in the *Commedia* to ancient literature. It is from this perspective, for instance, that we hear John Lockhart, the great nineteenth-century bi-

ographer of Walter Scott, describing Boswell's role as narrator
in terms which remind us of a modern critic discussing Lemuel
Gulliver: "Never did any man tell a story with such liveliness
and fidelity, and yet contrive to leave so strong an impression
that he did not himself understand it . . . unconscious all the
while, of the real gist and bearing of the facts he is relating."[10]
Only Lockhart's assumptions about biography, which are
roughly the assumptions of Gray and Macaulay, convert so
promising an insight into a matter of perplexity.

At the same time, one may discover traces of these same
assumptions in modern Boswell criticism, and along with them
an underlying tension in discussions of Boswell's role as narrator. It is today a commonplace of Boswell criticism, for instance, to describe Boswell as an Everyman figure, and to
discover in the description a double significance. When under-
taken in the interests of literary interpretation, as in Paul Al-
kon's fine essay on aesthetic distance in the *Life of Johnson*[11] or
in Frank Brady's enlightening discussion of Boswell's manner
of self-presentation,[12] the description normally refers to some
aspect of what we have called the symbolic "ordinariness" of
the narrator in the *bios* tradition. More often, however, the
description is merely honorific, a twentieth-century reaction
against Macaulay's estimate of Boswell operating on nineteenth-
century assumptions, where to see Boswell as Everyman is to
see him as someone very much like the rest of us, and not
(unless we are all idiots) as the inspired idiot Macaulay described.

Any inquiry into the meaning of Boswell's role as narrator
will lead away from this kind of reasoning, and towards a fuller
consideration of the relationship between narrator and hero in
Boswell's three major biographical narratives. Here, as with
the figure of the naive narrator, Boswell found freedom through
compromise: writing in an age when the hero's participation
in an unseen world was no longer credible, and when the no-

10. Quoted in Joseph W. Reed, *English Biography in the Early Nineteenth Century* (New Haven: Yale University Press, 1966), p. 6
11. "Boswell's Control of Aesthetic Distance," *UTQ*, 38 (January
1969), 174–191.
12. In "Boswell's Self-Presentation and His Critics," *SEL*, 12 (Summer 1972), 545–555, Brady specifically describes Boswell as an *"ingénu."*

tion of a heroic inner world of subjective experience had not altogether emerged, Boswell managed to create a version of the *bios* form by portraying his heroes as figures living outside their time, existing within a private order of the moral imagination looking back to an idea of spiritual coherence associated with an earlier age. The subject of Boswellian narrative is in this sense the hero in an unheroic world, and such men as Paoli and Samuel Johnson appear in it as isolated beings in a time that, in Carlyle's phrase, denies the desirableness of great men.[13]

When we consider the symbolic structure of Boswell's narratives, then, we are dealing with the relation of the narrator as *naif* to the figure of the isolated hero. Thus the *Tour to Corsica,* which is sometimes described as Plutarchan, actually belongs in the *bios* category, for as it concerns Boswell the *Tour* is the story of an impressionable young man suddenly confronted with a hero who lives in the inward sphere of things, and gives us our earliest example of the Boswellian narrator, a speaker who looks through the hero not to an unseen world but to the possibility of an order of coherence unperceived by ordinary men. This is a symbolic situation retaining an element of the miraculous, though Boswell is sufficiently uneasy about relating such stories as that concerning Paoli's mysterious visions of future events, "knowing how much may be ridiculed in an age when mankind are so fond of incredulity that they seem to pique themselves in contracting their circle of belief as much as possible."[14] Paoli appears in the *Tour* as a hero in the Plutarchan mold, but only because Boswell's "naive" perception of the world provides an expanded circle of belief impervious to modern scepticism.

In the *Tour to the Hebrides,* where Samuel Johnson appears as a philosopher–hero traveling through a primitive world of ruined cathedrals and decaying castles, Boswell's role is in one sense purely normative, for he represents the ordinary traveler whose response to Highland scenes becomes the measure of Johnson's deeper and more contemplative response. Yet the

13. See my essay "The Boswellian Hero," *SSL,* 10 (October 1972), 79–93.
14. *Boswell on the Grand Tour: Italy, Corsica, and France,* ed. Frank Brady and F. A. Pottle (London: Heinemann, 1955), p. 194.

Tour is in a larger sense about Johnson's discovery of a forgotten world of faith and heroic endeavor, and the major theme
of the narrative may be seen as deriving from Boswell's naiveté,
which here takes the form of a romantic enthusiasm for memories of the Highland past, as when he describes his response
to the rebellion of '45: "The very Highland names, or the
sound of a bagpipe, will stir my blood, and fill me with a mix-
ture of melancholy and respect for courage . . . in short, with a
crowd of sensations with which sober rationality has nothing
to do."[15]

Throughout the *Tour,* Boswell's naive and emotional response
runs as a counterpoint to Johnson's more sober rationality,
supplying the symbolic perspective through which we come to
understand the meaning of Johnson's discovery of the heroic
past in relation to his spiritual dilemma as a hero isolated in
the modern age. At the beginning of the story, Boswell draws a
sketch of his own character which suggests both the normative
and the *ingénu* aspects of his role as narrator: "He had thought
more than any body supposed, and had a pretty good stock
of general learning and knowledge. He had all Dr. Johnson's
principles, with some degree of relaxation. He had rather too
little, than too much prudence; and, his imagination being lively,
he often said things of which the effect was very different from
the intention" (V, 52). This Boswell is similar to the one who
speaks to us in the *Tour to Corsica,* a young and ingenuous
narrator whose voice is in one aspect the voice of ordinary
mankind in relation to the extraordinary man, in another the
voice of a *naif* unconscious of living in an age that denies the
desirableness of great men.

In the *Life of Johnson,* where Johnson appears as a hero
isolated from his society and age, Boswell's role as a normative
figure is more complicated. In one aspect, for instance, the *Life*
contains a *Citizen of the World* motif, for Boswell tells his
biographical story as a Scotsman viewing English society from
the outside, and discovering a disturbing configuration of events

15. All parenthetical references to the *Tour to the Hebrides* and the
Life of Johnson are to the Hill-Powell edition: *The Life of Johnson,* ed.
G. B. Hill, rev. L. F. Powell, 6 vols. (Oxford: Oxford University Press,
1934–1964). This passage occurs in vol. V, p. 140.

and impulses that confirms his idea of Johnson as a moral hero. In the same way, Boswell coming down from Edinburgh on his annual excursion to London resembles a provincial visitor to ancient Rome, for England represents for him not a country merely but a cultural and imaginative ideal, and it is with this — the England of Shakespeare and Milton and Magna Carta — that he identifies Samuel Johnson. This symbolic perspective allows us to see Johnson as a hero whose orthodoxy and Tory-ism belong to a private realm of embattled faith, and whose periods of melancholy and despair represent the spiritual paraly-sis of a mind for which the illusion of coherence has tempo-rarily failed.

Once again, our perception of Johnson as hero of the *Life* derives from what we have been calling Boswell's naiveté, in this case an impulse toward veneration that transforms ordinary scenes into symbolic episodes and reminds us of the earlier hero in the *bios* tradition: "the orthodox high-church sound of the MITRE, — the figure and manner of the celebrated SAMUEL JOHNSON, — the extraordinary power and precision of his con-versation, and the pride arising from finding myself admitted as his companion, produced . . . a pleasing elevation of mind be-yond what I had ever before experienced" (I, 401). At such moments, ordinary reality is replaced by something more mys-terious, for Boswell speaks as a narrator who has found an actual great man existing within the improbable confines of eighteenth-century London, and who discovers within the magic circle of his presence a moral certainty belonging to an earlier age.

When we consider symbolic structure in Boswell's three major biographical narratives, then, we are simultaneously consider-ing the phenomenon of scepticism or unbelief as possessing a double significance in the opposing worlds of narrator and hero. In portraying Paoli and Johnson as figures existing out of their time, Boswell creates around his heroes a private world of the moral imagination in which the rational scepticism we associate with the Enlightenment, the noble and emancipating weapon of the *philosophes,* is seen in the dark and pessimistic light in which Carlyle would describe it in the early nineteenth century: "not intellectual doubt alone, but moral doubt; all sorts of infidelity, insincerity, spiritual paralysis." This is, as Carlyle saw, the spiritual paralysis of an age that denies the very possibility of heroism.

In Paoli's identification with the heroes of antiquity, or in Johnson's Toryism and orthodoxy and monarchial principles, we thus have a notion of the past as spiritual refuge, and a concept of the hero as an isolated figure surrounded by invisible forces of moral anarchy. This is why the eighteenth century as portrayed in Boswell's narratives appears always in a double perspective. As a world of ordinary men with ordinary concerns, it is the busy, optimistic, confident world of the *philosophes,* the secular, low-mimetic realm of Fielding or Smollett or the comic scenes in the *Life of Johnson.* Within the larger circumference of this world, however, exists the separate world of Boswell's heroes, and it is as we gaze through one to the other that we perceive the age in its darker aspect, as a time when "old opinions, feelings — ancestral customs and institutions are crumbling away, and both the spiritual and temporal worlds are darkened by the shadow of change."[16]

Yet Boswell as a narrator in the *bios* tradition belongs not to the separate spiritual and imaginative world of his heroes but to the ordinary world beyond its perimeters — the eighteenth century of London shopkeepers, country squires, pamphleteers and freethinkers and *philosophes.* In this symbolic situation lies the meaning of what we have called the paradox of Boswellian narrative, for as a narrator representing ordinary mankind Boswell appears in his own works as a creature of the world he portrays, a speaker wholly subject — as his heroes are not — to the norms of his society and age. In this world, which is the world of Enlightenment rationalism, scepticism is the ironic detachment of Hume or Gibbon or Voltaire, an intellectual attitude that smiles at veneration and mocks enthusiasm, and makes a *naif* of the biographer whose temper does not answer to its own.

If we see Paoli and Johnson as heroes living in an unheroic world, maintaining their private visions of coherence in an age

16. The phrase is from Edward Bulwer Lytton's *England and the English,* quoted in Walter E. Houghton, *The Victorian Frame of Mind* (New Haven: Yale University Press, 1957), p. 2.

of spiritual crisis, we see Boswell as a narrator whose preoccupation with great men is part of his own struggle to discover faith and order amid the moral disarray of the later eighteenth century. This is the final meaning of Boswell's naiveté, for when belief in a transcendant order is universal, men fall down before Poseidon or worship Christ as a matter of course, and excesses of awe or veneration are not excesses. When coherence has disappeared, we have the detached scepticism of Hume or Gibbon or, in biography, of Lytton Strachey. But in a period of transition — the eighteenth century as portrayed by Boswell or Burke, the nineteenth as seen by Arnold or Yeats — the Everyman narrator of the *bios* form is himself an odd and inconsistent figure, a *naif* as out of place in the modern age as his heroes are, but on the ordinary or comic level, and unable to sacrifice his veneration of great men to a bleak ethic of ironic detachment.

When we approach such works as the *Tour to Corsica* and the *Life of Johnson* as self-contained worlds of image and speech and action, we thus arrive at something like the perspective that has allowed modern criticism, in its moments of genuine insight, to bring into our possession a kind of meaning belonging to literature alone. This is the context in which the problem of Boswell's role as biographical narrator may be taken to represent the problem of biography, and of the rich tradition of nonfictional narrative that remains to be explored by scholars interested primarily in its literary or symbolic meaning, only incidentally in its representation of such dates and names and other data as we take to be historical facts. "The critic's function," Northrop Frye has said, "is to interpret every work of literature in the light of all the literature he knows, to keep constantly struggling to understand what literature as a whole is about." The struggle becomes worthier when we include in what we mean by literature the works we call biographies.

KENNETH MARC HARRIS

Transcendental Biography: Carlyle and Emerson

Carlyle and Emerson were biographers before they were trans-
cendentalists. Carlyle served his apprenticeship writing unsigned
encyclopedia articles, mostly on biographical subjects, and published a *Life of Schiller* several years before he began to write
Sartor Resartus. Emerson's taste for biography dates back to a
childhood love of Plutarch, and he delivered a series of biographical lectures the year before he completed *Nature* (1836).
Both remained biographers all their lives. Carlyle lost his
health and much of his effectiveness as a writer during the
dozen years before 1865 when he labored on his mammoth
biography of Frederick the Great. Emerson's last public reading
was probably the talk on Carlyle he gave in February 1881, a
few days after his friend's death and some fifteen months before
his own.

After the heyday of transcendentalism in the 1830s, Carlyle
and Emerson renewed their interest in biography and history,
almost as if the comforts of historical certainty compensated
for the hazards of metaphysical speculation. In the great works
of their youth, *Sartor Resartus* and *Nature,* they had struggled
with the final questions beyond life and death — "whence?"
and "whither?" — without discovering any satisfactory solution:
there were no answers to these questions or, what amounts to

the same thing, the answers, like the questions, seemed to them nothing more than so many words. Words had meaning only as a part of human life, and only in the course of human life could such questions be meaningfully asked and answered.

Carlyle, who already had abandoned transcendentalism by the time he and Emerson met in Scotland in 1833, grew increasingly impatient with the latter's speculative writings, which he regarded as evidence of spiritual isolation at best and at worst mere moonshine. "You *tell* us with piercing emphasis that man's soul is great," he wrote Emerson in 1839, after reading the Divinity School Address, "*shew* us a great soul of a man, in some work symbolic of such: this is the seal of such a message, and you will feel by and by that you are called to this."[1] Carlyle himself felt the call to preach about great souls the very next year with his lecture series *On Heroes, Hero-Worship, and the Heroic in History* (pub. 1841). Emerson got the message, but several years passed before he let Carlyle know, in part because he wanted to avoid looking like another man's disciple. In the winter of 1845–46 Emerson also lectured on great men, but he waited until he had given part of the series in England during his second European tour before publishing the lectures in 1850. *Representative Men* in effect endorses Carlyle's claim that biography must supersede transcendentalism, or, as Emerson put it, "the questions of Whence? What? and Whither? and the solution of these must be in a life, and not in a book."[2] This declaration appears in the chapter on Swedenborg, whose ideas a decade earlier had inspired Emerson the transcendentalist.

"Transcendental biography" is not a very satisfying description of *Heroes and Hero-Worship* and *Representative Men,* and not only because of the difficulty of knowing how much the authors were still influenced by transcendentalism when they wrote those books. They were Men of Ideas as well as Men of Letters, but they were never ideologues, and there is no reason to interpret their biographical and historical writings as illustrations of abstract concepts or theories, whether transcendental

    1. Joseph Slater, ed., *The Correspondence of Emerson and Carlyle* (New York: Columbia University Press, 1964), p. 215.
    2. *The Works of Ralph Waldo Emerson,* Centenary Edition, IV, 94.

or of some other variety. As biographers, they had a genuine interest in the people about whom they chose to write, and in their better work they displayed the knack of all skillful biographers to make their subjects "come alive." Their philosophical ideas and attitudes acted as undercurrents, creating waves but rarely breaking the surface.

Some efforts to differentiate the biographical practices of the two writers are plausible enough but shallow and misleading. Thoreau, who regarded Carlyle and Emerson as "the complement of each other," distinguished Carlyle's sympathy with "men of action" from Emerson's preference for "thinkers."[3] Thoreau's "broad and rude distinction" is obviously right and obviously wrong; both authors wrote about both active and contemplative subjects. Another distinction, of greater depth but more misleading, contrasts the two men politically, opposing Emerson's "democratic cult of greatness" (to borrow a phrase from Stephen Whicher) to Carlyle's attitude, which is usually, though not invariably, considered more elitist or authoritarian. The political biases of biographers necessarily color their work, especially with portraits of "great men," but the main concern of good biography is a particular person, and not politics.

In any case we should resist the temptation to use protean words like "democracy" and "equality" as shibboleths to divide instantly and permanently one writer from the other. The egalitarianism of *Representative Men* is most explicit in the final part of the opening chapter, "Uses of Great Men," where Emerson questions the value of great men vis-à-vis "the masses." If Emerson is responding directly to Carlyle's book, which seems likely, he is attacking hero worship rather than heroism. "Why are the masses," he asks, "from the dawn of history down, food for knives and powder? The idea dignifies a few leaders . . . but what for the wretches whom they hire and kill?" His answer rejects the notion that most people are inferior to some people: "There are no common men. All men are at last of a size . . . Ask the great man if there be none greater. His companions are." History itself becomes "democratic," the col-

3. Henry David Thoreau, "Thomas Carlyle," in *The Works of Thoreau*, Walden Edition, IV, 345–346.

lective achievement of all, not the accomplishments of a few. "The genius of humanity is the real subject whose biography is written in our annals."[4]

Heroes and Hero-Worship offers a different theory of history. "Universal History," Carlyle explains in his opening lecture, "is at bottom the History of the Great Men who have worked here." Not only are Carlyle's heroes the "leaders" and "modellers" of the masses; they are even "in a wide sense creators of what soever the general mass of men contrived to do or to attain."[5] Carlyle seems to be on the other end of the scale from Emerson, but Emerson is capable of sounding precisely the same note. In "Self-Reliance" he equates "all history" with "the biography of a few stout and earnest persons."[6] And Carlyle, on the other hand, in the article "On History" (1830), proposes a definition of history fully in tune with Emerson's egalitarianism: "Social Life is the aggregate of all the individual men's Lives who constitute society; History is the essence of innumerable Biographies."[7] To confuse matters further, in *his* essay "History" Emerson advances the same conclusion: "There is properly no history, only biography."[8]

Much of the confusion among these clashing historical theories arises from imprecise terminology rather than from real contradiction. Philip Rosenberg's resolution of the dilemma for Carlyle is equally applicable to Emerson: "The idea that history should be the biography of great men and the idea that it should be the essence of the biographies 'of all the individual men . . . who constitute society' were alternative forms of the same truth."[9] The "elitist" Carlyle would no more characterize humanity as a mass of sheep with an occasional shepherd than would the "democratic" Emerson suggest that all should be chiefs and none should be braves. The titles of their books deserve much of the blame for such misconceptions. *Heroes and*

4. Emerson, *Works,* IV, 30–32.
5. *The Works of Thomas Carlyle,* Centenary Edition, V, 1.
6. Emerson, *Works,* II, 61.
7. Carlyle, *Works,* XXVII, 86.
8. Emerson, *Works,* II, 9–10.
9. Philip Rosenberg, *The Seventh Hero: Thomas Carlyle and the Theory of Radical Activism* (Cambridge: Harvard University Press, 1974), p. 193.

Hero-Worship is a particularly unfortunate title from a twentieth-century perspective. The words can easily conjure a hideous two-headed monstrosity, with some popular vision of Nietzsche's *Übermensch* facing down some repulsive Nazi fiction of an *Untermensch*. Carlyle had nothing of the sort in mind, nor did he even intend his two terms to be taken as antitheses. He wanted everyone to recognize and follow great men not for the glory of the hero but to overcome the paralysis of withdrawing into oneself. Hero worship, like heroism, was for Carlyle an expression of self-denial. The true hero was worthy of worship or emulation because of his greater self-denial. Hero and hero-worshipper were engaged in the same undertaking; their roles were mutually supportive and perhaps, as Rosenberg shrewdly suggests, even interchangeable in a sense.[10] Carlyle's hero might well agree with Emerson's great man that their "companions" are greater.

Emerson also encouraged emulation of great men, not in pursuit of self-denial but for the opposite purpose of self-aggrandizement. As he explained in *Representative Men,* because everyone is "self-defended," emulation of others will never lead to self-surrender; "you are you, and I am I, and so we remain."[11] Emerson's answer to hero-worship is implicit in the title of his opening chapter, "Uses of Great Men." The great man should be *used;* he is not worthy of being worshipped merely for his power, since the power he possesses, like the power anyone possesses, does not come from an act of the will. The great man does not even deserve the gratitude of those his "greatness" benefits, for "all mental and moral force . . . goes out from you, whether you will or not, and profits me whom you never thought of" (pp. 13–14). Neither great thoughts nor great actions are attributable to volition. "The power which they communicate is not theirs. When we are exalted by ideas, we do not owe this to Plato, but to the idea, to which also Plato was debtor" (p. 19). The words "representative men," especially in comparison with the title of Carlyle's book, sound very democratic, like the lower house of Congress, but democracy had little to do with the forces Emerson's representa-

10. Ibid., pp. 200–203.
11. Emerson, *Works,* IV, 28.

tive men actually represented. "He is great who is what he is from nature" (p. 6). In the same way, Carlyle's distaste for democracy had little to do with the heroism of his heroes or the reverence of the heroes' worshippers.

Emerson's determination to withhold from the great man the responsibility for his greatness clearly contradicts Carlyle, who was equally determined to award the hero the full credit for his heroism. In 1832 Carlyle wrote an article called "Biography," which was designed as part of an essay on Boswell's *Life of Johnson*. (The subject provided Carlyle with a unique opportunity for developing his biographical theories, since he regarded Johnson as a hero and Boswell as an illustration of the ennobling virtues of hero worship.) He commended the "poetic" aspect of biography for revealing the "struggle of human Freewill against material Necessity, which every man's Life, by the mere circumstance that the man continues alive, will more or less victoriously exhibit." Rather than "use" great men in Emerson's sense of a direct transfer of assets, Carlyle's "earnest Lover of Biography" drew inspiration from the great man's example in order to "expand himself on all sides, and indefinitely enrich himself."[12] Like the hero himself, the hero-worshipper must vitalize his own power, for he too must take part in the universal battle of "Freewill" against "Necessity."

Carlyle vehemently denied that the great man, or any man, acquires power from sources outside his will. In the first *Heroes* lecture he mocked those "critics" who, when shown a great man, "begin to what they call 'account' for him; not to worship him, but take the dimension of him." They make the hero a mere product of circumstances and conditions; they say that "the Time called him forth, the Time did everything, he nothing — but what we the little critic could have done too!"[13] The outside forces to which Emerson attributed human greatness are of course far loftier than the mechanical explanations ridiculed in Carlyle's diatribe, but a crucial distinction separates the two writers. Carlyle sought to preserve the great man's free will. Emerson gave all the credit to forces beyond human volition.

12. Carlyle, *Works,* XXVIII, 44–45.
13. Carlyle, *Works,* V, 12.

In actual practice, the distinction was not always discernible in the events of a subject's life or in the interpretation the biographer brought to those events. Neither man would superimpose theories onto realities. Emerson was quick to praise an act of courage; he could speak without hesitation of Martin Luther's "indomitable Will" in standing alone against the world. In "The Hero as Prophet," Carlyle solemnly defined the essence of Islam (and Christianity as well) as both "Denial of Self" and unquestioning submission to God or "Necessity," while in "The Hero as Poet" he described the great man as a "Force of Nature."[14] Carlyle and Emerson chose their language with care, but they felt no compulsion to use even their most significant terms with rigorous consistency from one work to the next. Ultimately, the true differences between them are best seen in their art, not in their philosophy, for it was in the actual process of narration, in a biographical piece, that each man revealed the true nature of his convictions. The biographical methods they chose reflected their beliefs more than the particular life stories they chose to record.

Carlyle always strove for identification with his subject, and the greater his sympathy, the more completely he tried to merge himself with his hero. Emerson maintained his detachment even when his passions were most aroused. Emerson's restraint can be observed in an early lecture on Luther, the best in the "Biography" series of 1835. Three years earlier, Emerson had thought of Luther when he resigned from the Second Church; after preaching his farewell sermon, he copied in his journal a paraphrase of Luther's defiant speech to the Diet of Worms.[15] (Unknown to Emerson, the unsigned article in *Fraser's Magazine* from which he borrowed was by Carlyle.) As he prepared his talk on Luther, he must have relived the day when he had nailed theses of his own to the church door, but a listener ignorant of Emerson's own history would scarcely suspect the extent of his emotional involvement with his subject:

> He deemed himself the conspicuous object of hatred to Satan and his kingdom, and to be sustained against their malice by

14. Ibid., pp. 56–57; p. 112.
15. Ralph L. Rusk, *The Life of Ralph Waldo Emerson* (New York: Columbia University Press, 1949), pp. 164–165.

special interpositions of God. This is the secret of his indomitable Will. No man in history ever assumed a more commanding attitude or expressed a more perfect self-reliance. His words are more than brave, they threaten and thunder. They indicate a Will on which a nation might lean, not liable to sullen sallies or swoons, but progressive as the motion of the earth.[16]

With an almost scientific objectivity, Emerson identified the sources of Luther's courage and the reasons for his ultimate victory. Luther's "perfect self-reliance" came from his trust in an external power that can raise nations and topple kingdoms. The perils Emerson faced in his battle of conscience were a little less awesome than the temporal and supernatural potentates confronting Luther, but in his isolation the young American preacher may have felt as great a need for sustenance as the young German monk. The spiritual bond Emerson felt with Luther can be seen in his quiet fervor.

Carlyle was also attracted to Luther. In 1830 he contemplated a full-length biography of him, though little came of it. In 1839 John Sterling's adulatory review article on Carlyle, which pleased its subject immensely, ended with an extended comparison of Carlyle and Luther. But Carlyle had not undergone a personal experience comparable to the crisis that led Emerson to draw consolation and strength from Luther's example; yet in "The Hero as Priest" his identification with Luther amounted to a virtual metamorphosis. At one point, without warning, the pronouns change their antecedents:

I, for one, pardon Luther for now altogether revolting against the Pope. The elegant Pagan, by this fire-decree of his, had kindled into noble just wrath the bravest heart then living in this world. The bravest, if also one of the humblest, peaceablest; it was now kindled. These words of mine, words of truth and soberness, aiming faithfully, as human inability would allow, to promote God's truth on Earth, and save men's souls, you, God's vicegerent on earth, answer them by the hangman and fire? You will burn me and them, for answer to the God's-

16. Stephen E. Whicher and Robert E. Spiller, eds., *The Early Lectures of Ralph Waldo Emerson* (Cambridge: Harvard University Press, 1959), I, 136.

message they strove to bring you? *You* are not God's vicegerent; you are another's than his, I think! I take your Bull, as an emparchmented Lie, and burn *it*. You will do what you see good next: this is what I do.[17]

Carlyle was an animated lecturer, especially when excited, and the audience must have found it rather unsettling to see the speaker, abruptly transformed into a fire-breathing Luther, upbraiding his listeners as though they had been transformed into the scarlet woman.

Emerson described how Luther's words "threaten and thunder"; Carlyle threatened and thundered. Emerson's Luther was sustained against his enemies; Carlyle's Luther took the Papal Bull and burned it. Emerson insisted on objectivity; Carlyle demanded intense emotional commitment.

The systematic objectivity of *Representative Men,* perhaps its outstanding quality, can be attributed to Emerson's dialectical approach to his subjects, which counters praise with detraction and in the end tries to "strike the balance" (as he puts it in the chapter on Shakespeare).[18] Perhaps he felt compelled to adopt so rigid a method in order to restrain his own impulse to identify with his heroes, and in this regard it may be significant that he omits Luther entirely. His procedure assures detachment and reinforces the message in the introduction that great men should be "used" and not worshipped, but it also demands that he cut his subjects down to size.

Writing to Emerson in 1850, shortly after the simultaneous English and American publication of the book, Carlyle offered his congratulations and hopes for its immediate success and praised the quality of the "portraitures." He "generally dissented," however, "a little about the *end* of all those Essays; which was notable, and not without instructive interest to me, as I had so lustily shouted 'Hear, hear!' all the way from the beginning up to that stage."[19] Since Emerson usually concentrated his negative judgments "a little about the end," we can guess the source of Carlyle's annoyance. It was not just a mat-

17. Carlyle, *Works,* V, 133.
18. Emerson, *Works,* IV, 216.
19. *Correspondence,* p. 460.

ter of undermining great men; Carlyle would have agreed that
some "great men" deserved to be undermined. But he knew
that most of the tarnished subjects of *Representative Men* were
figures whom Emerson greatly admired. He told Emerson in the
letter that he liked the Plato section the least. Carlyle was never
fond of Plato, so one might think that he would be pleased to
see Platonism dismissed as "a thing of shreds and patches."[20]
But he knew that Plato was one of Emerson's favorite thinkers;
yet here and throughout the book Emerson disparages his own
heroes. Swedenborg's work is a rotting corpse complete with
"charnel-breath" (p. 144); Montaigne the skeptic becomes an
amoral cynic, "content with just and unjust, with sots and fools,
with the triumph of folly and fraud" (p. 183); and Shakespeare,
a "Priest of Mankind" to Carlyle in "The Hero as Poet," is
accused by Emerson of leading "an obscure and profane life,
using his genius for the public amusement" (p. 218). Carlyle
would have expected some criticism of Goethe (for he and
Emerson had been arguing about Goethe since the beginning of
their correspondence) and he may actually have been surprised
by the generosity of Emerson's assessment. But why must Emerson deliberately reduce the stature of the great men most dear
to him? Carlyle could only wonder, for his methods were quite
different from the cool dialectics of Emerson.

In *Heroes and Hero-Worship* Carlyle successively parades
his heroes according to his own biographical formula: a hero
is named; Carlyle's passions are ignited and he *becomes* the
hero; the flame dies and Carlyle moves on to ignite another.
As with Emerson, the pattern of exposition reflects his beliefs.
His utter rejection of the idea that "the Times" produce the
hero inspires in the first lecture an image of the Times as "dry
dead fuel, waiting for the lightning out of Heaven that shall
kindle it. The great man, with his free force direct out of God's
own hand, is the lightning."[21] Carlyle is trying to have it both
ways with the "free force direct out of God's own hand" (how
could it then be "free"?), but the point is that the lightning,
and not the "dry mouldering sticks," creates the fire. To capture the power of the hero, the hero-worshipper must overcome

20. Emerson, *Works,* IV, 77.
21. Carlyle, *Works,* V, 13.

his own deadness and burst into sympathetic flame. And in lecture after lecture, hero after hero, the lightning strikes Carlyle on schedule and he promptly flares up in enthusiastic identification until the flames subside. He was too good a craftsman to kill an image by working it to death, however, so he uses the actual lightning and fire sparingly. The obvious application to the Norse gods in "The Hero as Divinity" is repeated in "The Hero as Priest" where the child Martin Luther is described as "a Christian Odin, — a right Thor once more, with his thunder-hammer, to smite asunder ugly enough *Jötuns* and Giant-monsters" (p. 128). (Somewhat incongruously, in the very next paragraph young Martin's playmate Alexis is struck dead "by lightning, at the gate of Erfurt.") Similarly, the age of "Mahomet" in "The Hero as Prophet" was "as if a spark had fallen, one spark, on a world of what seemed black unnoticeable sand; but lo, the sand proves explosive powder, blazes heaven-high from Delhi to Grenada!" (p. 77). And of Rousseau, with whom Carlyle had little sympathy, he writes, "There is no good in emitting *smoke* till you have made it into *fire,* — which, in the metaphorical sense too, all smoke is capable of becoming" (p. 184). Apparently Rousseau fizzled out because of wet sticks or feeble lightning bolts.

At the end of *Heroes and Hero-Worship,* when Carlyle comes to Napoleon, "our last Great Man," the lightning image itself sputters out, or what is worse, becomes a sort of ignis fatuus: "Napoleon's working, accordingly, what was it with all the noise it made? A flash as of gunpowder wide-spread; a blazing-up as of dry heath. For an hour the whole Universe seems wrapt in smoke and flame: but only for an hour. It goes out: the Universe with its old mountains and streams, its stars above and kind soil beneath, is still there" (p. 242). Instead of attaining greatness through self-denial, Napoleon betrayed his own heroism through "untruth of heart," or just plain egoism. "*Self* and false ambition had now become his god: *self*-deception once yielded to, *all* other deceptions follow naturally." Hence his proverbially false bulletins. Furthermore, instead of ennobling his followers through true hero-worship, he used them for his own selfish ends: "He believed too much in the *Dupeability* of men; saw no fact deeper in man than Hunger and this!"

Because of his failure to embody in himself and inspire in others the qualities of self-denial, he lost everything. "Like a man that should build upon cloud; his house and he fall down in confused wreck, and depart out of the world" (p. 241).

Compared with Carlyle's ideal ruler, Oliver Cromwell, Napoleon was really a little man; Carlyle does not forbear ridiculing the physical shortness of his hero *manqué*. Napoleon's hemispheric conquests, though much greater than the insular victories of Cromwell, nonetheless "are but as the high *stilts* on which the man is seen standing; the stature of the man is not altered thereby" (p. 237). In keeping with his Germanophilism, the "palpable tyrannous murderous injustice" for which Carlyle judges Napoleon rightly doomed is the execution of "that poor German Bookseller, Palm," rather than the crime which weighs more heavily in other British treatments of Napoleon (such as those of Scott and Hazlitt), the killing of the Duc d'Enghien. What surprises most in Carlyle's brief glance at Napoleon is its objectivity, its almost Emersonian detachment. Carlyle allows Napoleon his virtues, mainly his fidelity to the reforming spirit of the French Revolution, and he condemns his faults without exorbitant denunciation. Even his language takes on an Emersonian coolness. "What Napoleon *did* will in the long-run amount to what he did *justly;* what Nature with her laws will sanction. To what of reality was in him; to that and nothing more. The rest was all smoke and waste" (p. 242). Only in the pity and sadness with which the lecture concludes does something of Carlyle's emotional intensity survive. Napoleon "had gone that way of his; and Nature also had gone her way. Having once parted with Reality, he tumbles helpless in Vacuity; no rescue for him. He had to sink there, mournfully as man seldom did; and break his great heart, and die" (p. 243). Napoleon seems more real than Carlyle's other heroes because Carlyle recognizes how much of him was false. For once, the thundering big man becomes a little man on stilts.

Carlyle must have been pleased with Emerson's "Napoleon, or, The Man of the World," which represents essentially the same stilt-walker, although Emerson found more to admire. The phrase "man of the world" suggests both sides of Emerson's dialectic: the irresistible world conqueror and the ambitious upstart who knew how to get ahead. Emerson's Napoleon was well in tune with his fate, at least at first. "He respected the power of nature and fortune, and ascribed to it his superiority, instead of valuing himself, like inferior men, on his opinionativeness, and waging war with nature." In other words, Napoleon agreed with Emerson about the source of his greatness; "he pleased himself, as well as the people, when he styled himself the 'Child of Destiny.' "[22] Like Carlyle, Emerson admired Napoleon's antiaristocratic spirit, though he stressed the bourgeois and democratic aspects of Napoleon's reforms to a greater degree than would have pleased Carlyle. And whereas Carlyle had simply ignored the Duc d'Enghien affair, and one of Emerson's mentors, William Ellery Channing, had condemned the murder in terms as strong as Walter Scott's, Emerson approvingly repeated Napoleon's own answer to the charge of spilling noble blood: "Neither is my blood ditchwater" (p. 242).

The Napoleon piece may have been the only chapter in *Representative Men* whose ending Carlyle could genuinely admire; except for the first sentence, Emerson's conclusions about Napoleon's downfall were in accord with Carlyle's own: "It was not Bonaparte's fault. He did all that in him lay to live and thrive without moral principle. It was the nature of things, the eternal law of man and of the world which baulked and ruined him . . . Every experiment, by multitudes or by individuals, that has a sensual and selfish aim, will fail" (p. 258). Carlyle would not have agreed that it was not Bonaparte's fault, and he might have accused Emerson of being unfair to Napoleon and of lacking compassion, even for the murderer of Palm the bookseller. When all responsibility is placed on nature and destiny, the criminal is exonerated, but he is robbed of the pity that the guilty may sometimes extract from the innocent.

For all the talk of sincerity in *Heroes and Hero-Worship,* Carlyle's technique of total identification with his subjects sometimes creates an undesirably theatrical, if not fraudulent, impression. The passage from "The Hero as Priest" where Carlyle metamorphoses into an indignant Luther is a good example of the strengths and weaknesses of his methods. The device is

22. Emerson, *Works,* IV, 231.

effective to the extent that we are able to forget about the historical Luther and accept the speaker for what he unquestionably remains: Carlyle himself as a modern-day Luther indignantly burning the Papal Bulls of another era. Only those would object who actually wanted to hear Carlyle speak about Luther rather than just to hear Carlyle. (The *Heroes* book is best appreciated today when the reader imagines it being delivered in its original form, as lectures.) Carlyle's biographical writings may succeed as literary productions by Thomas Carlyle, but they often fail as the representations of other people. "We are left half-convinced," wrote A. O. J. Cockshut recently of a danger endemic to the entire genre, "that the man really was the man the biographer saw"; but with Carlyle this problem was largely irrelevant, since the man the biographer saw was usually himself.[23] And the irony is that Carlyle turned to biography in the first place to escape the shadow of himself through hero worship of someone greater.

Because for once his subject was not someone greater, to be worshipped as a hero, but a friend and equal, to be loved as a brother, Carlyle's *Life of John Sterling* (1851) is his most successful life study, one of his best books of any kind, and a minor masterpiece of Victorian biography. In writing Sterling's life, Carlyle reversed his usual procedure: instead of creating a hero for ordinary people to emulate, he presented an interesting but not extraordinary man whose "Pilgrimage through our poor Nineteenth Century" was intended to remind the great and all who would be great of their common humanity with everyone else. "I have remarked," he wrote in the first chapter, recalling a passage in his old essay "Biography," "that a true delineation of the smallest man, and his sense of pilgrimage through life, is capable of interesting the greatest man"; and he

23. A. O. J. Cockshut, *Truth to Life: The Art of Biography in the Nineteenth Century* (New York: Harcourt, Brace, Jovanovich, 1974; paper rpt. New York, 1976), p. 12. Even on its own terms, Carlyle's method may work only in short pieces like the *Heroes* lectures and not in sustained, full-length biographies. That might help explain Carlyle's inability to produce a life of Cromwell and the monumental morass he slowly sank into with *Frederick the Great*. The earlier *Life of Schiller* and the *Life of Sterling* were written in a different manner, while the fictionalized autobiography in *Sartor Resartus* is a separate case altogether.

added that "each man's life" is "a strange emblem of every man's."[24]

Along with Tennyson's friend Hallam and Hurrell Froude, the older brother of Carlyle's own biographer, John Sterling belonged to a class prominent in nineteenth-century England: talented men who died young, leaving behind them little more than unfulfilled promise. Carlyle felt drawn to Sterling, who was eleven years his junior, because few people understood Carlyle so well and also because, as he practically admitted, few of his other friends would so readily stand up to him in private conversation, oppose his obstinate harangues, and tell him when he was wrong. Sterling was never Carlyle's disciple or his hero-worshipper. Carlyle was "secretly" grateful for Sterling's favorable *Westminster Review* piece on him because "for me Sterling, often enough the stiff gainsayer in our private communings, was the doer of this." Perhaps Carlyle saw reflected in Sterling his own capacity for "holding out his last position as doggedly as the first: and to some of my notions he seemed to grow in stubbornness of opposition, with the growing inevitability, and never would surrender" (p. 192). But the essence of the book is not Carlyle's personal identification with Sterling. The assumption of such an identification may account for the common misreading of the best-known chapter, the devastating satire on Coleridge, as a repudiation by Carlyle of his own youthful transcendentalism. But Carlyle's aim was to reveal a typical life in which the reader can see something of himself, and not, as in a *Heroes* lecture, to impersonate a superhuman marvel and to lose himself in lightning-struck awe. In this book there is restrained emotion but no lightning and fire (although at one point there is a hurricane).

Sterling led a varied life, and Carlyle emphasized the variety in order to establish the universality of Sterling's experiences. And although Carlyle drew on his own recollections of Coleridge in depicting Sterling's visits to Highgate, the episode probably has no more autobiographical significance than any other event in the narrative. Carlyle recounted Sterling's involvement in a desperate conspiracy of Spanish exiles, his unsuccessful management of a plantation in the West Indies, his attenuated

24. Carlyle, *Works,* XI, 7.

career in the ministry, and his failure as a poet, along with the
Coleridge encounters (and even the Carlyle encounters) as il-
lustrative of the difficulties faced by an honest man trying to
live a decent life in "as mad a world as you could wish." The
variety of Sterling's life also supported Carlyle's poetic explanation for its brevity, that "it was the very excess of *life* in him that
brought on disease" (p. 123). For Sterling, character was fate.

Emerson also had a friend whose death seemed to him a consequence of her excess of life, although Margaret Fuller died
in a shipwreck rather than from consumption. Emerson dif-
ferentiated Fuller from himself by contrasting their respective
temperaments:

> When I found she lived at a rate so much faster than mine, and
> which was violent compared with mine, I foreboded rash and
> painful crises, and had a feeling as if a voice cried, *Stand from
> under!* — as if, a little further on, this destiny was threatened
> with jars and reverses, which no friendship could avert or con-
> sole. This feeling partly wore off, on better acquaintance, but
> remained latent; and I had always an impression that her energy
> was too much a force of blood, and therefore never felt the
> security for her peace which belongs to more purely intellectual
> natures. She seemed more vulnerable. For the same reason, she
> remained inscrutable to me; her strength was not my strength, —
> her powers were a surprise.[25]

Character was destiny for Fuller, too, which accorded not only
with Emerson's philosophy but with Fuller's own "faith more
or less distinct in a fate, and in a guardian genius" (p. 219).
Notwithstanding her "inscrutability," Emerson's Fuller sometimes seems to embody tendencies present in Emerson himself,
but which he insisted on keeping in check. She becomes an emotional Emerson, an Emerson without detachment, an Emerson
with greater "force of blood." She had "a certain pathos of
sentiment, and a march of character, threatening to arrive presently at the shores and plunge into the sea of Buddhism and
mystical trances." Emerson, of course, was very interested in
Eastern religions and in mysticism, but he never experienced

25. R. W. Emerson, W. H. Channing, and J. F. Clarke, *Memoirs of
Margaret Fuller Ossoli* (1852; rpt. New York, 1972), I, 228.

the "ecstasy" claimed by Fuller. He refused to accept her descriptions of her new "frame of mind" as "profound or permanent," and he ascribed her anger at his "want of sympathy" to "a certain restlessness and fever, which I did not like should deceive a soul which was capable of greatness" (pp. 308–309). The relationship between the two, in short, was as dynamic in its way as the friendship of Carlyle and Sterling. Fuller stood as an equal before Emerson. At one point he recalls "congratulating myself on the solid good understanding that subsisted between us," only to be "surprised with hearing it taxed by her with superficiality and halfness" (p. 288).

Margaret Fuller did not become a surrogate Emerson, though Emerson brought to his memoir of her a sense of personal involvement rare in his biographical writings on historical figures. Nor did she become a nineteenth-century pilgrim, though at the end Emerson praised her, simply, as "a right brave and heroic woman" (p. 300). Had Emerson attempted an independent, full-scale biography of Margaret Fuller, rather than confining himself to the ten years when he "knew her intimately," he might have produced an Emersonian *Life of Sterling*.[26] Carlyle's book was surely in Emerson's mind as he prepared his contribution to the Fuller memorial volumes, not only because of the similarities between Fuller and Sterling, but also because Emerson was a friend of both the woman and the man.

Carlyle and Emerson turned to biography from transcendentalism because they had decided that the most important questions are best answered in a life and not in a book; and on the whole they declared their convictions on freedom and fate, on self-denial and self-reliance, more forcefully, if not more convincingly, in their biographical writings than in their essays. The histories of heroes and representative men, when read for the philosophical ideas that underlie them, attain a dramatic intensity seldom achieved in strictly philosophical writing. The

26. Emerson admired the *Life of Sterling*, especially the quality of the writing; "this living narration," he wrote in his journal, "is daguerreotyped in his page." But, he added, Carlyle does not "very much uncover his secret mind." Cf. Emerson's *Journals*, ed. Edward Waldo Emerson and Waldo Emerson Forbes, VIII, 261–262. It should be mentioned that Emerson and Sterling never met in person.

philosophy does not overwhelm the biography because both authors had the simple ability to bring life to characters in a book, a talent observable in its pure form, free of didactic strategies, in the lives they wrote of their friends. Perhaps the questions are most fully answered both in a life and in a book.

JEAN STROUSE

Semiprivate Lives

Famous people are the subjects of most biographies. They become famous, usually, because they do interesting things: write novels, formulate theories about gene codes, rob banks, rule empires, scale peaks, get burned at the stake. Their lives become public, visible — other people watch what they do, where they go, whom they see — and their fame alone, regardless of their achievements, distinguishes them from people whose daily activities are essentially private. Looking at the lives of people who were famous tells us a great deal about the past, but it only tells certain kinds of things. Kings had different experiences of the Middle Ages than peasants had; cabinet ministers and ladies' maids saw different Queen Victorias. And since the kings and the cabinet ministers were more likely than the peasants or the ladies' maids to influence world events and to have biographies written about them, what we know of history (which H. G. Wells called "the chronicles of wars and kings") has been largely shaped by the careers of famous men.

The experiences of ordinary, not-famous people provide other kinds of information about history as it was lived day to day, about work, about life's conditions in distant times and places. In recent years students of social history and women's history have begun to look at the lives of people who did not do the

113

kinds of things that Napoleon, Marie Curie, and Thomas Jefferson did, and who did not live in the limelight of great events and public renown. The sources for this kind of history are quite different from the sources turned to by biographers of the eminent. A social historian looking at the recent past has the invaluable resource of oral history, but if his or her subject is older than living memory, the available information is usually impersonal and indirect — census reports, institutional records, demographic studies, economic data, birth and marriage records, membership lists.

"To live over people's lives is nothing," wrote Henry James, "unless we live over their perceptions, live over the growth, the change, the varying intensity of the same — since it was *by* these things they themselves lived."[1] It would be impossible to "live over" in this sense the life of an ordinary eighteenth-century London housewife unless the woman and the people who knew her had kept extensive diaries and written detailed letters all their lives, and unless all that material had been saved and passed on through two hundred years of succeeding generations — in which case she would not be ordinary at all.

At one extreme, then, are exemplary historical figures whose lives take on mythic proportions in the floodlights of public recognition, and at the other are census figures made out of obscure lives that now seem exemplary precisely because they were commonplace. In between is a twilight zone, a semiprivate realm occupied by minor poets, lesser dignitaries, hands that rocked important cradles, single flashes of success or fame, and the friends, relatives, and disciples of great men and women. There is a particular group within this large category of the semi-obscure that is made up of women: the wives, daughters, sisters, mothers, and lovers of people who did do things that made them famous.[2] Looking at the lives of individuals in this

1. Quoted as the epigraph to Leon Edel's *Henry James, The Untried Years: 1843–1870* (Philadelphia: Lippincott, 1953).

2. There are of course men who lived in the vicinity of greatness without large achievements of their own: Stanislaus Joyce, Robertson and Garth Wilkinson James, Tom Mitford, Pen Browning, Branwell Brontë. Their experiences were undoubtedly as interesting and difficult as women's, but they were probably quite different and deserve to be looked at separately.

group enables us to examine two dimensions of history at once, both the public arenas of great figures and events, and the hidden dramas of ordinary private life.

Many of these women were themselves intelligent and talented — for instance, Jane Carlyle, Lou Salomé, Alma Mahler, Alice B. Toklas, Zelda Fitzgerald, the Countess of Pembroke, Dorothy Wordsworth, Alice James, Mary Lamb, Marian Adams, Elisabeth Nietzsche, Jennie Churchill, Augusta Leigh, Eleanor Roosevelt. Whether they grew up with, married, gave birth to, or made love with the men (or, rarely, the women) who made what we now think of as history, they shared that history, were shaped by it, and had their own perceptions of it. Records of some of these perceptions have been preserved, either because (and this seems unlikely) the observations were seen to have a value of their own, or, more probably, because someone thought they might contribute to the understanding of great men. Whatever the reasons, where there are records it is possible to catch images and shadows, as if through partly closed blinds, of these half-illumined lives.

Alice James (1848–1892), the younger sister of Henry and William James, did not become famous and did not produce any lasting work except a diary of the years 1889 to 1892. Printed after her death in a private edition of four copies in 1895, the diary was published commercially in an abridged version in 1934, and finally in its entirety in 1964 with notes and an introduction by Leon Edel. Alice James's journal and letters display a rare gift for language, sharp wit, psychological acumen, and an intuitive grasp of political and economic realities. F. O. Matthiessen compared her "wealth of inner resources" with Emily Dickinson's, and Henry James wrote to William that their sister's journal constituted a "new claim for the family renown."

Alice James's story is interesting for what it tells us about a particular life and also for what it says about Victorian American women, about the James family, and about the phenomenon of neurasthenia in nineteenth-century America. The conflicts in Alice's ostensibly quiet life were intense: between natural intelligence, energy, and curiosity on the one hand and the passive virtues of genteel femininity on the other; between the teasing adoration of the male Jameses and her sense of exclusion from their intellectual world; between an extravagantly loving, permissive, childlike father and a firm, practical, managerial mother; between the "sensuous education" in Europe that Henry James, Sr., provided for his children and a New England morality of self-control. Like many other upper- and middle-class women and men of her time, Alice James turned her social and personal conflicts inward and became "neurasthenic," subject to nervous attacks and exhaustion, to fainting spells, dizziness, neuralgias, and mysterious aches and pains with no discernible physical causes. Some Victorians managed to alleviate their suffering in marriage, writing, or "good works." Others succumbed to invalidism and spent virtually their whole lives in bed. The experience and transcendence of this condition were the stuff of Alice James's life. Contending with her "nerves" for thirty years, she managed to keep her head, her comic sense, interests in the outside world, personal attachments, and a fierce integrity, and she never gave way to self-pity. If she had not been Henry and William James's sister, we would know nothing about her, but since she was, it is possible to see what an achievement she made of her life and to take a look at its conditions.

Special kinds of problems confront biographers of female, not-famous members of eminent families. Some of these difficulties arise in the search for sources, and others have to do with the question of biographical method.

There are at once too few and too many sources of information about a life that was obscured by famous others, too little direct evidence about the life itself and too much in the way of oblique or merely passing reference.

Indirect resources provide material for all historians, but they serve different functions in different kinds of biography. Where there is a plethora of documentary data in the first person singular, an observer needs other voices and substantiating views and information in order to gain perspective, fill out the historical picture, and see past the subject's own consciousness. E. M. Forster has a cautionary note about reliance on autobiographical sources in the preface to his biography of Goldsworthy Lowes Dickinson when he asks, "To what extent can a man be trusted

to review his own past? Something must always be discounted."
In Dickinson's case it was a "thin veil of melancholy which in-
terposed between him and the paper as soon as he sat down to
type."[3] Using secondary evidence to help figure out what has
to be discounted is very different from using it to tell the
story of a life: the author of an obscure life often has to fashion
the narrative itself out of passing reference, fading memory,
hundred-year-old gossip — out of a sense of what was going on
around the particular life rather than at its center.

Most biographies begin with the ancestors: who first came to
whatever country the family ended up in, who made or failed to
make the money, who begat whom, and so on. These facts have
been well documented in the various books by and about William and Henry James and their robust, eccentric, obsessively
adoring, passionately religious Swedenborgian father, Henry
James, Sr. But the ancestral line traced by the James biographers is the male ancestral line. What if one looked at the family
history through the women? What would it have been like to be
a James and a girl? These are interesting questions, but they
cannot be answered in any detail because there is so little information about the James and Walsh women. The genealogies
are patronymic. Information about the women is confined to
whose daughters, sisters, wives, and mothers they were. Personal recollections, mostly by sons and grandsons, offer some
clues. For instance, there are Henry James's fine evocations in
A Small Boy and Others and *Notes of a Son and Brother* as he
wanders in memory through "the very air of long summer after-
noons — occasions tasting... above all of a big much-shaded
savoury house in which a softly-sighing widowed grandmother,
Catherine Barber by birth, whose attitude was a resigned consciousness of complications and accretions, dispensed an hos-
pitality seemingly as joyless as it was certainly boundless."[4] Or
as he looks back at his mother's cousin, Helen Wyckoff: "I see
in her strong simplicity, that of an earlier quieter world, a New

3. E. M. Forster, preface to *Goldsworthy Lowes Dickinson* (New
York: Harcourt, Brace and World, 1934), p. vii.
4. Henry James, *A Small Boy and Others* (New York: Charles
Scribner's Sons, 1913), p. 4.

York of better manners and better morals and homelier beliefs,
the very elements of some portrait by a grave Dutch or other
truth-seeking master . . . I note with appreciation that she was
strenuously, actively good, and have the liveliest impression
both that no one was ever better, and that her goodness somehow testifies for the whole tone of a society, a remarkable cluster
of private decencies."[5]

These impressions are as tantalizingly vague as they are finely
drawn, and Henry James was no less liable to the distortions
and contradictions inherent in fond backward glances than are
less articulate observers. Catherine Barber James had a passion
for "the 'fiction of the day' " — Mrs. Trollope, Mrs. Gore, Mrs.
Marsh, Mrs. Hubback — which she used to read by the light
of a candle placed between the page and her eyes; she grew
peaches in her Albany yard, had ten children by an immigrant
Irishman who made three million dollars in business and real
estate, and she died at the age of eighty-seven. That is about
the sum of what we know about her. There are few letters or
papers by any of these women, few shreds of evidence docu-
menting their daily lives (equivalents of the men's business
records, sermons, or public awards), and too few eyewitness
accounts to add up to anything like a full picture. Their lives
were private; their achievements — children, good homes, ripe
peaches, warm quilts — were not the stuff of history.

What can be known about these women, then, is seen for the
most part through the eyes of men. The task of a woman's biographer might not be easier if the balance of documentary evidence were tipped toward the female, but it would be distinctly
different. The kinds of things we learn about women from men
are different from the kinds of things we learn about them from
other women, just as wives and brothers give us different kinds
of information about men. To fill in the complex dimensions of
a real life — male or female, famous or obscure — it is necessary to see the life from both vantage points, same and other.
Since women have been so profoundly the "other" throughout
history and literature, it should come as no surprise that most
sources of information about them gives us women as seen by

5. Ibid., 122.

men. Still, if one is specifically trying not to perpetuate that condition of otherness, trying to see the life from the inside out, it is especially discouraging to find so few female perspectives.

Turning from the female ancestors to the female friends of Alice James, one finds a similar scarcity of documents. The James family lived at the social and intellectual center of Victorian Boston and Cambridge. In the card catalogues of the various manuscript collections in the Boston area there are, of course, numerous entries for William and the two Henry Jameses, for Charles Eliot Norton, Henry Adams, Emerson, Howells, James Jackson Putnam, Oliver Wendell Holmes; but not many for Mary James, Susan Norton, Marian Adams, Edith Emerson, Mildred Howells, Marian Putnam, Fanny Holmes; and even fewer for women whose husbands, fathers, brothers, or sons did make the family name a collector's item. Having to check the catalogues twice for married women — under Sedgwick and Norton for Charles Eliot Norton's wife, under Emerson and Forbes for Emerson's daughter — is a minor but persistent problem; and not knowing who someone married may make it impossible to find her at all.

Women's history archives such as Radcliffe's Schlesinger Library, the Sophia Smith Collection at Smith College, and the Femina Collection at Northwestern University provide valuable resources; but such archives are new and few, and they depend not only on what people have happened to save but on what they have decided is worth giving to a library.

Fortunately, Alice James did come from a family with a collector's-item name, and some of her letters are preserved among the family papers at Harvard. Her voice, like her handwriting, is strong and clear after a hundred years, and the letters present vivid pictures of upper-middle-class nineteenth-century Cambridge and London:

> I have been struggling to like her [Lilla Cabot Perry, the wife of Henry James's old friend, Thomas Sergeant Perry] for a long period ... but it is a struggle that I can no longer keep up. I was thoroughly routed ... the last time. When she confined her wonder & admiration to her intellectual achievements I could

stand her, but now that she rams her moral perfections down your throat it's a little more than my imperfect digestion can stand. Sargy always had the capacities of a cormorant, so he is able to swallow her whole, not having to think about her as she is going down must make it easier.[6]

Nurse's little brother came home from school & said the Master made him 'exasperate' his *h*'s; must not this express the emotions of the *h* in its British vicissitudes?[7]

The party last night at Lizzy's was not eminently successful owing to rather a scarcity of the male sex, to which on social occasions, whether we have the vote or not, we are and shall always be slaves ... What a pity it is that Mr. Charley Atkinson always thinks it necessary to talk nothing but nonsense at parties, it's dreadfully tiresome ... The poor fellow looks thin and pale, I wonder whether it is still Miss Loring. Why is it that love affairs appeal so much less in real life to one's sympathy than they do in the silliest novel, even in a double-column Harper's reprint?[8]

What have you been reading lately? Have you read that prettiest of stories, "La Neuvaine de Colette"?[9] It quite captivated me because it comes after one or two of the pagan, miasmatic, exquisite Loti ... I do not like to blow the fraternal trumpet, but Harry's article in the Fortnightly on Guy de Maupassant is most brilliant ... I wish he did more of that kind of thing, but he thinks it unworthy, I believe.

Isn't the German situation most dramatic? To think of the death of that hoary old sinner[10] with his hymns and his bastards reducing us all to such "Grief." I suppose the cast-iron an-

6. Alice James to Sara Darwin, March 25 [1874?]. Quoted by permission of Alexander James and the Houghton Library of Harvard College Library.

7. Alice James to Francis Boott, June 23, 1889. Quoted by permission of Alexander James and the Houghton Library of Harvard College Library.

8. Alice James to Anne A. Richards, March 14 [1875?]. Quoted by permission of Alexander James and the Trustees of the National Library of Scotland.

9. A novel by Jeanne Schultz, published in Paris in 1888 and serialized anonymously in the *Revue des Deux Mondes* in the fall of 1887.

10. William I, Emperor of Germany and King of Prussia, who died in March, 1888. His grandson, William II, who was also the grandson of Queen Victoria, came to power in June 1888.

achronisms which he helped to build up will begin to totter in the hands of his grandson.[11]

But Henry, the family member who most appreciated Alice's writing and the one to whom she was closest, made a bonfire of letters toward the end of his life in what Leon Edel has called a "rage of privacy," and her half of their dialogue is silent, though it echoes in his carefully preserved responses. Alice's narration of her own life is interrupted for long periods by illness, Henry's fire, and whatever happens to all those letters that do not get saved. Undoubtedly more of what she wrote is missing than collected, and the diary covers only the last four years of her life. For great pieces of the life, then, it is impossible to obey Boswell's injunction to let the subject speak for herself. Other kinds of sources have to be found.

The richest second- and third-person primary source for Alice James, and probably for other women in this group, is the family correspondence. That the Jameses were inveterate travelers and prolific letter writers is a great advantage, since their correspondence is so full of articulate life. But this wealth of source material creates a new problem, a constant temptation to draw excessively on the accounts of the very significant others in the James family. The powerful and well-preserved voices of two of the American nineteenth century's best writers threaten to drown out their sister's less voluminous but nonetheless articulate account, just as the intellectual din at the family dinner table in the 1860s kept her quietly in the background.[12] Edward Emerson recalled meal times in the James household:

"The adipose and affectionate Wilkie," as his father called him, would say something and be instantly corrected or disputed by

11. Alice James to Sara Darwin, March 21, 1888. Quoted by permission of Alexander James and the Houghton Library of Harvard College Library.

12. In the various volumes of published letters by William and Henry James, the ellipses indicating passages omitted by the editors frequently signal comments in the originals about Alice. Sometimes the omissions are motivated by discretion, but often they seem to be based on judgments about what was interesting or historically significant. The first two volumes of *Henry James Letters* edited by Leon Edel (Cambridge: Harvard University Press, 1974, 1975) are welcome exceptions, as Edel prints every letter he includes in its entirety.

the little cock-sparrow Bob, the youngest, but good-naturedly defend his statement, and then, Henry (Junior) would emerge from his silence in defence of Wilkie. Then Bob would be more impertinently insistent, and Mr. James would advance as Moderator, and William, the eldest, join in. The voice of the Moderator, presently would be drowned by the combatants and he soon came down vigorously into the arena, and when, in the excited argument, the dinner knives might not be absent from eagerly gesticulating hands, dear Mrs. James, more conventional, but bright as well as motherly, would look at me, laughingly reassuring, saying, "Don't be disturbed, Edward; they won't stab each other. This is usual when the boys come home." And the quiet little sister ate her dinner, smiling, close to the combatants.[13]

This kind of eyewitness account provides useful information, as do books about the Jameses and their friends, histories of the period, studies of the climate of ideas in late nineteenth-century Boston, New York, and London, and descriptions of the cities themselves and their social groups and organizations. (Checking indexes becomes a real addiction, and one gets all too familiar with the alphabet of eminence on either side of the female James or Adams or Holmes whose name is all too frequently absent.) The archives of local historical societies turn up surprising things: records, for instance, of Alice's membership in the Banks Brigade, a group of Cambridge women who organized themselves at the start of the Civil War to sew shirts, bandages, and hats for the Union soldiers, and who kept on meeting and sewing, and writing memoirs of it all, until 1923. (After the war they made clothes for poor people in the Boston area.) And medical history provides another invaluable source of information about Alice: books and articles on neurasthenia and its treatments published by the doctors she consulted, records of the institutions she was in and the remedies prescribed, and general material by and about nineteenth-century physicians and their attitudes toward women, sexuality, nervous disorders, and madness.

The process of getting to know Alice James indirectly through the mediation of relatives, friends, records, and events is similar

13. Edward W. Emerson, *The Early Years of the Saturday Club* (Boston: Houghton Mifflin, 1918), p. 328.

to that of reading a late Henry James novel, where knowledge is in constant fluid motion between surfaces and depths, and where what happens is an opening out of perceptions about what exists only in the play and range of individual consciousness.

"Ignorance is the first requisite of the historian," wrote Lytton Strachey, claiming that the history of the Victorian age would never be written because we know too much about it, "ignorance, which simplifies and clarifies, which selects and omits, with a placid perfection unattainable by the highest art."[14] The bulk of information about the period and its eminents is even more staggering now than it was when Strachey first complained about it sixty years ago; yet ignorance about many aspects of a semiprivate life in Victorian America is inevitable. And since the "scrupulous narration" of nineteenth-century biography is neither possible nor desirable with an uncelebrated life, ignorance is the beginning of a method; omission and selection, freely chosen or imposed by circumstance, are its means.

For example, not much evidence is available about Alice James's relations with her mother. Since the drama of Alice's life is in many ways a private, interior one, the relations between mother and daughter are central to a full understanding of Alice, but they will have to come in at odd angles, through inference and isolated incident. Almost ten years after Mary James died Alice recorded in her diary: "Ever since the night that Mother died, and the depth of filial tenderness was revealed to me, all personal claim upon her vanished, and she has dwelt in my mind as a beautiful illumined memory, the essence of divine maternity from which I was to learn great things, give all, but ask nothing."[15] And in 1890, on rereading her parents' old letters, she found her "Mother's words breathing her extraordinary selfless devotion as if she simply embodied the unconscious essence of wife and motherhood."[16]

14. Lytton Strachey, preface to *Eminent Victorians* (London: Chatto and Windus, 1918), p. vii.

15. *The Diary of Alice James,* ed. Leon Edel (New York: Dodd, Mead, 1964), p. 221 (September 20, 1891).

16. Ibid., p. 79 (January 29, 1890).

"Extraordinary selfless devotion," "the essence of divine maternity," "give all but ask nothing." These phrases do not reflect the image of the practical, rather domineering figure who ran the tumultuous James household with a firm hand, who was described by a family acquaintance as "large, florid, stupid-seeming,"[17] and who (as Leon Edel points out) emerges in a series of terrifyingly powerful mothers in Henry's novels. But Alice was not alone in conferring sainthood on her mother. Henry Senior saw in his wife the personification of selflessness, which was the ultimate virtue in his moral pantheon. And the tyrannical mothers in the novels of Henry Junior were reserved for fiction; his language about his real mother is similar to Alice's: "She was patience, she was wisdom, she was exquisite maternity . . . It was a perfect mother's life . . . [to give herself for years to her family, and then when they no longer needed her] to lay herself down in her ebbing strength and yield up her soul to the celestial power that had given her this divine commission."[18]

To an only daughter whose own essence did not draw her naturally along the path of selfless devotion and who possessed a great deal of energy and curiosity and ambition, it must have seemed impossible to measure up against such a holy ideal of virtue. It was probably also impossible to know that the divine selflessness itself was something of a myth.

"It must have seemed . . ." Those can be dangerous words. Interpretation sometimes makes illuminating connections, but it can also reduce rather than enlarge, impose cloying fictions or ideological lessons, and suppress or distort whatever real experience has managed to come through the intervening years intact. Just how and when to weave one's own observations into the chronology are critical questions for all biographers, but they assume a different relation to the narrative when the reasons why the biography is being written at all are not self-

17. Lilla Cabot Perry, quoted in Van Wyck Brooks, *From the Shadow of the Mountain: My Post-Meridian Years* (New York: Dutton, 1961), p. 45.
18. *The Notebooks of Henry James,* ed. F. O. Matthiessen and Kenneth B. Murdock (New York: Oxford University Press, 1947), pp. 40–41.

evident. In the absence of familiar points of reference — a great novel, a theory of evolution — the question "Why is this person interesting?" looms as large for the writer in the imagined minds of potential readers as it does in the actual blank looks often encountered in conversation when one's subject is introduced: "Oh, and what did she do?"

One wants not to explain but to illustrate, to let the story's inherent interest do its own work. Still, the burden of proof rests somewhat heavily with the author of an uncelebrated life. A substantial amount of the material used in biographies of eminent people has to do with eminent achievements. What happened in the life becomes interesting because of what exists in the novels or philosophy, what took place on the battlefield or was discovered in the lab. Without that body of work, everything rests with the life itself and especially, therefore, on what the biographer sees and has to say about it. The reasons why any writer chooses a subject are bound to affect the work he or she produces, but those reasons probably come further into the open in presenting an obscure life, since the writer's interest and insights have to do the work that fame and great achievements do for other lives.

The best books about obscure lives (Geoffrey Scott's *Portrait of Zélide,* Vita Sackville-West's *Aphra Behn,* Henry James's *William Wetmore Story,* Forster's *Goldsworthy Lowes Dickinson* and his biography of his great-aunt, *Marianne Thornton*) make their subjects come alive through a combination of perfectly chosen detail and discreetly exercised critical intelligence. These books take their forms from the contours of the lives themselves and their value from the quality of the authors' perceptions; and the dramas they unfold are not diminished by the fact that they are often personal rather than historical in the conventional sense.

Strachey's warning in the preface to *Eminent Victorians* that "human beings are too important to be treated as mere symptoms of the past" applies to obscure as well as eminent lives.[19] In fact, where the subject of biography is not already well-known, the writer has to take special care not to turn Alice or

19. Lytton Strachey, preface to *Eminent Victorians,* p. viii.

Jane or Jennie into some kind of abstraction or case history. A superb piece of work in this genre is Elizabeth Hardwick's essay on Jane Carlyle in *Seduction and Betrayal*. Hardwick has brilliant things to say about Jane Carlyle in particular and about women generally, as she shows us precisely those dimensions of one person's experience that are larger and more interesting than private trouble.

> When Jane Carlyle was cleaning and sweeping and keeping the accounts within discreet limits she certainly did not set a price upon her actions. But, of course, there was a hidden price. It was that in exchange for her work, her dedication, her special if somewhat satirical charms, Carlyle would, as an instance, not go out to Lady Ashburton when she would rather he stayed at home. This is the unspoken contract of a wife and her works. In the long run wives are to be paid in a peculiar coin—consideration for their feelings. And it usually turns out this is an enormous, unthinkable inflation few men will remit, or if they will, only with a sense of being overcharged.[20]

Private trouble is not a sufficient subject for fiction or biography, although it often passes for one. As biography, once exiled by the New Critics, has come into its reputable own, as social history, family history, and women's history have become acceptable disciplines, and as sex and death and private experience have been turned into highly marketable commodities, there is a danger that we will merely substitute one set of historical distortions for another. The literature of confession and complaint, the exegesis of the personal, does have a point to make about what has been left out of history and literature, but it often makes boring reading. What passes for innocence in a number of tales that claim to tell, at last, the truth about sex, or women, or relationships that fail, is willful ignorance, a programmatic helplessness that takes no account of history, psychological complexity, or anything as difficult as motive.

Private trouble does not work as a central theme, but it is a presence in the kinds of lives under discussion here; Eleanor Roosevelt, Jane Carlyle, Zelda Fitzgerald, Alice James, and the

20. Elizabeth Hardwick, *Seduction and Betrayal* (New York: Random House, 1974), p. 173.

rest had to bear great pain, and the ways in which they managed to do so are partly what distinguish them. Heroism has to do with the struggle to endure and transcend the circumstances that make us who we are. Often, in these women's lives, the struggle took place in the realm not of action but of consciousness; it had to do with what Hardwick calls "Stoicism, growing to meet the tyrannical demands of consequence."[21] Alice James's bravery was remarked on by all who knew her, and the way she faced her approaching death (of breast cancer at the age of forty-four) is one of the most interesting aspects of her difficult life. She wrote to William six months before she died: "It is the most supremely interesting moment in life, the only one in fact when living seems life, and I count it the greatest good fortune to have these few months so full of interest and instruction in the knowledge of my approaching death. It is as simple in one's own person as any fact of nature, the fall of a leaf or the blooming of a rose, and I have a delicious consciousness ever present, of wide spaces close at hand, and whisperings of release in the air."[22]

From the distance of a hundred years, and from a time that is at last taking a long serious look at women's experiences in the past and present, it is tempting to dwell on personal struggles with madness, infidelity, invalidism, and betrayals. A spirit of protest enters inevitably into the process of looking closely at what Diane Johnson, in her book about George Meredith's wife, called "lesser lives."[23] Still, it is as great a mistake to view eighteenth- or nineteenth-century women's conflicts in the light of twentieth-century experience as it is to read the passionate, sentimental correspondence of nineteenth-century women as evidence of lesbianism. That the terms and the times were different is obvious. Yet the pressures toward assimilating the past to the present work in subtle ways, and it seems particularly important just now for contemporary female biographers of women to find ways of paying careful attention to their intuitions about their

21. Ibid., p. 208.
22. Alice James to William James, July 30, 1891. Quoted by permission of Alexander James and the Houghton Library of Harvard College Library.
23. Diane Johnson, *Lesser Lives* (New York: Knopf, 1972).

subjects' lives while at the same time maintaining a critical distance from those reactions.

A final difficulty with regard to method is the problem of dealing with the eminent other (in this case, others) in a semi-private life. In the biographies of Henry and William James, Alice is a significant but minor character, whereas both brothers and their father had major roles in her life, just as Carlyle did in Jane's, and Franklin in Eleanor's. Can these men, who seemed in many ways larger than life while they lived and seem even more so now, take on supporting roles in someone else's drama without taking over the stage? It is a complicated problem. One tends not only to rely too heavily on the James men's abundant and entertaining versions of the family saga, but also to be overwhelmed by the sheer weight of material about William and the two Henrys in their own works and biographies. How are these enormously complex and interesting lives to be fitted into Alice's story without disastrous oversimplification?

These dilemmas reflect the historical imbalance that women's history and this kind of biography are attempting to correct, and there are no abstract or general solutions to them. In *Zélide* Geoffrey Scott tells the eighteenth-century love story of Madame de Charrière (Zélide) and Benjamin Constant as if he were writing a novel. He uses history when it fits into the tale of these two passionate, brilliant, self-dramatizing figures; but James Boswell, Madame de Staël, and the French Revolution remain on the periphery as the central characters play out their captivating private drama. Scott, led more by intuition than history, relies more on irony than scholarship, and the portrait he has drawn is a work of art. And since it tells us about the intersections of intellectual and private life, about the changing climate of ideas in eighteenth-century Europe and the ways in which the changes were experienced in personal life and love, *Zélide* is also useful as history. Lytton Strachey's *Portraits in Miniature* does the same thing. Strachey gives us special insights into history from odd angles, through deft biographical sketches of such unlikely people as the Abbé Morellet, Mary Berry, Sir John Harington, and Madame de Sévigné's cousin.

For Alice James the central drama is not, like Zélide's, a love story, but a struggle of character and spirit. Shortly before she died Alice wrote to William apropos of the neurasthenia that had plagued most of her adult life, "When I am gone, pray don't think of me simply as a creature who might have been something else, had neurotic science been born."[24] That is a useful plea to keep in mind, with reference not just to "neurotic" illness (Alice used the term in its pre-Freudian sense, to mean nervous disorder) but to the whole range of circumstances that kept many lives from being "something else." Alice would not have been Henry and Jane Carlyle would not have been Thomas even if they had been born boys and in another century, and lingering over the "what ifs" does all of them an injustice. Who and what these women were is interesting enough in itself.

Semiprivate lives are different from famous lives. They offer new ways of looking at the intersections of public and private experience without the obfuscation of myth. They give us not an official version of history as the chronicles of wars and kings, nor literary biography's illuminations of the "mysterious and magical process of creation";[25] they provide instead glimpses of ordinary life, private drama, personal success and failure, sometimes heroism, sometimes the underside of fame — and a sense of the past as no more confined to a single version than the present is. History is not an alibi. It defines life's terms in certain ways but it does not explain genius or love, heroism or pain. Fully to live over, in Henry James's phrase, "the growth, the change, the varying intensity" of perception in an obscure life is to use all the versions and exigencies of the past to approach the truth of private experience.

24. Alice James to William James, July 30, 1891. Quoted by permission of Alexander James and the Houghton Library of Harvard College Library.
25. Leon Edel, *Literary Biography* (London: Rupert Hart-Davis, 1957), p. 3.

MICHAEL T. GILMORE

Eulogy as Symbolic Biography:
The Iconography of Revolutionary Leadership,
1776–1826

Eulogy has been called the oldest form of biography. In eulogy, however, the concrete details that make up the life of a particular person, details essential to even the most uncritical biography, tend to vanish as a result of the didacticism of the genre. The deceased appears less as an individualized figure than as an emblem or symbol contrived for the purpose of instructing an audience. Although the lives described turn out to be much the same, they nevertheless have value as a revelation of character. By treating the dead as a kind of cultural ideal, the eulogist seeks in effect to compose the collective biography of an entire people. Thus, the true subject of the eulogy is the speaker and his community rather than the character and career of the person nominally portrayed. For just this reason, the eulogies delivered for American revolutionary leaders during the first half-century of the republic's existence yield valuable insights into the ideological and emotional issues that engaged successive generations of their countrymen.

Two systems of allusion were available to American orators who commemorated the illustrious dead: the language of classi-

cal antiquity as received through the Commonwealthmen or
radical Whigs; and the evangelical or millennial vocabulary re-
vitalized by the Great Awakening. Each tradition had its models
of what a leader should be, and each helped to shape American
values and standards of conduct. Hopeful that the new nation
would be, in Samuel Adams's words, "the *Christian* Sparta,"
Patriot leaders themselves regularly drew inspiration from both
traditions. Patrick Henry was appealing to this dual inheritance
when he uttered his famous warning to King George at the
height of the Stamp Act crisis: "Tarquin and Caesar each had
his Brutus, Charles the First his Cromwell."[1]

Men do not simply inherit their vocabularies; they also revise

1. Adams quoted in Gordon S. Wood, *The Creation of the American
Republic, 1776–1787* (1969; rpt. New York: Norton, 1972), p. 118;
Henry quoted in H. Trevor Colbourn, *The Lamp of Experience: Whig
History and the Intellectual Origins of the American Revolution* (1965;
rpt. New York: Norton, 1974), p. 150. On the background and evolu-
tion of republican ideology, see, in addition to Wood and Colbourn,
Bernard Bailyn, *The Ideological Origins of the American Revolution*
(Cambridge: Harvard University Press, 1967); J. G. A. Pocock, *The
Machiavellian Moment: Florentine Political Thought and the Atlantic
Republican Tradition* (Princeton: Princeton University Press, 1975);
and Caroline Robbins, *The Eighteenth-Century Commonwealthman:
Studies in the Transmission, Development, and Circumstance of English
Liberal Thought from the Restoration of Charles II until the War with
the Thirteen Colonies* (Cambridge: Harvard University Press, 1959).
On the evangelical tradition, see Alan Heimert, *Religion and the Amer-
ican Mind: From the Great Awakening to the Revolution* (Cambridge:
Harvard University Press, 1966); Heimert and Perry Miller, eds., *The
Great Awakening: Documents Illustrating the Crisis and Its Conse-
quences* (Indianapolis: Bobbs-Merrill, 1967), pp. xiii–lxi; and Richard
L. Bushman, *From Puritan to Yankee: Character and the Social Order
in Connecticut, 1690–1765* (1967; rpt. New York: Norton, 1970). For
the general proposition that Enlightenment ideas were modified in
America and made compatible with Protestant Christianity, see Henry
F. May, *The Enlightenment in America* (New York: Oxford University
Press, 1976), esp. pp. 153–357. By revolutionary leaders I mean those
individuals who played a prominent part in the War for Independence
in either a civilian or a military capacity. It should be stressed at the
outset that only a few orations for such men were published prior to
1800, and that the eulogists themselves were members of the American
leadership. This study is obviously based on a sampling rather than
a comprehensive survey of elite opinion. I believe, however, that the
emphases isolated here were reflective of broader currents within American culture.

and transform them. The meanings of particular words may be radically altered by the speaker who employs them, or by the context in which they appear. The appeals to Puritan Christianity and classical paganism made by patriotic eulogists in 1776 meant something different by the turn of the century. Originally used to justify revolt against Britain, these appeals were later invoked to legitimize the newly established American state. To speak in terms of the familial imagery then prevalent in political discourse, they were placed at the service of paternal authority, and severed from their previous connection with filial dissent. As American Sons of Liberty became the Founding Fathers, there emerged a rhetorical synthesis of the two traditions that was more appropriate to the celebration of an empire than an authentic republic.

The funeral orations pronounced during the war years naturally took as their theme the justice and glory of the American cause. The orators, in praising their fallen leaders, accordingly dwelt on the revolutionary implications of the two pasts they had inherited. Declaring that war and rebellion were preferable to slavery, they upheld the right of resistance to unjust authority on the basis of republican precedent and their reading of Scripture. They portrayed their subjects as both heroes and saints, martyrs to the rights of Englishmen and the truths of the Christian religion, and they enjoined their hearers to emulate the dead by displaying a similar zeal in defense of virtue and liberty.

The opening salutation commonly set the mood of these early eulogies. William Smith, speaking before the Continental Congress in memory of General Richard Montgomery, began in typical fashion when he addressed the assembled delegates as "Fathers, Brethren, and Countrymen!" Smith's greeting, which recalls the opening lines of Mark Antony's eulogy from *Julius Caesar* (a play well-known to Americans for its portrayal of the decisive moment in Roman history, the transition from the Republic to the Empire), was based on the stylistic convention, the tricolon: an arrangement of words or phrases in a group of three that was perfected in classical antiquity by teachers of rhetoric and popularized in English by writers seeking to repro-

duce the cadences of Ciceronian Latin.[2] Adopted by orators
throughout the revolutionary period, it was a fitting device to
introduce a eulogy that treated its subject as a figure worthy of
comparison with the greatest heroes of Greece and Rome.

Smith's eulogy was typical in other respects as well. Reminding the Congress that *amor patriae,* "the love of our country,"
was the most exalted of virtues, he combed two thousand years
of history for examples of antique republicans and radical Whigs.
Not only did he liken Montgomery to such legendary ancients
as Regulus and Cincinnatus — the latter, like his American
counterpart, "a *General* from the *plough!*" — he also ranked
him with two of the brightest luminaries in the Commonwealth
galaxy, John Hampden and Algernon Sidney. Smith's use of the
classical past was highly selective, in accordance with the bias
of the English libertarians, whose translations and commentaries
were the chief source for the American cult of antiquity. The
ancient authors he cited most frequently — Cicero, Horace, and
Livy — had endeared themselves to the eighteenth century by
contrasting the corruption and decay of the Roman Empire with
the idealized purity of the early Republic — that golden age of
austere morality that had seemingly vanished forever when Caesar crossed the Rubicon to march upon Rome.[3]

2. William Smith, *An Oration in Memory of General Montgomery
and of the Officers and Soldiers Who Fell with Him, December 31, 1775,
before Quebec; Drawn Up (and Delivered February 19th, 1776) at the
Desire of the Honourable Continental Congress* (2nd ed.; Philadelphia,
1776), p. 1. On the tricolon, see Gilbert Highet, *The Classical Tradition:
Greek and Roman Influences on Western Literature* (1949; rpt. New
York: Oxford University Press, 1970); pp. 112–113, 334–335. For
evidence of American familiarity with *Julius Caesar,* see Francois Xavier
Martin, *A Funeral Oration on . . . Major-General Richard Caswell* (New-
bern, N.C., 1790), pp. 3–4. Martin quotes directly from Antony's eulogy
for Caesar as rendered by Shakespeare.

3. Smith, *An Oration,* pp. 3, 20, 12, 11, 4–5, 31, passim; Carl L.
Becker, *Everyman His Own Historian: Essays on History and Politics*
(New York: F. S. Crofts, 1935), p. 49. See also, in general, Meyer
Reinhold, ed., *The Classick Pages: Classical Reading of Eighteenth-
Century Americans* (University Park, Pa.: The American Philological
Association, 1975). For further evidence of the juxtaposition of ancients
and Commonwealthmen, see Perez Morton, *An Oration; Delivered at
the King's Chapel in Boston, April 8, 1776, on the Re-Interment of the
Remains of the late Most Worshipful Grand-Master, Joseph Warren,*

A comparable world, in the view of Smith and his fellow revolutionists, had been reborn on American shores in the persons of men like Montgomery, himself of Irish origin, who had served with the British forces in Canada and been captivated by "our simplicity of manners, yet uncorrupted by luxury or flagrant vice." How admirable that Montgomery should choose to settle on the banks of the Hudson, and to pursue in rustic retirement "the life of a country gentleman, deriving its most exquisite relish from reflection upon past dangers and past services." To an audience steeped in the classics, such words evoked the Horatian ideal of a rural retreat to which disinterested patriots could retire after a lifetime spent in devotion to country and duty. Clearly America was the place where those agrarian virtues characteristic of the greatest days of the Roman Republic could flourish.[4]

The American setting was also congenial to the cultivation of true religion and piety. Montgomery, according to Smith, was a devout Christian as well as an antique Roman, a man who had taught his heart to "beat *unison* with the harmony of heaven!" Although Smith himself happened to be an Anglican priest with little sympathy for the evangelicalism of the Great Awakening, his celebrations of frugality, industry, and "pure benevolence" could well have been uttered by the Calvinist clergy. He confidently turned to the Bible for proof that the prophets were no less opposed than the ancients to rule by tyrants, and he quoted at length from Isaiah foretelling the downfall of Babylon: "How hath the oppressor ceased! The Lord hath broken the staff of the wicked! He that smote the people in wrath — that ruled the nations in anger — is persecuted, and none hindereth!" Smith even appended a footnote to his published oration in which he quoted an English prelate as saying that "true religion, virtue, and liberty are more intimately connected than men commonly

Esquire . . . (Boston, 1776). "In Fine, to compleat the great Character," Morton said of Warren, "like HARRINGTON he wrote, like CICERO he spoke, like HAMPDEN he lived, and like WOLFE he died," p. 12.

4. Smith, *An Oration*, pp. 18–19. The Horatian ideal is discussed by Howard Mumford Jones, *O Strange New World: American Culture, The Formative Years* (1964; rpt. New York: Viking, 1968), pp. 245–247.

consider." The corresponding theme of his own remarks, he added, was "the reward of *heroes,* in the *Christian's heaven.*"[5]

For both Christians and pagans, Smith declared, the purpose of the eulogy was to encourage the living to imitate the dead — not to worship or deify them. Since men were more prone to imitate than to be instructed, "eminent characters" had "a stronger influence than written precepts." Montgomery's countrymen could show their respect for his memory by consecrating their own lives to the revolutionary cause. "Rome in all her glory would have decreed honors," Smith told his audience; the Congress in justice could do no less.[6]

Smith's oration, apparently the first delivered for an American officer killed in combat, went into a second edition within a matter of months. Although Smith still retained some hope that England would mend her ways,[7] his speech was otherwise representative of the several eulogies for Patriot leaders that have survived from the war years. Chaplains with denominational affiliations less bound to the royal establishment differed little in their choice of models. Israel Evans, an evangelical and militant awakener,[8] saw no conflict between Edwardsean Calvinism and classical republicanism when he commemorated General Enoch Poor of the New Hampshire Brigade in 1780. Dissolving the private man into the public image, Evans also resorted to the ancient authorities as well as the gospel in dignifying his subject. He opened his address with a tricolon — "Friends, Country-men, and Fellow-Soldiers; Favor me, I beseech you, with your attention and candor" — and hailed Greece and Rome as "those sublime patterns of republican wisdom, virtue, and valor." Like others of the revolutionary generation, Evans's understanding of ancient history was thoroughly "Whiggized." Cato the Younger, who had committed suicide at Utica to avoid capture by Caesar, stirred his enthusiasm. Paraphrasing directly from Thomas Gordon's translation of Sallust, the Roman historian who had mercilessly dissected the moral decay of the

5. Smith, *An Oration,* pp. 18, 13, 10, 7–8.

6. Smith, *An Oration,* pp. 10, 36.

7. As it turned out, the Congress considered Smith's position too moderate and voted down a motion to thank him for his address.

8. Evans is mentioned in Heimert, *Religion and the American Mind,* pp. 498, 531. A brief biographical sketch appears on p. 558.

late Republic, Evans told his audience that "Cato fled from fame, but she pursued him with the greater speed. He chose to be virtuous rather than appear so."[9] Evans also drew on Joseph Addison's tragedy *Cato* (1712), the most popular play in eighteenth-century America. In his peroration, he reproduced Addison's words with only slight variation:

> 'Tis not in mortals to command success,
> But we'll do more my friends, we will deserve it.[10]

The example of Poor, who sacrificed private interest to public welfare, suggested comparison to another hero of the classical pantheon, the great Roman patriot Cicero. In his celebrated orations, Cicero had championed resistance to tyrants, and he had saved the Republic by exposing and crushing the Catiline conspiracy. Evans, in praising Poor, declared that the General's selfless conduct "shall procure for him the glorious name of a FATHER to his country" — the title, according to Plutarch, which Rome had given to Cicero for his service in the cause of liberty.[11]

Poor's patriotism, Evans assured his listeners, was nurtured by his religion. "True piety to God" strengthened his resolution in battle, and enabled him to shun intemperance, profanity, and avarice — the besetting vices of armies, equally hateful to virtuous pagans and practicing Christians. His life exemplified

9. Israel Evans, *An Oration, Delivered at Hackinsack, on the Tenth of September, 1780, at the Interment of the Honorable Brigadier Enoch Poor, General of the New Hampshire Brigade* (Newburyport, 1781), pp. 3–6, 9. Sallust is excerpted in Reinhold, *The Classick Pages,* pp. 101–106. The relevant quotation appears on p. 105: Cato "aimed not so much to appear, as to be, a virtuous Man; So that the less he courted Renown, the faster it followed him."

10. Evans, *An Oration,* p. 36. Compare the lines by Portius, Cato's son, from I.ii.44–45: "'Tis not in mortals to command success,/but we'll do more, Sempronius; we'll deserve it." Addison's play was also an important influence on George Washington, Patrick Henry, and Nathan Hale. See Fredric M. Litto, "Addison's *Cato* in the Colonies," *William and Mary Quarterly,* 23 (1966), 431–449.

11. Evans, *An Oration,* p. 27. Cf. Plutarch, *The Lives of the Noble Grecians and Romans,* trans. John Dryden, rev. Arthur Hugh Clough (New York: The Modern Library, n.d.), p. 1054. The so-called Dryden translation (actually by several hands) was first published in 1683.

the lesson "that religion and true courage are no ways inconsistent with each other, but being united, mutually promote
dignity and true glory." By imitating the example of Poor, who
combined moral goodness with love of country, the soldiers of
the American army could be sure of purchasing not only "the
glorious titles of heroes and patriots," but also "a passport . . .
to the regions of eternal happiness."[12]

To the revolutionary eulogists, then, religion and republican
ideology were equally instrumental in preparing the colonists to
depose the British rulers who had infringed upon their liberties.
The two traditions raised up an intrepid leadership and supplied
the vocabularies with which patriotic orators vindicated the
legitimacy of the American cause. Should representatives of
the Crown protest that rebellion was disloyalty to the king,
Americans could answer in the words of Addison's Cato: when
asked, "What is a Roman, that is Caesar's foe?" Cato replies,
"Greater than Caesar; he's a friend to virtue" (II.ii.40–41).
Should Tory clergymen such as Jonathan Boucher assert that
the Scriptures taught passive obedience to rulers, Patriot clergymen could respond in the strains of Isaiah, exulting over the
fall of tyrants. Among the eulogists, it was Israel Evans who
made the most dramatic use of this dual inheritance when he
closed his funeral oration for General Poor with a liturgical
formula and a Latin quotation from Horace:

> Now to God the Father, Son, and Holy Spirit, be ascribed, as is
> most due, all praise, might, majesty and dominion, from ever-
> lasting, and to everlasting. Amen, and Amen.
>
> GLORIA EST PRAEMIUM VIRTUTUS.
> DULCE ET DECORUM EST PRO
> PATRIA MORI.[13]

The two systems of allusion employed by eulogists for Patriot
leaders were supplemented by a mode of political discourse
habitual to Englishmen on both sides of the Atlantic. At home
and in the colonies, they were accustomed to speak about po-

12. Evans, *An Oration,* pp. 13–14, 26–27, 31–32, 36, passim.
13. Evans, *An Oration,* p. 36.

litical obligation in terms of analogy to the family. The history of the familial metaphor in Western political thought has only recently begun to be studied; its ancestry dates back at least to the ancient Athenians.[14] For seventeenth-century Englishmen, the authority of the metaphor was based on the Word rather than on classical precedent. Their catechisms had taught them that all civil, religious, and natural callings were covered by the biblical injunction to "honor thy father and thy mother." As John Flavel explained in 1692, the Fifth Commandment applied to magistrates and their subjects, ministers and their flocks, household heads and their children, and masters and their servants. Every member of the community at large was expected to act as a godly father toward his subordinates and a dutiful son toward his superiors.[15]

It took Sir Robert Filmer to translate these general sentiments, shared by Puritans and Anglicans alike, into a full-blown defense of the divine right of kings. According to Filmer, all political authority had evolved from the family, and rulers were therefore entitled to the same absolute obedience that children owed to their parents. Adam, in Filmer's view, had been the original father, and his power, descending through the Hebrew patriarchs to the English kings, was sanctioned by God. Filmer's patriarchalism elicited an outspoken response from John Locke in his *Two Treatises on Government* (1689–1690). According to Locke, parenthood was a trust and a duty founded on the weakness of children; parental authority was not absolute because children had rights of their own. Indeed, Locke's contention that consent and contract rather than parenthood were the true foundations of the body politic wholly repudiated the political significance of the Fifth Commandment. Although patriarchalism gradually fell into disfavor as a political doctrine, Locke's warning against reasoning analogically from fami-

14. Gordon J. Schochet, *Patriarchalism in Political Thought: The Authoritarian Family and Political Speculation and Attitudes Especially in Seventeenth-Century England* (New York: Basic Books, 1975), pp. 20–24. Schochet's study is the fullest treatment of the subject, and I am indebted to his book in this and the following paragraph.

15. Flavel is quoted in Schochet, *Patriarchalism in Political Thought,* p. 81.

lies was either forgotten or ignored, and Englishmen writing on politics continued to employ the familial metaphor.[16]

It has been shown that this analogical habit of thought was in fact a staple of polemical literature in the period surrounding the revolutionary conflict. Jonathan Mayhew described British kings as "the political FATHERS of their children, and the people their CHILDREN"; John Dickinson urged his countrymen to "behave like dutiful children, who have received unmerited blows from a beloved parent"; Thomas Paine attacked King George as a "wretch . . . with the pretended title FATHER OF HIS PEOPLE"; and John Adams compared England to "a cruel Beldam," capable, like Lady Macbeth, of plucking her nipples from America's toothless gums and dashing out the brains of the infant.[17] These examples suggest the important differences between the filial, paternal, and maternal images used by the colonists.[18] England, the country, was always likened to a mother or parent, never to a father; and womanhood, as a figure of speech, was applied to the nation or land rather than political authority as such. It was George the Third, the pretended father of the empire, who represented the political power of the state. When that power was unjustly exercised, the otherwise dutiful colonists, now transformed into insurgent Sons of Liberty, had the right to oppose and reject it. Sonship, in the context of the Revolution, signified a challenge to, or defiance of, political

16. Schochet, *Patriarchalism in Political Thought,* pp. 115–158. See also Edwin G. Burrows and Michael Wallace, "The American Revolution: The Ideology and Psychology of National Liberation," *Perspectives in American History,* 6 (1972), 167–189.

17. Burrows and Wallace, "The American Revolution," pp. 196–197, 214, 194, 292; generally, pp. 190–306. Quotations are from Mayhew's *The Snare Broken* (1766); Dickinson's *Letters from a Farmer in Pennsylvania* (1768); Paine's *Common Sense* (1776); and the writings of John Adams, who thought so much of the comparison that he used it several times.

18. The differences have been explored from a psychoanalytic point of view by Bruce Mazlish, "Leadership in the American Revolution: The Psychological Dimension," in *Leadership in the American Revolution* (Washington, D.C.: Library of Congress, 1974), pp. 113–133. See esp. pp. 122, 124. Also relevant is Winthrop D. Jordan, "Familial Politics: Thomas Paine and the Killing of the King, 1776," *Journal of American History,* 60 (1973), 294–308.

authority. In the Declaration of Independence, the colonists expressed their "filial" disobedience by addressing their grievances directly to the king. The authors of that document compiled a lengthy list of the crimes committed by the British government, each prefaced by the pronoun "he" — "He has refused," "He has dissolved," "He has ignored," "He has plundered."

Hence the American leaders of 1776, eulogized as heroes and saints, were also described metaphorically as revolutionary sons. And it was precisely the fact of their seditious "sonship" that created problems for patriotic eulogists in the period after independence.[19] Some of these problems can be traced to republican theory, others to events occurring at home and abroad in the 1780s and 1790s.

To Americans whose view of antiquity was colored by the pessimism of the Latin historians, the fates of Greece and Rome underscored the frailty of republican governments. The mixed constitution extolled by Polybius and revered by the Commonwealthmen had not prevented the downfall of Rome, while England offered contemporary proof that no people was safe from degeneracy. The cyclical reading of history, a story of the rise and decline of nations, conditioned Americans to believe that their own republic was dangerously vulnerable to decay and corruption. As they recalled the warnings and lamentations of Sallust and Tacitus, as they brooded on the tragic deaths of Cato and Cicero, Americans could not help but fear for the survival of the republican experiment.[20]

These fears seemed amply confirmed by the turmoil of the eighties and nineties, particularly by the erosion of social and political deference. The Revolution, in the opinion of many,

19. The revolutionists themselves believed they were being "loyal" to their political fathers by upholding the rights of freeborn Englishmen. The fact remains, however, that they were in revolt against established authority. For a discussion of this point from a psychoanalytic perspective, see Mazlish, "Leadership in the American Revolution," p. 124.

20. See John R. Howe, Jr., "Republican Thought and the Political Violence of the 1790's," *American Quarterly,* 19 (1967), 147–165; Wood, *Creation of the American Republic,* pp. 393–429; and Marvin Meyers, "Founding and Revolution: A Commentary on Publius-Madison," in Stanley Elkins and Eric McKitrick, eds., *The Hofstadter Aegis* (New York: Knopf, 1974), pp. 3–35.

had emboldened ignorant and unqualified men to aspire to positions of dominance traditionally reserved for their betters.[21] Growing economic unrest, furthermore, culminated in two armed insurrections within the space of a decade: the uprising of agrarian debtors led by Daniel Shays of Massachusetts in 1786, and the so-called Whiskey Rebellion mounted by farmers in western Pennsylvania in 1794. News from abroad only heightened the anxieties of those who interpreted such occurrences in light of the history of the ancient republics. By the turn of the century, even the warmest friends of the French Revolution saw in its excesses the inevitability of the Polybian cycle of constitutions. The Reign of Terror had created the chaotic conditions essential to the ascendance of Napoleon, a new Caesar who climaxed his rise to power by assuming the title of emperor.[22]

This widespread uneasiness over the future of republican government was reflected in the funeral orations delivered after the war. Eulogists responded to the fears they shared with many of their countrymen by recasting the symbolic lives of the Patriots and altering the public image of American leadership. To be sure, continuities remained between the eulogies delivered in 1776 and those pronounced over the course of the next fifty years. The eulogist for Robert Treat Paine, who had signed the Declaration of Independence, was repeating a commonplace when he observed of his subject in 1814 that "he bore successive bereavements as a man and a christian, he died like a hero and a saint."[23] Officers, signers, and other prominent leaders were as likely as ever to be praised for their piety and compared to republican ancients. A 1792 eulogy asserted that Benjamin

21. Wood, *Creation of the American Republic*, pp. 471–518.

22. On the American response to the French Revolution, see Gary B. Nash, "The American Clergy and the French Revolution," *William and Mary Quarterly*, 22 (1965), 392–412; Richard Buel, Jr., *Securing the Revolution: Ideology in American Politics, 1789–1815* (Ithaca: Cornell University Press, 1972), pp. 1–240; and Eric Foner, *Tom Paine and Revolutionary America* (New York: Oxford University Press, 1976), pp. 253–261.

23. John L. Abbot(?), *Sketch of the Character of the Late Hon. Robert Treat Paine, LL.D.: Extracted from a Sermon, Delivered at the First Church in Boston, the Sabbath after His decease* (Boston, 1814), p. 4. Cf. David Ramsay, *An Euloqium upon Benjamin Rush, M.D.* (Philadelphia, 1813), p. 108.

Franklin outshone Lycurgus as a lawgiver and doer of good and, blandly disregarding Franklin's skeptical deism, attributed to him a belief "in divine Revelation." Samuel Adams's eulogist gilded his character with appropriate quotations from Cicero, Plutarch, and the gospel of St. Matthew. And the orator who commemorated General Charles Cotesworth Pinckney in 1825 spoke for all the eulogists, past and present, when he entreated the living to honor the dead by copying the qualities "which form the incorruptible Patriot, the gallant Soldier, the accomplished Statesman, and the liberal, sincere Christian."[24]

Despite the persistence of these familiar rhetorical strategies, shifts of intention and emphasis began to appear by the middle 1780s. In the eulogies dating from around the time of the Shaysites, traditions previously invoked on behalf of rebellion were used in defense of the public tranquillity — to keep the sons in their place, so to speak, and to buttress paternal authority. Orators appealed to classical antiquity and the Bible in order to reprove ambitious upstarts and to bewail the sins of a restless and seemingly ungovernable people. Even as they continued to praise the Patriots for forcefully resisting "a servile submission to the wills of a few," the eulogists inserted admonitions against less disinterested men who had also toppled authority by resorting to force. The speaker honoring General Nathaniel Greene contrasted his subject with the many who "have waded through seas of blood to the gratification of a lawless ambition, and arrived to the height of power over the ruins of their country . . . Such are the Alexanders, the Caesars, the Tamberlanes, and Koulikhans of history." A decade later, eulogizing the Federalist governor of Connecticut, Azel Backus poured scorn on "those general thieves and butchers, called Heroes and Conquerers," who were taking America on the road of the French Revolution. "The Aristides," he fumed, "the Numa Pompiliuses, the Alfreds, and the Manco Capacs, seem

24. William Smith, *Euloqium on Benjamin Franklin* (Philadelphia, 1792), pp. 7, 37; Thomas Thacher, *A Tribute of Respect to the Memory of Samuel Adams* (Dedham, Mass., 1804), pp. 23–24, 9; Alexander Garden, *Eulogy on General Chs. Cotesworth Pinckney, President-General of the Society of the Cincinnati, Delivered . . . on Tuesday, the First of November, 1825, at St. Philip's Church* (Charleston, S.C., 1825), p. 37.

to be forgotten, in the noise made by the Pericles, the Syllas, the Mariuses, the Catilines, and the Caesars of later ages."[25]

A new note of the jeremiad began to sound in the funeral orations of the eighties and nineties, and still could be heard in the following century. The traditional biblical text reintroduced by conservative divines to preface their eulogies often revealed a partiality for the books composed before and after the Babylonian captivity — books full of reproach for the backsliding Israelites. Audiences were reminded that Israel's history between the reigns of David and Solomon and the exile in Babylon was "little more than a narrative of the most distinguished vices." Pessimistic Federalists like Fisher Ames, who clung to the cyclical interpretation of history, gloomily turned their hands to composing classical jeremiads. When Ames eulogized George Washington in 1800, he compared the first President to Epaminondas in "the purity and ardor of his patriotism . . . There, it is to be hoped, the parallel ends: for, Thebes fell with Epaminondas." Four years later, with the Jeffersonians in power, Ames wrote off the republic completely in his eulogy for Alexander Hamilton. "Our Troy has lost her Hector," he lamented, without bothering to qualify the parallel. His audience did not have to be told of Troy's fate after the death of Hector.[26]

Although Ames and Backus were conservative Federalists, the concerns they voiced in their eulogies were exceptional only in degree. And those concerns were dramatically magnified by the realization that the leaders whose lives they commemorated

25. William Hillhouse, *An Oration in Commemoration of General Nathaniel Greene, Delivered before the Connecticut Society of the Cincinnati, at New Haven, September 12, 1786* (Brooklyn, N.Y., 1886), pp. 4–5; Azel Backus, *A Sermon, Delivered at the Funeral of His Excellency Oliver Wolcott, Governor of the State of Connecticut* (Litchfield, Conn., 1797), pp. 11, 17. Wolcott was also a signer of the Declaration of Independence.

26. Backus, *A Sermon*, p. 3; Fisher Ames, *An Oration on the Sublime Virtues of General George Washington, pronounced . . . on Saturday, the 8th of February 1800*, in Franklin B. Hough, ed., *Washingtoniana: Or, Memorials of the Death of George Washington* (Roxbury, Mass., 1865), II, 52; Ames, *A Sketch of the Character of Alexander Hamilton*, in *A Collection of the Facts and Documents, Relative to the Death of Major-General Alexander Hamilton* (1804; rpt. Boston: Houghton, Mifflin, 1904), p. 249. For a good study of the Federalist literary mind, see Linda K. Kerber, *Federalists in Dissent: Imagery and Ideology in Jeffersonian America* (Ithaca: Cornell University Press, 1970).

had been revolutionaries themselves, disloyal sons to their political father George the Third, the symbolic head of the British Empire. Hence the eulogists were involved in the paradoxical situation of upholding public order in the name of men who had subverted it. Contemporary rebels like Daniel Shays could not have been far from their minds when they called the roll of classical demagogues. Yet Shays, too, could claim — as his followers did claim — that he was opposing "a servile submission to the wills of a few" by championing the rights of countless yeoman farmers against a handful of oppressive creditors. What was to prevent disaffected veterans like Shays, or those other "new men" so despised by the ruling elite, from proclaiming themselves sons of liberty in their own right? "Happy the country," exclaimed the eulogist for General Greene, referring to the officers and soldiers of the Continental Army, "that can boast of such sons."[27] But sonship, in that era of American history, was associated with resistance to political authority; and the country was unhappy indeed in having such sons as Daniel Shays and the insurgents of the Whiskey Rebellion.

Azel Backus, for one, was unhappy with the actual youth of the nineties. In his eulogy for Oliver Wolcott, he blamed the waywardness of the rising generation for many of the problems of the American Israel. Wolcott's character had been formed in his youth, and his unblemished life confirmed the adage that the "shape of the sapling" determined the future tree. More representative of present-day youth, it seemed to Backus, was the biblical Ishmael, the outcast son of Abraham, "with his hand against every man, and every man's hand against him." Native-born Ishmaels (perhaps like the Francophile undergraduates at nearby Yale) were taking after their Old Testament namesake by abjuring the faith of their ancestors and "quarrelling not only with the laws of civil society, but the laws of God." Bewailing the sins of the young had been a favorite pastime of the Puritan clergy almost since the settlement of Massachusetts Bay. In the context of the 1790s, however, such lamentations could be read as a kind of political shorthand in which filial disobedience stood for political unrest and disaf-

27. Hillhouse, *An Oration*, p. 4.

fection from the newly established American state. The eulogist for John Hancock, speaking in 1793, certainly invited this inference when he informed his listeners that "some must be in authority and others must obey." The people, he added, in words addressed to a new generation of Americans, "may please themselves with the fancy of being superior to restraint, and retaining their own majesty, yet if there are not rulers among them, and these rulers are not honored and obeyed, there can be neither public peace nor private happiness."[28]

These and similar pronouncements implicitly posed the fateful question confronting the American leadership. Was perpetual revolution to become the "lawless law" of a land in which the state rested for its legitimacy on the right to revolution — on "the Right of the People," as enshrined in the Declaration of Independence, "to alter or abolish ... any Form of Government?"[29] Given the implications of the familial metaphor in American politics, how could the state erected by revolutionary sons command the permanent loyalty of future generations?

Patriotic eulogists devised two related solutions to this troubling dilemma. They created the mystique of the Founding Fathers by holding up the revolutionary leaders to the youth of the country not as insurgent sons but rather as symbols of paternal authority. And while they continued to rely heavily on classical allusions, they turned increasingly to the use of biblical models, particularly to Moses, in order to bind the millennial hopes aroused by the Great Awakening to the new American government. In sum, they transformed the Sons of Liberty into deified Founding Fathers, and they equated the American republic with the kingdom of God on earth in the process of realization.[30]

28. Backus, *A Sermon*, pp. 5, 8; Peter Thacher, *A Sermon Preached to the Society in Brattle Street, Boston, October 20, 1793, and Occasioned by the Death of His Excellency John Hancock Esq.* (Boston, 1793), p. 7.

29. See Meyers, "Founding and Revolution," pp. 24–25. The phrase "lawless law" is used by Meyers.

30. Ernest Lee Tuveson calls this combination of ideas "apocalyptic Whiggism" in *Redeemer Nation: The Idea of America's Millennial Role* (Chicago: The University of Chicago Press, 1968), p. 24. See also Pocock, *The Machiavellian Moment*, pp. 511–512.

The most sustained effort to revise the image of the Patriot leadership, and thus to rewrite, as it were, the collective biography of the early Republic, occurred in the three months following Washington's death on December 14, 1799.[31] In eulogy after eulogy, orators vied with each other in elevating "the first, the greatest of Columbia's sons" to "the distinguished father of his country." The first chief magistrate of the nation was repeatedly hailed as the father of his adoring but often unruly children, a father who composed their quarrels, protected their safety, and accepted with thanks their expressions of filial gratitude. "The father, under God" of our sacred liberties, in the phrase of one eulogist, he was even said by Gouverneur Morris to have had no biological children so that he might claim paternity over the entire American people.[32] Such tributes reaffirmed the political relevance of the Fifth Commandment: their source of inspiration was not an ancient like Cicero, but rather the Hebrew patriarchs of the Old Testament. In the words of one admirer, "Heaven's high decree was that he should be the ruler, the father of that family, which he had rescued from bondage. Having led you in war, he must also conduct you in peace, and roll his vigilant parental eye over you, his beloved children." This passage comes closer in sentiment to the patri-

31. Well over four hundred eulogies have survived from this period. Although Republicans may have been less likely than Federalists to exalt Washington as a symbol of the state, eulogists included members of both parties, and orations were delivered in all sections of the country. Useful studies of the Washington cult have been made by Robert P. Hay, "George Washington: American Moses," *American Quarterly,* 21 (1969), 780–791; Lawrence J. Friedman, *Inventors of the Promised Land* (New York: Knopf, 1975), pp. 44–78; Seymour Martin Lipset, *The First New Nation: The United States in Historical and Comparative Perspective* (1963; rpt. Garden City, N.Y.: Anchor Books, 1967), pp. 18–26; William Alfred Bryan, *George Washington in American Literature, 1775–1865* (New York: Columbia University Press, 1952); and Marcus Cunliffe, *George Washington: Man and Monument* (Boston: Little, Brown, 1958).

32. Peter Van Pelt, *An Oration, in Consequence of the Death of General George Washington* ... (Brooklyn, 1880), pp. 3, 16; John M. Mason, *A Funeral Oration on General Washington* ..., in Hough, ed., *Washingtoniana,* II, 170; Alexander MacWhorter, *A Funeral Sermon, Preached in Newark, December 27, 1799* ... *for the Universally Lamented, General Washington* (Newark, 1800), p. 16; Gouverneur Morris, *An Oration upon the Death of General Washington* ..., in Hough, ed., *Washingtoniana,* II, 140.

archalism of Filmer than to the contractual theory of Locke; it
suggests that by the turn of the century elements of divine right
absolutism had resurfaced in the Washington cult. Washington,
the titular head of the Federalist party, was no more. He had
become the Founding Father who personified the authority of
the American state.[33]

Indeed, the orators of 1800 equated filial piety to Washington's memory with patriotism itself. All civil and political instruction, according to the Reverend Aaron Bancroft, will
henceforth "be comprised in one sentence, GO, IMITATE OUR
WASHINGTON." Since America was now a "fatherless orphan
country," it was imperative to the nation's survival that the
young be taught to cherish and emulate Washington's exemplary qualities. "O! like him," implored a representative eulogist, "be thou, brave, prudent, temperate and just. O! Be thou,
like him, thy country's shield in war, its ornament in peace."
Henry Lee, in the most famous of all the funeral orations,
summed up the fondest hopes of his countrymen when he pic-
tured Washington guiding future generations with words of
advice delivered from heaven. Shun factionalism, Lee imagined
Washington as saying, "reverence religion," and above all, "be
American in thought, word, and deed."[34]

Lee's Washington address contained perhaps the most celebrated tricolon in the history of American oratory: "First in
war — first in peace — and first in the hearts of his countrymen." Subsequent eulogists eager to present the first president
as the equal, if not indeed the superior, of any ancient often
repeated Lee's words. He was, the eulogists concurred, a Fabius
in prudence, a Cato in integrity, an Aristides in patriotism, and
"another Cincinnatus, returning to the plough." It was incum-

33. Van Pelt, *An Oration*, p. 16.
34. Aaron Bancroft, *An Eulogy on the Character of the Late General
George Washington* ... (Worcester, Mass., 1800), p. 12; William Clark
Frazer, *A Funeral Oration ... in Memory of ... George Washington*
(Wilmington, Del., 1800), p. 15; James Madison, *A Discourse on the
Death of General Washington* ... (Richmond, Va., 1800), p. 24
(Madison was Bishop of the Protestant Episcopal Church in Virginia
and President of William and Mary College); Henry Lee, *Eulogy on
Washington, Delivered at the Request of Congress*, in Hough, ed.,
Washingtoniana, I, 73.

bent upon all Americans to publicize the matchless virtues "which have raised our WASHINGTON'S, above every Grecian and Roman name." One speaker confessed himself "strangely mistaken" if Washington's epistolary style did not altogether overshadow that of Pliny or Cicero, and he added that the exploits of Epaminondas "can scarcely form spots in his unclouded SUN." Although Washington prepared for war by studying the tactics of ancient generals like Camillus and Emilius, his mind "soared above imitation," and the orators were certain that "he was himself destined to be a high example to mankind."[35]

Just how high an example became apparent from the construction placed by the eulogists on the precept to "reverence religion" — Washington's parting wisdom, as imagined by Lee (and as actually enunciated in his Farewell Address).[36] Convinced as they were of republicanism's fragility, the eulogists turned to the Puritan past to give a religious sanction and coloring to the American polity, and thus to exempt it from the classical cycle of rise and decay. And finding no divine sanction for patriotism in the annals of the pagan republics, they appropriated the eschatology of the colonial Puritans and proclaimed themselves latter-day Israelites, the people chosen by God to usher in the millennium. Just as the Puritans had likened their own leaders to Old Testament patriarchs, the eulogists of 1800 deified Washington as an American Moses. As a typical speaker explained, using a fittingly familial image, Washington "has been the same to us, as Moses was to the Children of Israel." One zealot even went so far as to hail Moses as "the Washington of Israel." Statements like these, recurring in scores of orations, strengthened the conviction that the American Israel was the eternal republic envisioned but never

35. Lee, *Eulogy,* in Hough, ed., *Washingtoniana,* I, 72: Joseph Story, *Eulogy Delivered at Marblehead, Mass. . . . ,* in Hough, ed., *Washingtoniana,* II, 83; Samuel Stanhope Smith, *Oration upon the Death of George Washington . . . ,* in Hough, ed., *Washingtoniana,* II, 179; Joseph Blyth, *An Oration on the Death of General George Washington . . . ,* in Hough, ed., *Washingtoniana,* II, 123; MacWhorter, *A Funeral Sermon,* pp. 4, 11; Madison, *A Discourse,* p. 7.

36. Washington stated there that "reason and experience forbid us to expect that national morality can prevail in exclusion of religious principle."

achieved by the ancients. For "if God be for us," the eulogists demanded rhetorically, "who can be against us?"[37]

Still other eulogists interpreted Washington's terrestrial appearance as the second coming of Christ. They enjoined youthful auditors to worship at his tomb and acclaimed the departed leader as "the savior of his country, the messiah of America!" The first president was a kind of mortal god whose character exhibited no flaws, and who had died only after completing his mission of bringing the gospel of freedom to a worshipping nation. "The picture of man in him was perfect," asserted the Reverend Bancroft, "and there is no blot to tarnish its brightness." According to David Tappan, he deserved "to be ranked among Earthly Gods," for he came nearer to "the EXPRESS IMAGE of divine glory" than any other mortal. As late as the 1830s, Gustave de Beaumont could report after visiting this country that "Washington, in America, is not a man but a God."[38]

The patriotic orators who promoted Washington to divine status in order to legitimize the newly instituted government whose authority and power he symbolized did not create a national church. What they did create was a national religion whose cardinal tenet was the divinity of the American republic.[39] They differed, in this respect, from Jonathan Edwards and his fellow awakeners, who had tapped the revolutionary potential in millennialism by turning it against the authority of the colonial churches. Edwards himself, disillusioned by the failure

37. Thaddeus Fiske, *A Sermon, Delivered . . . Immediately Following the Melancholy Intelligence of the Death of General George Washington . . .* (Boston, 1800), p. 10; Eli Forbes, quoted in Hay, "George Washington: American Moses," p. 788; Madison, *A Discourse,* p. 17.

38. Mason, *A Funeral Oration,* in Hough, ed., *Washingtoniana,* II, 117–178; Frazer, *A Funeral Oration,* p. 6; Friedman calls Washington "an immortal mortal" in *Inventors of the Promised Land,* p. 59; Bancroft, *An Eulogy,* pp. 15–16; Tappan is quoted in Bryan, *George Washington in American Literature,* p. 62; Beaumont's *Marie, or Slavery in the United States* is quoted in Lipset, *The First New Nation,* p. 22, n.6.

39. For a thorough and perceptive treatment of American "civil religion" in the revolutionary period, see Catherine L. Albanese, *Sons of the Fathers: The Civil Religion of the American Revolution* (Philadelphia: Temple University Press, 1976).

of the revival, eventually abandoned his faith in the special destiny of the American people. In 1747, for example, he spoke of the worldwide community of believers and identified the "one holy nation" as the universal church of Christ. Yet even in the headiest days of the Great Awakening, Edwards staked his hopes on the country rather than the magistracy, the land rather than the existing state. When he uttered his renowned prophecy of the imminent kingdom, he referred to America as "she," the daughter of Europe:

> The other continent hath slain Christ, and has from age to age shed the blood of the saints and martyrs of Jesus, and has often been as it were deluged with the church's blood: God has therefore probably reserved the honor of building the glorious temple to the daughter, that has not shed so much blood, when those times of the peace and prosperity and glory of the church shall commence, that were typified by the reign of Solomon.[40]

Also at the height of the Great Awakening, Gilbert Tennent denounced the established clergy as "an unconverted ministry." The attacks of Tennent and other evangelicals helped to undermine habits of deference and to weaken "filial" subordination on the part of the people. Sixty years later, in contrast, the Washington eulogists, enjoining the young to be faithful to the "God of our fathers," renewed the covenant in the name of paternal authority. The orators of 1800 who enlisted religion to support the republic neutralized the radical impulse in Edwardsean Calvinism.[41]

One has to go back to the original Puritan theocracy to discover a native equivalent for the union of state and religion proclaimed by the Washington eulogists. When John Winthrop delivered his lay sermon aboard the *Arbella,* he compared himself to Moses as the chief magistrate of a new race of Israelites. Cotton Mather, writing in the waning days of the theocracy,

---

40. Edwards, *The Visible Union of God's People,* in Heimert and Miller, eds., *The Great Awakening,* pp. 565, 567; Edwards, *Some Thoughts Concerning the Revival,* in Edwards, *The Great Awakening,* ed., C. C. Goen (New Haven: Yale University Press, 1972), p. 355. See also Heimert, *Religion and the American Mind,* pp. 126–127.
41. Mason, *A Funeral Oration,* in Hough, ed., *Washingtoniana,* II, 177.

repeated the analogy by ascribing to Winthrop "a Mosaic Spirit," and he pronounced the first governor of Massachusetts Bay "the Father of New-England." In verses composed in memory of Sir William Phips, Mather even anticipated the famous tribute of Gouverneur Morris: "Write Him not Childless, whose whole People were / Sons, Orphans now, of His Paternal Care." Like the eulogists of 1800, Puritans such as Winthrop and Mather employed familial imagery in speaking of rulers and subjects, and they sanctified paternal authority by variously hailing the New England governors as a Moses, Nehemiah, or King David *redivivus*. The prodigiously learned Mather also ransacked antiquity for apt parallels to the colonial magistracy and declared Winthrop the superior of either Lycurgus or Numa as a lawgiver. The hagiologies of the *Magnalia,* however, were those of an embattled theocrat, not a republican, and hardly suitable for eighteenth-century revolutionists who had cast off the imperial yoke. On the contrary, as applied to the Patriot leadership, they were more appropriate for the rulers of the Roman Empire than the heroes and martyrs of the Roman Republic.[42]

In fact, there was a profound historical irony involved in the excessive veneration of Washington's memory. Although the eulogists failed to realize it, they were effectively duplicating the cult of the Caesars, a cult that had only arisen after the loss of republican freedom. The "divine Julius," upon destroying the Roman Republic, sought to found an absolute monarchy and to legitimize his kingship by having the Senate decree him a god. Under the Empire established by Augustus, Caesar's nephew and appointed heir, it became standard practice to worship the divinized sovereign and formally to acknowledge his godhead after his death. Claiming to be the anointed leader of an elect people, Augustus promulgated the doctrine that Rome had been summoned by providence to civilize the world and inaugurate an earthly millennium. Like their American counterparts, the imperial Romans raised patriotism to a national religion and proclaimed the eternality of their city on a

---

42. Cotton Mather, *Magnalia Christi Americana* (Hartford, 1853), I, 118–119, 230.

hill.[43] They did so, moreover, while going through the motions of restoring the Republic and presenting themselves as defenders of Roman tradition. The emperors even assumed the title originally bestowed upon Cicero for having risked his life to preserve republican liberty. In Charles Rollin's *Roman History,* the most popular shortcut to the classics of the revolutionary era, Americans could read that "Father of his Country" was "a title afterwards affected by the Emperors, but which Rome, whilst free, gave to no body except Cicero."[44] These were words of ironic relevance for the orators who eulogized Patriot leaders between the death of General Poor in 1780 and that of George Washington two decades later. Although the phrase "father of his country" was itself unchanged, the context had utterly altered its meaning, and the men who spoke it, in imperial Rome as well as America, had betrayed their ideals by making the state an object of worship.

By the turn of the century, then, American eulogists had combined the vocabularies of Christianity and classical paganism with the paternal metaphor to create an iconography of leadership appropriate for a republic on the verge of becoming a continental empire. They employed the identical rhetoric in eulogizing John Adams and Thomas Jefferson when the second and third presidents died — miraculously, it seemed to their countrymen — on July 4, 1826. Following the practice of their predecessors of 1800, the funeral orators who commemorated the two Founders likened them to illustrious ancients and Com-

43. Throughout this paragraph I am indebted to Lily Ross Taylor, *The Divinity of the Roman Emperor* (Middletown, Conn.: American Philological Association, 1931); Charles Norris Cochrane, *Christianity and Classical Culture: A Study of Thought and Action from Augustus to Augustine* (1940: rpt. New York: Oxford University Press, 1972), pp. 1–176; and Moses Hadas, *Hellenistic Culture: Fusion and Diffusion* (1959; rpt. New York: Norton, 1972), pp. 249–263. Cochrane remarks that "the organized society of the empire is the Graeco-Roman counterpart to the New England Kingdom of the Saints; subject, it may be added, to limitations and threatened by dangers which confront all societies in which consecrated egotism (*amor sui*) disguises itself as the love of God" (p. 65).

44. Charles Rollin, *The Roman History from the Foundation of Rome to the Battle of Actium* (London, 1754), XI, 396. This volume was actually written by Mr. Crevier and is described as "the Continuation of Mr. Rollin's Work."

monwealthmen and acclaimed them as the Mosaic deliverers
of a millennial people. As William Wirt put it, after enrolling
"our Great Fathers" in the ranks of Aristides, Cato, Sidney,
and Locke, "they moved all heaven and all earth besides, and
opened a passage . . . through the great deep." The extraordinary coincidence of their joint departure on the fiftieth anni-
versary of freedom's inception was unanimously construed as a
sign that the republic was under the guidance of "an All-seeing
Providence." The God of Israel was the God of America, Wirt
asserted, and all the orators assigned the responsibility of keeping the covenant to the present generation. America's youth
were exhorted to imitate Adams and Jefferson "as models of
human perfection," and to demonstrate their filial allegiance by
worshipping at the "graves of our political parents." Persuaded
of heaven's approbation as their countrymen pushed westward
toward the Pacific, patriotic eulogists paradoxically affirmed
their republicanism by making father deities out of former
revolutionaries and perpetuating the Augustan cult of the state.[45]

James Madison, one of the last surviving Founding Fathers,
died on June 28, 1836, at the age of eighty-six. On September 9
of that same year Ralph Waldo Emerson published his famous
essay *Nature,* usually regarded as the first major statement of
the American Renaissance. The almost simultaneous occurrence
of the two events points toward a reinterpretation not only of
Emerson's work but of American romanticism in general. For
the celebrated opening sentences of *Nature* could only have been
written in an age saturated with familial rhetoric, an age in
which the most sacred duty imposed on the young was to keep
the faith of the fathers.[46] "Our age is retrospective," Emerson

45. See, in general, *A Selection of Eulogies, Pronounced in the Several
States, in Honor of Those Illustrious Patriots and Statesmen, John
Adams and Thomas Jefferson* (Hartford, 1826). References are to the
eulogies by William Wirt, pp. 394, 385, 401–402; Samuel Smith, p. 88;
William F. Thornton, p. 346; and William Wilkins, p. 350. The most
thorough treatment of this subject is Robert P. Hay, "The Glorious
Departure of the American Patriarchs: Contemporary Reactions to the
Deaths of Jefferson and Adams," *The Journal of Southern History,* 35
(1969), 543–555.

46. For extensive evidence of the persistence of the familial metaphor
in American political discourse, see Rush Welter, *The Mind of America,
1820–1860* (New York: Columbia University Press, 1975), pp. 3–74.

noted. "It builds the sepulchres of the fathers. It writes biographies, histories, and criticism. The foregoing generations beheld God and nature face to face; we, through their eyes. Why should not we also enjoy an original relation to the universe? . . . Let us demand our own works and laws and worship." While Emerson's essay, like the comparable manifestos of the revivalists a century earlier, was religious in tenor, it was also an expression of filial revolt, and filial revolt in America has historically signified political dissidence. The Great Awakening transformed the political landscape of colonial America; and the publication of *Nature,* whatever its author's intentions, had definite political (not to mention artistic) consequences. For the hallmark of the writers who were influenced by Emerson — most notably Thoreau, Hawthorne, and Melville — was their dissent from, and criticism of, the social and political realities of contemporary America.

The attacks on the fathers found in the writings of all these artists, and so often interpreted in recent studies as an index of psychological disorder,[47] can be explained as a conscious protest against existing political authority. Thoreau, Hawthorne, and Melville quarreled with the fathers because the fathers were synonymous with the state, and the state regularly justified its measures in the language that rightfully belonged to its critics — the two systems of allusion that originally inspired the Revolution. In order to articulate their filial dissent, therefore, the American romantics had to recover the revolutionary implications of the dual inheritance appropriated by patriotic orators. They had to perform the radical act of turning Christianity and classical paganism against paternal authority, and to liberate the rhetoric of the Revolution from its current function of reinforcing political loyalty. It was this act of opposition, as carried out in their imaginative literature, that makes the nineteenth-century romantic authors the true successors to the insurgent sons of 1776.

47. For example, Frederick C. Crews, *The Sins of the Fathers: Hawthorne's Psychological Themes* (New York: Oxford University Press, 1966); Quentin Anderson, *The Imperial Self: An Essay in American Literary and Cultural History* (New York: Knopf, 1971); and Edwin Haviland Miller, *Melville: A Biography* (New York: George Braziller, 1975).

One thinks, for instance, of that opening paragraph of *Nature,* with its explicitly millennial language — its reference to beholding God face to face and its hope of regaining paradise through an original, that is to say, an Adamic, relation to the universe. Or "Civil Disobedience" (1849), where Thoreau declaims in the accents of an eighteenth-century Commonwealthman against standing armies and the imperialism of Manifest Destiny, and demands that his compatriots complete the Revolution by abolishing slavery and resisting a tyrannical government, namely their own. Or *The Scarlet Letter* (1850), where the rulers of the Puritan theocracy, with the exception of Arthur Dimmesdale, are all described as elderly men, incapable "of sitting in judgment on an erring woman's heart." In his preface to the romance, Hawthorne points out that the inhabitants of the Salem Custom-House, which displays the heraldry of the federal eagle and symbolizes "Uncle Sam's government," are just as aged as their seventeenth-century counterparts. He thus suggests that in both epochs political authority is paternal if not patriarchal, and that the men who administer the state in America wield the power of figurative fathers over the people.

One thinks, most of all, of Melville, who almost paraphrases Emerson when he writes in *Redburn* (1849) that "the thing that had guided the father, could not guide the son," and whose eponymous hero discovers that the world of the fathers is built on a system of social injustice and oppression. In this early novel, Melville calls for an extension as well as a renewal of the revolutionary heritage, and he postulates a new fraternal order based on the principle that "there is no true sympathy but between equals." Repeatedly alluding to classical ancients and radical Whigs, and employing the language of native millennialism, he makes his case in the very rhetoric used by patriots to sanctify existing institutions. He speaks, for example, of the "unmatchable Tacitus," fondly recalls a childhood history of Rome (presumably Livy's), and praises Cincinnatus, Seneca, Addison, and Socrates, the last of these for having "died the death of a Christian." He mentions, too, the biblical promise of a restoration to Eden, and even accepts the special destiny of the American people; but he rebukes the notion, so dear to his countrymen, that the republic is already the latter-day kingdom. He refers, like Edwards before him, to the New World rather than the current authorities when he utters his own millennial prophecy:

> The other world beyond this, which was longed for by the devout before Columbus' time, was found in the New; and the deep-sea-lead, that first struck these soundings, brought up the soil of Earth's Paradise. Not a Paradise then, or now; but to be made so, at God's good pleasure, and in the fullness and mellowness of time. The seed is sown, and the harvest must come; and our children's children, on the world's jubilee morning, shall all go with their sickles to the reaping.

Melville's *Israel Potter* (1854) establishes beyond question the link between paternal authority and the sovereignty of the state in the work of the American romantics. While recounting the history of Israel's early adventures, Melville emphasizes "the tyranny of his father" in opposing the hero's desire to marry. He spells out the analogy between filial and political rebellion by observing that "ere on just principles, throwing off the yoke of his king, Israel, on equally excusable grounds, emancipated himself from his sire." The legendary fathers of the American republic, Benjamin Franklin and John Paul Jones, are shown to be hypocrites who exploit and abandon Israel Potter; while Ethan Allen, a Roman and a Christian who represents the authentic revolutionary spirit, is seen literally bound in chains. When Israel returns to the "Canaan beyond the sea" after his fifty years of exile, he is almost run over by a "patriotic triumphal car" in a procession honoring the soldiers who fought at Bunker Hill. Melville's dedication "To His Highness the Bunker Hill Monument" clearly indicates that Americans, having made an idolatry of patriotism, have forsaken their republican principles. In light of the iconography of Patriot leadership, it becomes a detail of more than passing interest that Israel Potter comes home on July 4, 1826 — the date of the deaths of Adams and Jefferson.

ANDREW DELBANCO

Thomas Shepard's America:
The Biography of an Idea

Self-examination was a Puritan imperative. The sermons insisted
on it. The diaries recorded it at growing length, if sometimes
with diminishing candor. The poets sang both the sanctity and
squalor of the individual soul — in such veiled confessions as
Milton's, or in Taylor's secret lyrics. In documents where the
self was not consciously put forward, scholars have reconstructed it through the ideas it generated or in its civic manifestations. The several minds that Perry Miller subsumed in
his vision of the "New England Mind" are gradually yielding
their individuality. Some still resist. In a society of perpetual
self-scrutiny, the published writers were wary of subjectivism,
an impulse both demanded and damned in the Puritan balance
between cultivating the self and abhorring it.

Among his contemporaries, Thomas Shepard spoke more
than most on the subject of the self. Yet of the first great triad
of New England ministers, he remains least known.[1] His relative
volubility both tantalizes and frustrates a prospective biogra-

1. Despite Michael McGiffert's valuable edition of the personal
writings, *God's Plot* (Amherst: University of Massachusetts Press: 1972),
the larger outline of Shepard's intellectual development has not been
traced.

pher, since his inner life is not to be found solely or even reliably where he says he has revealed it. It cannot be contained within his few explicitly confessional pages; to force it into those boundaries now would be to distort it, to accept uncritically a man's account of himself. Shepard lived a true life of the mind, a mind engaged, not disembodied. For him, ideas generated events, and events altered ideas. Haunted by the moral crisis of migration, he struggled in the face of divine judgment to distinguish between departure and desertion; he refused a second move deeper into the wilderness, and his acts had consequences — large ones — for the early American mind of which he was a chief architect. His memoir and journal do more than flesh out one man; they show, if not always consciously, the identity of idea and feeling for the Puritan sensibility. Still, to reconstruct Shepard's mental life is finally a matter of reading the sermons as if they were literary works; for to reach the deepest assumptions of a culture it is necessary to hear how men speak as well as what they say.[2]

In 1608 the town of Towcester, England, where Shepard was born three years earlier, experienced an epidemic. The son of a grocer, "youngest and best beloved" of his mother, he was removed for safety to his grandparents' home at Fossecut, a "most blind town" where, in time, he was put to "keep geese and other such country work."[3] Later he moved to the home of an uncle, where he was trained to "sing and sport as children do . . . and dance at their Whitsun Ales."[4] Even Sunday revels were commonplace, since the king encouraged frolic as a wedge to break the discipline imposed by a ministry hostile to the crown.

Thirty-three years later, in Newtown (now Cambridge), New England, Shepard commenced one of the first great intellectual efforts in American history, the *Theses Sabbaticae,* an attempt to shore up the sabbath, to keep it shared and solemn, to make

2. Inaccuracies in early editions of the English sermons troubled Shepard; he supervised subsequent printings, but the American sermons were posthumously transcribed from his notes. Accordingly, I have tried not to build arguments on a punctuation mark here or a phrase there.
3. Shepard, *Autobiography,* in *God's Plot,* ed. McGiffert, p. 38.
4. Ibid., p. 38.

of it a tool for social cohesion. That book was the culmination of his decision to migrate to a New World. But long before, his childhood flight from the plague at Towcester had revealed the pattern that would inform the life of his mind. When he returned home, aged four, his mother was lately dead, or she was dying.

The Puritan sense of destiny rested on God's word no matter how quietly he spoke it. Audible not only through scripture or from the pulpit, that word sounded through God's visitations in this world. Shepard always felt its power and he fought sometimes with others, sometimes with himself, to fix its meaning: with himself when he lost his child during the ocean passage; again when he lost his wife to a consumption contracted aboard the ship to which he led her.

Contending with his manifold disloyalty, Shepard presages the New England experience. The forced separation from his mother is least consciously apprehended; the "desertion" of the mother country quite openly confronted; but most important is his disloyalty to the cardinal Calvinist assumption about the nature of man. Shepard's battle with the idea of depravity is his ultimate struggle, and the same conflict consumes most significant American minds after his. He dared, like America herself, to test humanity in freedom. And like so many after him, he shrank from what he saw. To show how he translated that revulsion into promise is the burden of this study.

Speaking of himself in the conventional terms that many Puritans used in referring to their dissolute youth, Shepard tells of his rebirth while listening to the masterly John Preston. He had scurried to "gaming and bowling and drinking" and "awakened late on the Sabbath and sick with [his] beastly carriage";[5] desolate, he had hidden in the cornfields outside Cambridge. But now, his ears "bored" through by "the most searching preacher in the world," he was ripped out of sin.[6] Eventually ordained, the young man took a lectureship at the village of Earle's Colne where the townspeople, defying Archbishop Laud

5. Ibid., p. 41.
6. Ibid., pp. 41–42.

who almost suffered apoplexy when he faced their minister, raised hell and money to keep him.[7] So, at twenty-five, in tenuous possession of a pulpit and with Canterbury fuming, he began to preach the sermons that survive as *The Sincere Convert* and *The Sound Believer*.

One feels in these pages a land suffocating, not under particular tyranny — for the diffuse nature of evil is the heart of his dilemma — but under the weight of moral confusion. Flexing their muscles in the 1620s, Englishmen grew respected abroad, potentially convulsive at home; they saw king and nobility court the country while Parliament — increasingly representative of urban, merchant interests — now bristled, now bridled, as the actuality of its power outstripped the pace of institutional change. Closer to Jonson than to Marlowe, Shepard does not celebrate the exhilaration of a newly potent nation; the rash of opportunity for his parishioners grants only license: "[There is] no greater sign of God's wrath than for the Lord to give thee thy swing, as a father never looks after a desperate son, but lets him run where he pleases."[8]

The admonition rests on anguish at social dissension; the individual Englishman is a beast gone mad, threatening to infect his fellows. England through Shepard's eyes is a madhouse of debtors fleeing creditors, a recurrent simile for sinners fleeing Christ:[9] "If the Lord of hosts can catch you, you . . . shall feel with horror of heart that which you fear a little now" (*SC,* 71). While the present spins in moral vertigo, God's will on earth fades into a far future: "Because this attribute suffers a total eclipse almost, now, there must come a day wherein it must shine out before all the world" (*SC,* 39). If Shepard honors any social reality, it is not the business ethic that the Max Weber– R. H. Tawney analysis of Puritan origins would claim, but

7. John Albro, *Life of Shepard,* in *The Works of Thomas Shepard* (Boston, 1853), I, lxxi–lxxvi. Future citations to the *Works* are to this edition, also available in reprint from AMS Press, New York, 1967. Quotations have been uniformly modernized and discrepancies with seventeenth-century editions silently corrected.

8. *The Sincere Convert,* in *Works,* I, 33. Cited hereafter in the text as *SC.*

9. Ibid., pp. 70–71.

rather the poor and "lowly," those ensnared by a new economy. "God bestoweth the best fruits of his love upon mean and weak persons" (*SC,* 49).

These are the key assumptions. The objective is to dismantle the illusions of his hearers and render them sensitive to the insidious substitutes for real security with which English society bombarded them. Terror tactics appear, including a harbinger of Edwards' spider: "Thou hangest but by one rotten twined thread."[10] The torment, however, comes not by falling into the hands of Satan, into flames, but in the tardy recognition of forsaken beauty, out of the hands of God: "Thou art a runagate from the face of God . . . O, but God, the greatest good, is lost" (*SC,* 33). This distinction underlies the central assumption of the English period: that man *can* replenish his lost grace; for in Shepard's naturalistic theory of conversion, grace is retrievable without radical regeneration. Even at his least merciful he cannot blot its last glimmer: "If thou has any good thing in thee, it is but as a drop of rosewater in a bowl of poison, where fallen it is all corrupted" (*SC,* 28). This is the quintessential Shepard; his horror lies in the disappearance of the dividing line between pure and foul. Fighting to hold the distance between his congregation and the mass around it, he would immunize against contagion by "opening" the meaning of an imperially proud society just as he would open a sentence of scripture. To barricade against evil is the task. The rationale for migration is born here.

"Secret whoredom, self pollution, speculative wantonness, men with men, women with women" are among the sins that he imputes to his congregation. Reminded of the sexual sin, dissembling in the pews, staring at the pulpit or more likely the floor, they must have tasted hypocrisy thick in the air. This "soul-ravishing"[11] minister has driven them to the first corollary of self-love: self-deception. Typically, Shepard insinuates rather

10. *Sincere Convert,* p. 35. For Shepard's influence on Edwards, see John E. Smith's introduction to the *Religious Affections* (New Haven: Yale University Press, 1959), pp. 52–57.

11. Edward Johnson, *Wonder-Working Providence* (1653; New York: Barnes and Noble, 1967), p. 94.

than accuses, a rhetorical gambit aimed toward refashioning the social relations of his audience. Such a goal forbids contempt; he must not foreclose the exculpatory state of feeling victimized. For this becomes the safety valve when dealing with a more explosive contagion, money, a commodity whose manipulation for purposes of its own procreation was already linked in the mind of his time with sordid sexual metaphor, famously in a Puritan document of the 1630s: "Beauty," Comus pleads, "is Nature's Coin" and "must be current" (lines 739–740). Practicing a truly Miltonic program of education by temptation, Shepard offers Christ as merchandise, then snatches him away from those who would spend anything less than their souls.

One of the remarkable accomplishments of the Puritan ministry was to foster fatherly relations with congregations that were the objects of such constant harangue. Among the future founders of Massachusetts, Shepard was prodigiously gifted in striking the balance between attack and what our jargon calls "ego-reinforcement." The motives for departure emerge again through this balance. For his perpetual enemy, self-satisfaction, has two social causes. First, there is the barely excusable but reparable variety, that which afflicts the "blockish, ignorant people" (*SC,* 69) whose days are a fight for survival. Largely blameless because of the *circumstance* of their existence, "they have no pilot — poor forsaken creatures" (*SC,* 69). We should raise our eyebrows at finding a Puritan who speaks of mitigating circumstance. It signals a critical shift from the orthodox way of thinking about sin.

But there is a second, unforgiveable strain: the "hollow professors," wily, haughty, up to their necks in the commerce of the land. Both share an ignorance of sin, but the nature of the blockage is crucially different. Money — the lack of it for one, the grasping after it for the other — is the shared agent of blindness, and, as with the litany of sexual sin, one can imagine Shepard's parishioner cowering at the recollection of the last "just" price he set or the interest rate he raised. One must sympathize as well with the parishioners' moral turmoil, that to which their minister is so sensitive. His Cambridge predecessor, William Perkins, had phrased the same dilemma as a question:

"How if I should have sold my corn cheap all this year, and nobody else, what good would this have done?"[12] This is the poignance of a captive ideal, the fear — in the special virulence of its post-Reformation strain — that the human will, after all is said and done, is finally puny. In a society whose collective will is depraved, what can one man do? It is not an antique question. What is so significant about Shepard's version is the urgency in his indictment of the circumstance that entices the sinner deeper into sin. He strikes a telling contrast with English Puritans, notably Richard Sibbes, who did not leave their native Sodom but stayed to face her chaos as a test for the sainthood of the saints: "Shall we leave his [God's] subjects and children for this or that fear?"[13] For Shepard, all turns to a single end: the revelation of the context of sin.

That context is finally England herself. She has declined from social unity (perhaps a myth from her pre-Norman past,[14] but a slipping ideal all the same): for now, "one man is taken up with suits in law, and another almost eaten up with suretyship, and carking cares how to pay his debts" (*SC,* 70). Nothing pains Shepard more than the spectacle of collapse in human relations; his heaven is a place of human contact, his hell a place of loneliness: "Thou shalt stand stripped of all friends, all comfort, all creatures" (*SC,* 37). Filled with suspicion, England is becoming that hell.

The migration is an effort to escape the moral pollution. This assertion may seem to run counter to the Puritan idea of natural depravity; evil is a matter not of place or institution but of the heart. But Puritanism stems also from a reform impulse whose first target was encrustation upon the church. The lineage is dual, and Shepard follows both strands — the first in his uncompromising search for the "bosom serpent" of sin; the second in his defense of a withering social ideal. He feels tender disappointment with the adolescence of mankind: "For beggars'

12. Perkins, *Works* (Cambridge, 1608–1609), III, 466.
13. Sibbes, *Works* (Edinburgh, 1863), IV, 320. I owe this reference, and a larger debt, to Ritchie Kendall.
14. See Christopher Hill, "The Norman Yoke," in *Puritanism and Revolution* (New York: Schocken, 1964), pp. 50–122.

children to live vagrants and poor is not so lamentable as for
a great prince's children to become such" (*SC,* 19–20). He will
not surrender that last remnant, that drop of rosewater. Man as
a vessel from which God has departed is the dominant image
in his evocation of the damned estate. As the possibility of
divine return dwindles in England, an idea of pursuit grows.[15]

Shepard longs, then, for the restoration of the father–son
relation between God and man. Significantly, the sonship of
Christ, perhaps a hazard to that relation, is not much celebrated.
His Christology offers the son, sometimes grotesquely, as trans-
portation to the father's house; the telling metaphor is Christ as
rowboat.[16] Uncomfortably aware of the diminution, Shepard
periodically disclaims the utilitarian view.[17] But his retrospective
dream of the unfallen state leaves little room for Christ, whose
very act of martyrdom denies the premise of that dream — an
unforsaken human creature who needs no surrogate to suffer for
his sin. A fascinating example of the problematic role of Christ
for a truly Protestant intellect, Shepard's Christology varies —
not serially, but in rough correlation — with his changing hope
for man's destiny. Now the son is merely means to the father;
now he is personally vibrant; now he is abstract, the divine will
working through human agency. In old England the vision focuses generally on the old Adam, the once-filled vessel, rather
than upon Christ, the new.[18] Despite this intellectual nostalgia,
Shepard fully rejects the prelapsarian relation of man and God:
the covenant of works. The whole force of his English writing
is to break the equation of sanctification and grace, to attack the
idea that righteous conduct assures salvation. For Shepard is
acutely aware that the definition of sanctified behavior depends

15. See Thomas Hooker, *The Danger of Desertion* (1631) in his
Writings in England and Holland, ed. G. H. Williams et al. (Cambridge:
Harvard Theological Review, 1975), pp. 228–252.

16. *Sincere Convert,* p. 106. The image shows Shepard's tentativeness,
as Christ falls almost accidentally into the identity.

17. Ibid., pp. 213–214.

18. See Jesper Rosenmeier, "New England's Perfection: The Image of
Adam and the Image of Christ in the Antinomian Crisis," *William and
Mary Quarterly,* 27 (1970), 435–459. Occasionally, early in the *Ten
Virgins,* Christ becomes a vivid, human presence, fully conceived in the
marriage imagery of the parable (for example, pp. 69–71).

on social consent, and society is going to the dogs. He has announced what will be a central theme of New England literature at least through Emerson.

On the eve of departure,[19] then, Shepard holds a peculiarly mixed theology: one which dreams of restoration to an Eden without the primacy of law, which cries the fiendishness of sin but feels it as a bridgeable gap, a space, between man and God, which tempers its own perfectionist impulse while yielding in *The Sound Believer* one of the most ecstatic visions of a communion of saints until Edwards' *God's End in Creation:* "Here shall be no imperfection of limbs, scars, or maims, natural or accidental deformities . . . their bodies . . . shall exceed the light and glory thereof, these being more compacted, and thence shining out in greater luster, that the eyes of all beholders shall be infinitely ravished to see such clods of earth as now we are advanced to such incomparable beauty and amiableness of heavenly glory."[20] Grim England could not accommodate this harmony. America, perhaps, could.

The central document of the period of decision is a contribution to the literature of casuistry, *Certain Select Cases Resolved.* The book was written in the winter of 1634–35, after a nearly fatal shipwreck had shaken Shepard's resolve to try the Atlantic.[21] His thinking turns here against the old call for self-scrutiny. Behind the obtuseness of the hollow professors looms a new danger: rampant solipsism, a retreat deep, too deep, into the self, away from the world of lucre. To combat this withdrawal, Shepard now recasts the final ecstasy of *The Sound Believer* into political terms. Bend your heads to earth, he urges, to find the beatific vision; Christ, the guide, is no longer to be found in England, where the "whole world [is] vanishing in . . . smoky thoughts of the glory of God."[22] In short, the only escape

19. Like *The Sincere Convert, The Sound Believer* was published when Shepard was in America, but internal evidence indicates its delivery in England; see esp. *Works,* I, 283.
20. *Works,* I, 269.
21. Albro, *Life of Shepard,* p. ci.
22. *Certain Select Cases Resolved,* in *Works,* I, 315.

from the prison of sin is an escape into fantasy. There must, he suggests in the *Select Cases,* be a better way.

That way is tested in the personal writings. It is agonizingly weighed: "I considered how sad a thing it would be for me to leave my wife and child (if I should die) in that rude place of the north where was nothing but barbarous wickedness generally, and how sweet it would be to leave them among God's people, though poor."[23] It was, we know, not he but his wife who died. It is a nasty irony. Still, one must confess that Shepard's account may be consciously designed to show discrepancy between expectations and experience — a plausible strategy in a narrative which, like Benjamin Franklin's, is a homily to a senior son. The recollection may even be tinged with pride in advertising the selflessness of its author's hopes. In any case, more than a touch of defensiveness sounds here, a need to purify in retrospect the motives for transplantation. One version of his guilt, only one, is his anguish at the loss of a wife toward whom he is always tender.

The charge of desertion marches now from the back to the fore of his mind. High on the Laudian enemies list, he went into hiding and saw his firstborn child sicken and die: "[He] was buried at Yarmouth, where I durst not be present lest the pursuivants apprehend me and I should be discovered, which was a great affliction and very bitter to me and my dear wife."[24] Implicit guilt becomes explicit; the paralyzed exile, unable to bury his own child, emblemizes the barriers between men that he was battering in Earle's Colne. Call it uncompromising service to his God, or call it social subversion, his principle cannot be assimilated into the social machine. Nowhere does the theme of isolation ring clearer than in this unmediated account of a father's failure.

Exposing the deepest roots of orthodoxy, his "own experience so sensibly confuting the freedom of the will,"[25] Shepard's personal writings are recast in the molds of his American polemics. Here, though in a less accessible idiom, the problem of desertion

23. *Autobiography,* p. 56.
24. Ibid., p. 61.
25. Ibid., p. 73.

will be not only confessed but confronted by the fullest powers of his mind.

"I do not cry the temple of the Lord, nor idolize order and churches; but I tell you what your privilege is."[26] Shepard uttered this disclaimer probably in early summer of 1636, now in Massachusetts Bay, near the start of what would mushroom into a four-year effort to open the parable of ten virgins. Nothing in early America reveals a greater sensitivity to the social impact of ideas; he begins with this apology only to end by attacking those to whom he had apologized. The work, in short, records reaction to the first great dissonance in the new commonwealth: the antinomian crisis.

The first year or so of sermons reflect not only a renewal but a heightening of the mystic impulse that closes *The Sound Believer*. His anti-institutional and antilegal position has hardened: "The soul," he declares, "must be divorced from the law."[27] This Shepard walks less gingerly now that he can fortify defenses against evil rather than work the grim work of treating the already tainted. The fright of the *Select Cases* seems to have been transitory, even to the extent that he can overlook his own complicities: "It is the great plot of the Arminians to make Christ a means" (*TV*, 38–39). Is a rowboat, we must ask, not a means? And the new-found rhythms of preaching for an ascendant cause turn to poetry: "The Lord hath no need of thee, or of thy love. He could raise up of stone children of praise . . . [he] can fetch his glory out of thy ruin . . . by all thy sins thou dost but throw stones against the wind, or snowballs against the sun" (*TV*, 46).

The new energy has one objective: to forestall the complacency that had addled the society he left. To recognize the enemy is to divert him, to keep him off the coast: "When England's lights and lamps are going out . . . Does not plenty of means make thy soul slight means? When you went many miles to hear, and had scarce bread at home, O, you thought,

26. *The Parable of the Ten Virgins*, in *Works*, II, 19. Cited hereafter in the text as *TV*.
27. *Ten Virgins*, p. 29. See page 22 for an expression of Shepard's zeal for church purity soon after arrival.

if once you had such liberties; but when they are made yours,
now what fruit? . . . O, love dies! . . . Thou mayst lament those
evils which peace breeds now" (*TV*, 92). Shepard would be sad,
but not surprised, to know that historians have called the great
migration a flight from a depressed wool industry, an adventure
in fur trade, an expression of land hunger. He would not grant
the sway of economic need over the human will. This is not to
say that he thought material motives irrelevant to the reading
of history; in fact, his plea that New Englanders remember and
relive the demands of a harsh past is nothing else than a call
for the will of a new society to oppose the record of the old —
to break the precedent of "progress." It is a recognition that
thought can govern action, that assumptions about the nature
of man can generate their own truth. It is also perhaps the first
American protest against the gross national product as an index
of national morality.

With Mrs. Hutchinson proclaiming the indwelling of the holy
spirit, Shepard weighs alternatives of Christian experience: first,
that which he himself has once called lukewarm, and second,
that which now feels too hot to his wary curiosity. This repri-
mand, for example, is surely addressed to himself as much as to
his hearers: "As a man on a mount is the same man, no taller,
only the mountain makes him so, so think of thyself" (*TV*,
109). Still, almost shyly, as if to a former intimate, Shepard
permits an extraordinary lapse of his own authority in contem-
plating Hutchinson's alternative, the mystic union of Christ and
Christian: "Quest.: How do the soul see him [Christ] as he is?
Ans.: I, in this case, rather desire to learn than teach" (*TV*,
124). At Hutchinson's trial he would reflect "that the vilest
errors . . . [are] brought in by way of questions."[28] But now,
as he once assaulted a notional awareness of sin — "A man
will not be afraid of a lion when it is painted only upon a
wall"[29] — he utters a remark which momentarily echoes the
anti-intellectualism that flirted with Hutchinson's movement:
"Saints do not only see things in letters and syllables and words,

28. David D. Hall, ed., *The Antinomian Controversy, 1636–1638: A
Documentary History* (Middletown, Conn.: Wesleyan University Press:
1968), p. 354.
29. *The Sound Believer*, p. 128.

but see things as they are in themselves."[30] There has always
been an impulse in Shepard to disdain the rustle of pages, to
play the raw, untutored enthusiast: "Jesus Christ," he had declared in England, "is not got with a wet finger" (*SC,* 64). How
he moved from these enticements to become one of "the most
vindictive prosecutors of Mistress Hutchinson" begins his history
as an American.[31] For his enmity was never unmixed with wonder: "Have we not fallen a-dreaming here . . . golden dreams of
grace . . . who would think that ever any should so fall by a
simple woman?"[32]

The fundamental restraints that lead him to thank God for
sparing him from her antinomian seductions — "I account it no
small mercy to myself that the Lord kept me from that contagion"[33] — are two. First, the antinomian position implies a
denial of his whole theory of psychology. It throws into confusion the hierarchy of the faculties and jumbles his orderly picture of the mind: "If faith close with the person of the Lord
Jesus, the same faith must first see that person . . . Did you ever
see any espoused together that did not first see and know each
other? . . . My meaning is there must precede this act of the
understanding, to see Christ, before a man can close with Christ
by his will . . . in order of nature it does precede, and absolutely
necessary it is" (*TV,* 120). Second, in Shepard's thought the
workings of one mind correspond to the development of the
collective mind; the preparatory experience of the Jews in exile,
for example, typifies preparation in the individual. And so the
sequential progress of truth through the mind has its social corollary: the governing reason why Shepard absolutely had to
suppress whatever antinomian sympathies he harbored was a
perception of their social consequences. The sudden effect of
this insight makes a dramatic cleavage in the *Ten Virgins.* The
hesitancy vanishes; the real danger of Hutchinsonianism ex-

30. *Ten Virgins,* p. 144. See Perry Miller, *The New England Mind:
The Seventeenth Century* (Boston: Beacon Press, 1961), pp. 76–88.
31. Miller, *The New England Mind: From Colony to Province* (Boston: Beacon Press, 1961), p. 57.
32. *Ten Virgins,* p. 377. See also the Shepard — Cotton correspondence in Hall, ed., *Antinomian Controversy,* pp. 24–33. In these letters
of 1636 Shepard is more exploratory than defiant.
33. *Autobiography,* p. 65.

plodes upon him: "It is strange to see what a faith some men have that can close with Christ as their end, and comfort themselves there. It is not means (say they,) but Christ; not duties, but Christ, and by this faith can comfort and quiet themselves in the neglect and contempt of Christ in means — as infallible a brand of God's eternal reprobation of such a soul as any I know. So that this is New England's sin" (*TV*, 171). To cope with this discovery — that the exultant lessons of social criticism which he preached in old England have been too well learned in New — Shepard postulates conspiracy: "There is a plot afoot to make you loathe ordinances, that so God may loathe you" (*TV*, 176). And as the ideological battle takes shape, he reasserts the vision of man restored to order: "The eye or mind of a man sits like a coachman, and guides the headstrong affections" (*TV*, 230). This statement conforms to the standard Puritan psychology as Miller describes it.[34] But it is more than rote recital; it comes from a man who sometimes seems the middle link between his teacher, Preston, and Edwards, in developing a more organic, less compartmental model for the mind. For Preston, regeneration had already begun to imply a change in perception, a fusion rather than mechanical cooperation of the faculties. Preston goes beyond the prevailing contemporary notion of grace as self-control: "[The saints] are able to discern things . . . their judgment is another kind of judgment"; they "relish," "taste," where once they were numb.[35] And Shepard sometimes sounds this Preston–Edwards note: "There is a light of glory, whereby the elect see things in another manner" (*TV*, 235). To show the pallor of unregenerate knowledge he speaks of blind men trying to see sunlight or tasteless men trying to savor sweet honey — both images will fill Edwards' *Religious Affections*. In sum, Shepard's heart feels something that his intellect resists. It is too much to say that he actually propels the movement forward toward a vision of the mind as less a combine of gears and more a living whole, but there are sufficient rumblings to warrant an attempt to explain why he suppresses them.

At least the kernel of an explanation may be found in his

34. *The New England Mind: The Seventeenth Century*, pp. 239–279.
35. Preston, *The New Covenant* (London, 1629), p. 258.

new — newly American — contemplation of sin: "A man's master-sin may be changed; those sins that are his master-sins in his youth are not in his old age; those that are at one time, in one place, are not in another" (*TV*, 305). What is expressed here, and throughout the context of this passage, is an acutely heightened sensitivity to the invasive and chameleon nature of sin.[36] Sin has changed its tactics; in the old world it had been icy complacence; now it is the hysteria of evangelical pride — and in its new face Shepard can see his own. He is appalled. Evil moves and eludes now, where once it was plodding. The plant-root metaphor — sin offers boughs for excision while its roots remain concealed — joins the imagery of invasive disease, and with it a corresponding interdependence of the violated sectors of the soul. "He that escapes one sin, another shall slay him" (*TV*, 394). It is from this vision of unmanageable evil that Shepard recoils, and returns to the comforting metaphor of reason as groom and coachman for the unruly but breakable affections. As the soul can be filled with light, so it can be soaked with sin. To preserve a view of the mind that inhibits one is, for Shepard, to accept a limitation of the other. "Sudden work," says the man who once burned in Preston's converting fire, "is superficial" (*TV*, 346).

There is a tragic accent here as America perpetuates what Shepard fled: "wilderness sin," a longing after comfort, reveals itself to be the brother if not the twin of the "sin of prosperity" (*TV*, 166). Both conspire to make "ordinances and truths . . . sapless things unto us" (*TV*, 166). The tragedy lies in the failure of the journey; it is the force of that realization, the shock of finding the new social landscape too familiar, with only the single new twist that money-lust now breeds antinomian anarchy rather than Arminian moralism. Imagine the pilgrim's pain: "O New England! New England! . . . I dare not yet tell thee what Christ Jesus has to say unto thee!" (*TV*, 154).

The metaphors, chiefly of hollowness and rottenness, mix,[37] and to watch him struggle with them is to watch the agony of a man who feels his old conviction of sonship to God but who

36. For the contrasting sense of sin as a thing that can be pinpointed, see *The Sound Believer*, pp. 121–122.
37. *The Parable of the Ten Virgins*, pp. 282–283.

sees a deepening stain that cannot be washed away.[38] It has not been diluted even by an ocean's journey: "It is with the soul as with water, all the cold may be gone, but the native principle of cold remains still. You may remove the burning of lusts, not the blackness of nature, from a carnal heart, and the ground holds, nature is not changed" (*TV,* 307). This is not an inept craftsman mixing metaphor, but a man who cannot decide, or will not pronounce his decision — whether cold is an absence of heat or a positive property. With its seventeenth-century associations — death, the flight of the spirit; ague, the constriction of the humours; alchemy, the dwindling of the fire — cold is always a fading of heat, an essentially privative word. But Thomas Shepard in Massachusetts Bay in the late 1630s begins to feel the cold as a "native principle."

Sometimes the metaphors can be even more dramatically precise: "The profession of the faithful springs not from outward motives or principles of motion . . . life is an inward principle of motion of any thing in its own place; as the sun, and trees, and grass, and cattle. You may take a stone, or a millstone, or wheel, and move it, and yet they have no life, because this is not from an inward principle" (*TV,* 268–269). The "inward principle" of man has moved five thousand miles. Whatever proto-Rousseauian hopes this Puritan may have cherished when he set sail, he has found a familiar creature, mostly savage, in the civilization he left and in the state of nature to which he has come.

In November of 1640, with Hutchinson silenced and the *Ten Virgins* complete, Shepard received a letter from his father-in-law, Thomas Hooker, inviting him to lead his congregation on another journey — this time to Matabeseck, now Middletown, Connecticut, to which Hooker had moved in 1636. With immigrants scarce and money scarcer, Massachusetts was entering full-scale depression. In October corn had been declared legal tender; creditors, growing as nervous as they had ever been in Earle's Colne, sought authority to seize house, land, and cattle in fulfillment of unpaid debts. Shepard's journal records a sore temptation to move again.

38. Ibid., p. 306.

This essay is not the place to join the debate over Hooker's secession, but it should now be clear that his social thought had long prefigured a need to escape urban culture.[39] Hooker's English writing is remarkable for its sense of urban claustrophobia. Furthermore, the swelling imagery of nature in the redemption sermons confirms that his heart was in the country before his person.[40] Unspoiled Hartford was his second sanctuary. Shepard, still deliberating, remained in his first.

The instability of neighborly relations in England,[41] and a widespread sense if not the fact of overcrowding,[42] (with the need to propagate the gospel among the Indians) comprised the chief reiterated reasons for migrating in the key documents of the 1620s and 1630s. The moral ill-health of England had its physical corollaries, as in Winthrop's surmise that those who pined for home often contracted the scurvy,[43] or in John White's encomium on the robustness of the American native.[44] To one of its first ideologues, Hooker, its governor, Winthrop, its Christener and conscience, Cotton, the New World was a healthful ideal, a place for unthrottled energy, a place that would not hinder its social architects.[45]

Why, then, when Thomas Shepard found in this clean place the same affliction that more than any other had made him flee England — pressure for moral compromise to slake the worldly

39. See V. L. Parrington, *Main Currents in American Thought* (New York: Harcourt, Brace and World, 1927), I, 55–62, and Miller's response, "Thomas Hooker and Connecticut Democracy," rpt. in *Errand into the Wilderness* (Cambridge: Harvard University Press, 1956), pp. 16–47. For a recent view centering on Hooker's preparationism, see Norman Pettit, "Lydia's Conversion: An Issue in Hooker's Departure," *Cambridge Historical Society Proceedings,* 40 (March 1965), 59–83.

40. *Redemption: Three Sermons,* ed. Everett Emerson (Gainesville, Fla.: Scholars' Facsimiles and Reprints, 1956), p. 61.

41. See Robert Cushman, *Reasons and Considerations of Removing out of England into America* (1622), in Alexander Young, ed., *Chronicles of the Pilgrim Fathers* (Boston, 1841), pp. 246–247.

42. See John Cotton, *God's Promise to His Plantations* (1630), in *Old South Leaflets,* III, no. 53, p. 8.

43. Winthrop, *Journal* (1631), in Edmund S. Morgan, ed., *The Founding of Massachusetts* (New York: Bobbs-Merrill, 1964), p. 231.

44. White, *The Planter's Plea* (1630), in The Massachusetts Historical Society, *The Founding of Massachusetts* (Boston, 1930), pp. 160–161.

45. See Alan Heimert, "Puritanism, Wilderness, and the Frontier," *New England Quarterly,* 26 (1953), 361–382.

appetite — did he not move again? An answer lies in the self-abuse that floods the pages of his journal around the decision to remain: "When there was a church meeting to be resolved about our going away, I looked on myself as poor and as unable to resolve myself or guide others or myself in any action as a beast, and I saw myself in respect of Christ as brutish as a brute is in respect of a man."[46] This self-hatred may be spiced by his felt absence from what looked like Armageddon — old England on the edge of revolution. As the local issue is rehearsed, he confesses the prevailing motive to be transparently economic and his guilt takes on a retrospective sound; his mind is in England again. "I saw that if God's people could joyfully be content to part with all to the Lord, prizing the gain of a little holiness more than all their losses, that the Lord would then do us good."[47] He recoils now from his fellow men, extending his horror beyond himself: "My heart began to withdraw itself from my brethren and others."[48] This is a political man combatting an ugly popular mood. In the process he staggers in his cumulative perception of human nature. It is a tragic moment in American literature. For this man has enacted the great Renaissance dream of passage to a green world, to a place of limitless mystery and consent for man. It is the dream of Shakespeare's stage from *As You Like It* to *The Tempest,*[49] and like Prospero himself, who also fled the baseness of a European city, Shepard has finally accepted his complicity in the failure of retreat: "This thing of darkness I" — Caliban for Prospero, the restless self for Shepard — "acknowledge mine" (V.i.275–276). In rejecting Hooker's invitation, he has taken another step from an idea of evil external to the human soul. By the end of 1640 he was determined to deal with man as man. If the *Ten Virgins* sealed his skepticism of the ubiquity of the new Adam, he will begin his last effort equally determined not to seek the old Adam in a new Eden. He will face the monster now, and rather than relocate him, or even try to tame him, he will cage him. An Ameri-

46. Shepard, *Journal,* in *God's Plot,* ed. McGiffert, pp. 89–90.
47. Ibid., pp. 126–127.
48. Ibid., p. 113.
49. See Leo Marx, *The Machine in the Garden* (New York: Oxford University Press, 1972), pp. 34–72. Like Shakespeare, the Puritans found that the New World impelled the mind to confront the enemy within.

can tradition is about to begin that will culminate in *Billy Budd*. He who had warned against the reign of law will now embrace it as the last, best hope for man.

"Are these abstracted notions of a Deity (into the vision and contemplation of whose amazing glory — without seeing him as he is in Christ — a Christian, they say, must be plunged, lost, and swallowed up, and up to which he must ascend, even to the unapproachable light) the true and only Sabbath? . . . must the new light of these times be the dreams, and visions, and slavering of doting and deluded old monks?"[50] Though the free-grace preacher, John Saltmarsh, perhaps a proxy for Cotton, is the unnamed adversary, Shepard, as we have seen, had once felt washed by the same light. The final vision of *The Sound Believer* is so very close, sadly close, to what is being mocked here. From there to this scorn is an intellectual distance commensurate with the miles; he has come by the 1640s to fear the sensibility of his own youth.

Today, those former leftists who claim a monopoly of insight into the evils of radicalism may not recognize their precedents: for Shepard showed in 1640 that the best anti-antinomian is an ex-antinomian. His *Theses Sabbaticae* is a mass of reconsiderations; it calls experience, not revelation, its authority. It shows unaided reason its own insufficiency but warns against reliance on the misguided rhetoric of tricksters, of typology and hocus-pocus numerology: "Men's wits in imagining types and allegories are very sinfully luxuriant" (*TS*, 173). It turns instead to the tradition of law, once "engraven upon man's heart" (*TS*, 51), once on tablets of stone, now in the ordinances and the human conscience.[51] The *Ten Virgins* was a dramatic record of spontaneous retreat from the relentless old sins, first worldly greed, then spiritual greed. It invited, if not coerced, its audience to share in that recoil. The *Theses,* on the other hand, comprises an argument spun out of a need for intellectual anchor-

50. Shepard, *The Theses Sabbaticae,* in *Works,* III, 82. Cited hereafter in the text as *TS.*
51. See also *Subjection to Christ* (1641), in which a severe and punitive Christ eclipses the mild comforter: "If Christ's laws cannot bind, Christ's chains must," *Works,* III, 287.

age; it is the product of an older mind that has made and
recognized mistakes. It leaves the Pauline flashes behind and
moves instead to a patiently pedagogical God: man is a student
now where once he was a wide-eyed disciple. In prose, but not
prosaic, the *Theses* falls in the tradition from the *Mutabilitie
Cantos* to the *Four Quartets;* it is a personal search, as well as
a political program, for a way to transcend time.

In denying the sabbath as mere symbol, Shepard recasts it
as an experience permitting the growth of mutual knowledge
between man and God, "a sign of our communion with God,
and God with us" (*TS,* 173). The book can sound almost Johnsonian in its studied moderation: the sabbath must be kept with
neither "gross profaneness nor pharisaical strictness" (*TS,* 256).
As Shepard opposes excessive allegorizing, so he opposes paralyzed literalism. Thus the duration of the sabbath should follow
the sun and New Englanders need not, as it were, synchronize
their Accutrons with their brethren across the sea: "God hath
... appointed the sun for times and seasons"; so "our countrymen in Old England begin their Sabbath above four hours before us in New ... yet both ... observe the same day" (*TS,*
185). The new vision of history dampens the apocalyptic theme;
one feels a relation between Christian and Jewish dispensations
as refinement to crudity; some ceremonial days, some dietary
laws, remain. History becomes less a bursting into bloom than
a pruning.

Indeed, the *Theses Sabbaticae* sometimes more than anticipates an Enlightenment sensibility; it states it: "If the daylight be
the measure of the Sabbath, those that live in some part of the
Russia and East Land must have once a year a very long Sabbath, for there are some times of the year wherein they have
daylight a month together" (*TS,* 218). One can fairly hear his
Harvard audience chuckling. In such moments of cool mockery,
Shepard heralds the rationalism that another Harvard preacher
would assault two hundred years later in a more famous Divinity
School address.

But of course this book is more than the expression of a
maturing temperament, for Shepard is speaking within a white-
hot controversy. Much more than changing fashion, the rise of
a weekly sabbath and decline of periodic saints' days in late

sixteenth- and early seventeenth-century England manifested a shift in social dominance from country to city.[52] For time, on any day, was money to a tradesman, while the seasonal rush to seed and harvest took the erratic as its norm. In countenancing the Maypole, King Charles, like the king of Shepard's childhood, was making futile resistance to the Puritan use of the Sunday sabbath for purposes of community control. The great irony — for Shepard a chilling one — is that while the Puritans had fought in Jacobean England for a uniform and stringent sabbath on behalf of a new economic class as well as in the name of piety, now, in safely Puritan New England, that same class is disowning even the weekly sabbath, and doing so with the old Anglican argument of the illegibility of scripture, and all in the name of liberty — the liberty to make money. For Shepard knows, or says, exactly with whom he is dealing: "The Anabaptists and rigid Separatists [that is, perfectionists in general] . . . prefer tradesmen before those whom God hath gifted."[53] He is indeed very explicit about identifying the merchants as those seeking to "spiritualize the sabbath out of the world" (*TS*, 17). "If any work be done for any worldly gain, profit, or livelihood . . . this is a servile work" (*TS*, 257). The hated past, his childhood past, condemns the present: "The liberty given in the reign of Episcopacy for sports, and pastimes, and May games, upon the Lord's day, was once loathsome to all honest minds" (*TS*, 264). The liberty to make gain in the congregational reign, especially in its obscene repetition of the past, is more loathsome still.[54]

Delivered by a politically powerful American intellectual before that phrase became an oxymoron, the *Theses* signals, quietly but unmistakably, a momentous change in American

52. See Christopher Hill, "The Uses of Sabbatarianism," in *Society and Puritanism* (New York: Schocken, 1967), pp. 145–218.

53. Shepard, *New England's Lamentation for Old England's Errors* (London, 1645), p. 2. For a demographic study that confirms Shepard's analysis of the social allegiances, see Emery Battis, *Saints and Sectaries: Anne Hutchinson and the Antinomian Controversy* (Chapel Hill: University of North Carolina Press, 1962).

54. Not only greed, but also the "abominable filthiness" of "fornication . . . [was] breaking in upon us." See Shepard's 1642 letter to John Winthrop in *The Winthrop Papers*, ed. S. E. Morison et al. (Boston: Massachusetts Historical Society, 1944), IV, 345.

political culture. Conciliation creeps into Shepard's tone; the ring of debtless authority is fading; he feels compelled to satisfy a quizzical Harvard audience, whose chins perhaps are resting on their fists. Some of them may even be making a "vocational choice" between ministry and marketplace. Before them, Shepard feels compelled to defend the sabbath as a law "commanded . . . because it is good . . . not . . . good because it is commanded" (*TS,* 30). This is a crucial wavering at the realization that the ethical content of the law may no longer be assumed but must be explained. It is an epochal concession for the history of the American mind.

But when Shepard looked into time he could not see the ironies of history. He could not see, for example, a Sabbatarian movement spearheaded in the 1820s by descendants of his enemies — a mercantile class far beyond the need for an extra day's leeway for commerce, and afraid of losing Sunday as a time to beat humility into a rumbling multitude.[55] He saw instead the sabbath as an emblem of future permanent communion with God: "Here our rest is but begun, there it is perfected" (*TS,* 27). Addressed to the earthly limbo of America in 1644, the *Theses* protects the mechanism for social commonwealth: the moral law. Its objective remains that celebrated in *The Sound Believer.* It is new, however, in its search for stable means to that vision; it fears its own historicism, confessing that man varies through time in his ostensible need according to his social circumstance, while insisting passionately that a principle of fastness must be maintained amid the changeability of nature and history. Its task is not to impose regularity in human affairs but to release that order which is divinely ordained, to let it unfold as the start of full harmony between man and nature's God. The graceful meditation on time adumbrates that unspeakable union:

> Time is one of the most precious blessings which worthless man in this world enjoys; a jewel of inestimable worth; a golden stream, dissolving, and as it were, continually running down by us, out of one eternity into another, yet seldom taken notice of

55. See Arthur M. Schlesinger, Jr., *The Age of Jackson* (Boston: Little, Brown, 1945), p. 138.

until it is quite passed away ... all inferior creatures, as they
come out of God, so their motion is toward man, for whom
they are nextly made, and they go straight from God forward ...
in a straight line toward man, to the last end and term of which
straight line they are come, in the service of man, they then can
not proceed any farther, and do therefore perish and cease to
be ... but man ... hath ... his motion so toward God as that
he returns immediately unto him again, and is not led in a
straight line, but led ... about in a circular motion, and hence
returning immediately to him ... Look, therefore, as when man
hath run his race ... so it is ordered by divine wisdom as that
he shall ... return unto and into his rest once at least within
the lesser and smaller circle of every week, that so his perfect
blessedness to come might be foretasted every Sabbath day.
[*TS*, 25–26]

By seeking the principle of stability in any sphere other than
this earth, man is either committing a blasphemy on behalf of
an extra day of income in "the counsels of lawyers ... or the
herring trade of fishermen" (*TS,* 256), or he is releasing, like
wild Master Saltmarsh, "a canker worm to fret and eat out the
heart and being ... of all duties and graces of God's spirit"
(*TS,* 81–82).

A high conservatism, Shepard's politics have their roots not
in a fraudulent but in a truly personal disenchantment with un-
fettered man. Echoed by some lapsed communists of our own
century and by many romantics of the last, they are sad politics,
but of fierce integrity. For the "heart and being" remains for
Shepard what it has been all his life: the knotty but potentially
beautiful relations of human beings on earth. His days were filled
with separations; death tested him so sorely because, while he
knew it delivered men to God, he felt that it tore them from
one another. The dissolution of civilized human relations is
what generates the grandeur and urgency of his work. He would
live on to fight for infant baptism, for the transmission of the
precious church covenant to his survivors.[56] But now, near the
end of a life of losses, he simply could not bear to relinquish his

---

56. Shepard, *The Church Membership of Children,* in *Works,* III,
491–540. This was published by his son in 1663, one year after the
adoption of the halfway covenant.

American dream, a dream of linkage between man as he is and
as he may become: "All the law," he promises, "is fulfilled in
love" (*TS,* 104). Later American thinkers, so many of whom
would also find their hope deferred, would long ponder and
longer envy the faith in God's condescension that saved him
from utterly abandoning that promise.

JOEL PORTE

Emerson in 1838: Essaying to Be

"There are some subjects which have a kind of prescriptive right to dull treatment."

For many readers, a discussion of Ralph Waldo Emerson would exemplify the truth of this quotation, so there is something amusing in the fact that Emerson himself was of all our writers perhaps the most aware that listening to a speech or reading an essay can be a deadly occupation. The quotation is actually the opening sentence of a discourse entitled "Politics" that Emerson delivered in 1840, and it suggests that he tried to anticipate the difficulty by beginning with a propitiatory gesture towards the demons of boredom and distraction with the hope of disarming them. Here is the whole first paragraph:

> There are some subjects which have a kind of prescriptive right to dull treatment. A sprightly book on the Civil Law or on Tithes or on Dogmatic Theology or on Liberty and Necessity would be presumptuous. The State and the Church guard their purlieus with a jealous decorum and the etiquette of these august courts as of palaces requires of all comers sleepy manners, half-shut or whole-shut eyes, and the rigorous exclusion of all wit. The ignorant reader in these profane days when all men take all books in hand with such impatient haste to get at their value and conclusion, may sometimes wonder where such massive

volumes found writers and where they found readers among mere mortals who must sometimes laugh and are liable to the infirmity of sleep.

We notice immediately that Emerson is playing a kind of game with us. Though he insists that it would be "presumptuous" to attempt to be sprightly on some subjects, such as the very one he is broaching, he does just that. His tone is facetious, and he moves nimbly between implying that writers are bores, on the one hand, and readers impatient and inattentive, on the other. Perhaps through his droll dialectic Emerson intends to remind us of the classic interchange between Hamlet and Polonius. The speech "is too long," complains the dull courtier. "He's for a jig or a tale of bawdry, or he sleeps," retorts the supercilious poet-prince.

But no, Emerson, implies, author and audience need not exist in an adversary relationship. Dullness is not required on either side of the lectern or page; indeed, it is the very negation of that exchange of hearts and minds which ought to constitute a literary transaction.

On July 15, 1838, Emerson had argued passionately at the Harvard Divinity School that contemporary preaching — at least of the Unitarian variety — was bankrupt precisely because it was devoid of human content. The true preacher, Emerson insisted (and by "preacher" he meant to imply any and every speaker) must "convert life into truth," deal "out to the people his life — life passed through the fire of thought." We may come to the meeting-house or lyceum hall out of habit or for want of anything better to do, Emerson concedes; but we remain, or continue to devote our attention, only if a true word is spoken — a word that brings the life of the speaker into vital connection with our own. In a very real sense, we long to see and hear some aspect of the speaker's life *enacted* before us.

That criterion of authenticity may mean no more for Emerson than sharing freely his anxiety about being dull if that is his liveliest emotion as he mounts the platform. But the logic of Emerson's argument, at its profoundest level, suggests a more comprehensive end: namely, to make his very lecture a reflexive act — an exposition and enactment of what he is becoming

through his speech. Writing in what he himself called "the age
of the first person singular," Emerson attempted what he praised
in Dante: "He dared to write his own autobiography in colossal
cipher, or into universality." Emerson's best work, the record
of a mid-life crisis and adventure, constitutes our first real portrait of the native genius in the act of creating itself, amid the
spiritual, vocational, and financial uncertainties of Jacksonian
America.

It is abundantly clear from his journals that Emerson, in the
difficult years immediately following the publication of his first
book, *Nature,* in 1836, had definite theories about lecturing and
great expectations for his own ability to perform in that role.
One year after the Divinity School Address, in July 1839, he
wrote: "A lecture is a new literature, which leaves aside all
tradition, time, place, circumstance, and addresses an asssembly
as mere human beings, — no more — it has never yet been
done well . . . But only then is the orator successful when he is
himself agitated and is as much a hearer as any of the assembly.
In that office you may and shall (please God!) yet see the elec-
tricity part from the cloud and shine from one part of heaven to
the other." As Emerson's editors point out, "He accepts this
new phenomenon not only as an expressive cultural fact but
also as his own medium." Perhaps it would be more accurate
to say that Emerson was determined to *make* it his own medium
precisely in the way we have noticed and find verified in this
entry: by taking his audience into his confidence, treating them
as his counterparts, anticipating their own anxieties and desires,
and conceiving of the experience as a joint experiment or voyage
of discovery. As Emerson avowed in another journal entry, he
intended to "lay himself out utterly, large, enormous, prodigal,
on the subject of the hour." Thereby he dared "to hope for
ecstacy and eloquence."

We know how Emerson's eloquent baring of his soul on that
Sunday evening in the summer of 1838 "agitated" his audience
— ecstatically in the case of the young and the transcendental,
apoplectically in the case of the orthodox guardians of the faith.
Unlike the "formalist" preacher, whom he pilloried in his talk,
Emerson had certainly bored no one. But, especially in view
of his own theory of the lecture as a form of self-culture, what

had Emerson done to or for himself? If, as is generally believed, Emerson's poem "Uriel" represents a wry treatment of the event, we may at least assume that he was somehow chastened by the stir he had caused, since he writes that

> A sad self-knowledge, withering, fell
> On the beauty of Uriel;
> In heaven once eminent, the god
> Withdrew, that hour, into his cloud.

What sort of cloud did Emerson's heretical overreaching (if, indeed, that is how he himself saw it) force him, or perhaps return him, to? Literally, at least, the statement seems inaccurate, since nine days after his performance at Cambridge Emerson delivered an address at Dartmouth College that he subsequently called "Literary Ethics."

Emerson scholars and critics have neglected this fascinating piece, perhaps because it lies so directly in the shadow of "The American Scholar" and Divinity School Address. Ralph Rusk, for example, in his still standard biography of Emerson, willingly disposes of the address in a few lines: "His oration at Dartmouth College, read some days after he had stirred up the hornet's nest at Cambridge . . . was on the subject of literary ethics, was a poor relation of the Phi Beta Kappa oration of the year before ["The American Scholar"], caused hardly a ripple of excitement, and was promptly forgotten by all but a few."

In many ways, I prefer "Literary Ethics" to "The American Scholar," and lest this seem perverse and uncritical, it should be noted that Emerson's friend and contemporary, the signally perspicacious Oliver Wendell Holmes, in his own biography of Emerson, devotes some fine pages to "Literary Ethics," reminding us significantly of the setting and audience for that address:

If any rumor of the former discourse [Divinity School Address] had reached Dartmouth, the audience must have been prepared for a much more startling performance than that to which they listened. The bold avowal which fluttered the dovecotes of Cambridge would have sounded like the crash of doom to the cautious old tenants of the Hanover aviary. If there were any drops of false or questionable doctrine in the silver shower of eloquence under which they had been sitting, the plumage of orthodoxy glistened with unctuous repellants, and a shake or two on coming out of church left the sturdy old dogmatists as dry as ever.

Holmes's humorous metaphor amounts to this: since the old birds on the Dartmouth faculty, and presumably the fledglings in the college as well, were all staunch Calvinists, they were effectively protected from Emerson's heresies by the imperviousness of their orthodoxy; whereas the Harvard Unitarians, by 1838 under attack from many quarters, had — to paraphrase Emerson — necks of unspeakable tenderness that winced at a hair. Emerson's own cut, from their point of view, was the unkindest of all and most resented because it effectively came from within the fold.

Unlike the Divinity School Address, of course, Emerson's oration at Hanover on the 24th of July was not explicitly theological in character. But I believe it was less startling for another reason — one that relates to a fundamental split, or antinomy, in Emerson's character, about which it may be useful to generalize a bit. As Erik Erikson has written, "Men, especially in periods of change, are swayed by alternating world moods which . . . could not exist without the highly exploitable mood cycles inherent in man's psychological structure. The two most basic alternating moods are those of carnival and atonement: the first gives license and leeway to sensual enjoyment, to relief and release at all cost; the second surrenders to the negative conscience which constricts, depresses." One might easily assimilate such a formulation to Marvin Meyers' paradoxical characterization of the Jacksonian spirit as being that of a "venturous conservative." And Meyers cites Tocqueville to good effect: " 'They love change,' Tocqueville's provocative formula for American democrats goes, 'but they dread revolutions.' " That could stand as a pretty fair description of Emerson's general attitude. But whether one opts for Erikson's psychological explanations or Tocqueville's cultural ones, the fact is that Emerson's own writings provide the most representative and finest expression of this curious alternation or division in American character. The view of Emerson as a shallow optimist who approved of, or indeed helped inspire, the mind-

less boosterism or go-getting spirit so frequently associated with
mid-nineteenth-century America is as false to Emerson as it is
to our national character.

It used to be said in Cambridge that when the new philosophy building — appropriately named Emerson Hall — was being completed in Harvard Yard early in this century, it was
proposed to Harvard's redoubtable president, Charles William
Eliot, that the frieze on the outside of the building be decorated
with these optimistic lines of Protagoras: "Man is the measure
of all things." But Eliot, sharply aware, it seems, both of the
origins of the college and the darker side of the Emersonian
spirit, is reported to have shaken his head and decided instead
in favor of the line from the Psalms that is actually to be found
on the building: "What is man, that thou art mindful of him?"
These alternative notions help to define the ebb and flow of the
Emersonian tide. Man may be potentially divine and omnipo-
tent, but as Emerson conceded in his first book, he "is a god
in ruins." A more personal expression is to be found in the first
series of essays that he published five years later:

> Our moods do not believe in each other. To-day I am full of
> thoughts and can write what I please. I see no reason why I
> should not have the same thought, the same power of expression,
> to-morrow. What I write, whilst I write it, seems the most natu-
> ral thing in the world; but yesterday I saw a dreary vacuity in
> this direction in which I now see so much; and a month hence, I
> doubt not, I shall wonder who he was that wrote so many con-
> tinuous pages. Alas for this infirm faith, this will not strenuous,
> this vast ebb of a vast flow! I am God in nature; I am a weed by
> the wall.

This lamentation over what we might call a manic-depressive
mood swing is the furthest thing from being simply academic
or merely perfunctory. To my ear, its tone is peculiarly intimate — as in the great essay "Experience," where Emerson
avows that he has set his heart on "honesty." The fiercely
sombre mood of that utterance is normally attributed to Emerson's despair over the death of his young son, but the truth is
that tragic event only exacerbated a tendency discernible in

Emerson's writings from the start — one that finds frequent expression in the six years or so between the publication of *Nature* and the death of little Waldo, and which may be said to culminate in, rather than to be initiated by, the essay "Experience." These years, stretching roughly between Emerson's thirty-third and fortieth birthdays and interestingly co-terminous with the very hard times that began at the end of Jackson's administration, were manifestly difficult ones for Emerson. His victories, such as they were, were clearly hard-won, for one finds in Emerson's journals and lectures of the period much evidence of low spirits, self-doubt, a nagging sense that time was swiftly passing and little had been accomplished.

In one lecture delivered at the beginning of 1839, Emerson argued — strangely, it might certainly be felt — that "the Fall of man is the first word of history and the last fact of experience." What, he asks,

> is the account to be given of this persuasion that has taken such deep root in all minds? What but this that it is an universal fact that man is always in his actual life lapsing from the Commandments of the Soul. There is somewhat infirm and retreating in every action; a pause of self-praise, a second thought. He has done well and he says I have done well and lo! this is the beginning of ill. He is encumbered by his own past. His past hour mortgages the present hour. Yesterday is the enemy of Today. His deed hinders him from doing, his thought from thinking; his former virtue is apt to become an impediment to new virtue.

This paralyzing sense that the soul is *not* competent to keep the heights it has gained — this horrible feeling of insecurity that both drains one's pleasure in what has been done and renders one incapable of further effort — was evidently Emerson's familiar companion at this time. In his next lecture of this series "Human Life," Emerson complained that life was dull, melancholy, and grief-ridden. Generalizing, he said: "It does seem too as if history gave no intimation of any society in which despondency came so readily to heart as we see and feel it in ours. As we see and know it, melancholy cleaves to the English mind in both hemispheres as closely as to the strings of an Aeolian harp. Young men, young women at thirty and even earlier have lost all spring and vivacity and if they fail in their first enterprizes there seems to be no remedial force in nature, no Roman recovery, but the rest of life is rock and shallow."

Lest we are tempted to read such a passage too impersonally, to take it as the detached observation of an objective historian placidly surveying the mid-nineteenth-century *Zeitgeist,* we might note that just a few years prior to this lecture Emerson wrote in his journal: "After thirty a man wakes up sad every morning excepting perhaps five or six until the day of his death." It is no wonder, then, that in his lecture Emerson described existence as a "defensive war; a struggle against the encroaching All, which threatens with certainty to engulf us soon, and seems impatient of our little reprieve. How slender is the possession that yet remains to us; how faint the animation! How the spirit seems already to contract its domain, to retire within narrower walls by the loss of memory, leaving what were its planted fields, to erasure and annihilation. Already our own thoughts and words have an alien sound." Here, as in the other passages we have examined, Emerson feels assaulted and weakened in two ways: his anxiety over the probable diminution of his powers in the future is deepened by his inability to believe in what he has already accomplished. In a sense, the bleakness of future prospects is allowed to cast a kind of retrospective pall over the past, as if in some perverse and self-punishing way Emerson's perpetual feeling of unworthiness obliged him to poison the well of past achievement so that he would not be tempted to drink there in dry times to come. One might say, however, that there *is* a harsh nobility in such a habit of mind which, though it conceives of the future as a desert or an empty room, is determined to live there, finding or making its opportunities out of the very barrenness of its premises. Emersonian self-reliance could hardly be put to a more stringent test.

To return to that refulgent summer of 1838, it seems clear that a cloud did settle over the brow of the presumably insolent and self-assured apostate who fluttered the dovecotes of Cambridge in his confident Divinity School Address. Characteristically, Emerson gave unequivocal signs of suffering the kick of his own gun following his stunningly assertive performance. Responding, for example, to a critical letter from his old friend and colleague Henry Ware, Jr., the distinguished Unitarian minister and member of the Harvard Divinity School faculty, Emerson began by insisting that he was not "a stock or a stone . . . and could not but feel pain in saying some things in that place and presence" which, he supposed, "would meet with dissent . . . of dear friends and benefactors." And though he stood firm in his convictions, he confessed himself sufficiently "admonished" by Ware's objections "to revise with greater care the 'address' before it [was] printed." Since the manuscript of Emerson's address as he delivered it has unfortunately never been located, it is impossible to know how much he may have toned it down for publication. Well into the fall of 1838, throughout this period of criticism and controversy, Emerson filled his journal with uneasy reflections on the affair, exposing his low spirits, acknowledging himself to be "sensitive as a leaf to impressions from abroad," and owning that he was "often inclined to take part with those who say I am bad or foolish, for I fear I am both . . . I know too well my own dark spots . . . A few sour faces, a few biting paragraphs, — is but a cheap expiation for all these shortcomings of mine." In another letter to Ware, Emerson described himself as "cruelly" treated and insisted that in the role of "heretic" — that is, a person "who is to make good his thesis against all comers" — he felt himself to be "the most helpless of mortal men." Though some have been tempted to argue that Emerson's tone in the letter is either coy or disingenuous — and, indeed, it wavers oddly between assertiveness and exaggerated humility — I believe he was simply being honest in calling himself helpless in the face of such sharp reactions. The whole affair tapped a deep fund of self-doubt.

Therefore, when Holmes, in his biography, affirms that "Literary Ethics," like "The American Scholar," was "written and delivered in the freshness of [Emerson's] complete manhood . . . at a time when his mind had learned its powers and the work to which it was called," he glides too easily over a significant rough spot in Emerson's development. The Dartmouth address is less startling, at least initially, than the one delivered at Harvard nine days before because Emerson seems to have com-

pleted it in a state of funk, his carnival mood at the Divinity
School having given way to one of atonement. Let us glance at
the opening of the talk:

> The invitation to address you this day, with which you have
> honored me, was a call so welcome that I made haste to obey it.
> A summons to celebrate with scholars a literary festival, is so
> alluring to me as to overcome the doubts I might well entertain
> of my ability to bring you any thought worthy of your attention.
> I have reached the middle age of man; yet I believe I am not less
> glad or sanguine at the meeting of scholars, than when, a boy, I
> first saw the graduates of my own College assembled at their
> anniversary. Neither years nor books have yet availed to extirpate
> a prejudice then rooted in me, that a scholar is the favorite of
> Heaven and earth, the excellency of his country, the happiest of
> men. His duties lead him directly into the holy ground where
> other men's aspirations only point. His successes are occasions of
> the purest joy to all men. Eyes is he to the blind; feet is he to
> the lame. His failures, if he is worthy, are inlets to higher
> advantages.

Even the most cursory comparison of this first page of Emerson's talk with the opening of either "The American Scholar"
or the Divinity School Address reveals two things: that Emerson's mood here is much more personal, even confessional; and
that he is beginning in a state of mind that is at least muted,
if not explicitly despondent.

There is no reason for believing that Emerson was being
merely conventionally self-deprecating in immediately sounding
the note of *non sum dignus;* his phrase about doubts that he
"might well entertain" of his ability seems curiously pointed
and, reinforced as it is by his mention of "failures" shortly after,
suggests that Emerson had a particular occasion in mind. Moreover, his pronouncement about having "reached the middle age
of man" — and indeed, he was just thirty-five — freighted as it
is with all the Dantean associations of the *mezzo del cammin,*
stands out with an odd kind of emphasis, drawing the hearer's
attention to this moment in the speaker's life as to a time of
spiritual crisis — a moment of disconsolateness or uncertainty
that will either cripple or provide an occasion for regeneration.

It is the *speaker* who seems to feel blind and lame, and who is exhorting himself to be his own savior by converting failures into opportunities for new self-creation. Here, I believe, is the exciting theme of Emerson's talk: we are invited to be present as this disheartened scholar demonstrates how hope, in Shelley's phrase, can create "from its own wreck the thing it contemplates."

Pausing briefly to generalize from his own experience, Emerson laments the fact that America has failed to fulfill "what seemed the reasonable expectation of mankind" — namely, to produce a race of literary Titans — and that "the diffidence of mankind in the soul has crept over the American mind." This diffidence, which he, at least fitfully, has shared, Emerson attributes, as we should expect, to a lack of self-trust; so as he proceeds to outline the resources and the subject of a literary career, it is not surprising that it all comes down finally and inexorably to the simple facts of our own despised being. As if to stir himself from his own torpor, Emerson willfully becomes heated in tone as he thinks that he has allowed "a false humility" to defraud him "of supreme possession of this hour." In the passage that follows, it is not difficult to hear in his flashes of anger Emerson's own reaction to the humiliating reception that his display of independent thinking had found in Cambridge:

> If any person have less love of liberty and less jealousy to guard his integrity, shall he therefore dictate to you and me? Say to such doctors, We are thankful to you, as we are to history, to the pyramids, and the authors; but now our day is come; we have been born out of the eternal silence; and now we will live, — live for ourselves, — and not as the pallbearers of a funeral, but as the upholders and creators of our age . . . Now that we are here we will put our own interpretation on things, and our own things for interpretation. Please himself with complaisance who will, — for me, things must take my scale, not I theirs. I will say with the warlike king, "God gave me this crown, and the whole world shall not take it away."

That last sentence draws a startling picture, suggesting that as he reshaped his experience, Emerson cast himself in the role of Napoleon thundering a fearful admonition to past and future detractors. But his crown is simply his own unique being. It is *that* which Emerson will put "for interpretation," building a literary career on the exposition of his own growth.

Though Emerson is fascinated, indeed obsessed, by great men — and Napoleon is notable among those he admired — he asserts characteristically that "the whole value of history, of biography, is to increase my self-trust, by demonstrating what man can be and do." He is hungry to read the story of his own potential greatness in the record of their development; not to marvel at what they achieved but to convince himself that such things may be done by mere flesh and blood. The greatest fortification of his hope Emerson naturally finds in three great writers. And speaking of this triumvirate whose work always lay so close to his heart, Emerson set down a sentence which, in its fine — I might say, stunning — verbal wit, establishes the terms of his whole literary project here and in what is to come:

> If you would know the power of character, see how much you would impoverish the world if you could take clear out of history the lives of Milton, Shakespeare, and Plato, — these three, and cause them not to be. See you not how much less the power of man would be? I console myself in the poverty of my thoughts ... by falling back on these sublime recollections, and seeing what the prolific soul could beget on actual nature; — seeing that Plato was, and Shakespeare, and Milton, — three irrefragable facts. Then I dare, I also will essay to be.

Emerson does not say he consoles himself in his dispirited moments by falling back on the *writings* of these three. What fortifies Emerson is the recollection that the prolific author begets on nature, creates out of his intercourse with the world, not simply what can be described as his works, but rather *himself* — the being he has achieved through that work. His writings, so to speak, are the commentary upon that process. And so Emerson utters his audacious sentence: "I also will essay to be." Anyone who doubts the intentionality of Emerson's vigorous and reverberating pun here should recall that this is the same Emerson who, in his first book two years earlier, described himself as a "transparent eyeball" through which the "currents of the Universal Being circulate" and then called man "the immortal pupil"! *Essaying to be* is the fundamental conceit of this greatest of American essayists. He too dares, endeavors, tries, attempts, essays — all these are the actual terms Emerson employs in the address — to create himself in the very process, in the very act, of setting the words on paper or uttering them aloud. In order to exist he must speak, for the speech validates itself — brings into being that which is envisioned or hoped for. "The man is only half himself," Emerson writes in "The Poet," "the other half is his expression." Not to speak, in this high Emersonian sense of speaking in the service of self-culture, is not to be; despair might be defined as the settled belief that one is unworthy to utter oneself. Note the passage that follows Emerson's sentence about essaying to be: "The humblest, the most hopeless, in view of these radiant facts [that is, Milton, Shakespeare, and Plato], may now theorize and hope. In spite of all the rueful abortions that squeak and gibber in the street, in spite of slumber and guilt, in spite of the army, the bar-room, and the jail, *have been* these glorious manifestations of the mind; and I will thank my great brothers so truly for the admonition of their being, as to endeavor also to be just and brave, to aspire and to speak." The incomplete creatures who squeak and gibber in the street are called "rueful abortions," not, I think, because of any fastidious Emersonian disdain for ordinary people, but because their trivial and degraded speech, issuing from a *rue*-ful spirit that is too ashamed of its condition to aspire and speak more nobly, simply fails to help them create themselves anew. They remain abortions, because their utterances, and therefore their lives, are not *informed* by a braver impulse.

Taking our cue from the mention of Shakespeare in this key passage, and noticing that the phrase "squeak and gibber" is drawn from *Hamlet,* we may pay particular attention to the insistency with which Emerson rings changes on verbs and nouns of *being* ("cause them not to be. See you not, instantly, how much less the powers of man would be? . . . seeing that Plato was, and Shakespeare, and Milton, — three irrefragable facts. Then I dare; I also will essay to be . . . *have been* these glorious manifestations of the mind; and I will thank my great brothers so truly for the admonition of their being, as to endeavor also to be"). Can there be any doubt that Shakespeare's conflicted poet-prince, and his most famous speech, are Emerson's monitory paradigms here?

In *Representative Men,* published some twelve years later, Emerson would say: "It was not until the nineteenth century, whose speculative genius is a sort of living Hamlet, that the tragedy of Hamlet could find such wondering readers. Now, literature, philosophy and thought are Shakspearized. His mind is the horizon beyond which, at present, we do not see." But to return to 1838, we remember that one year earlier, in his "American Scholar" address, Emerson had indeed invoked the noble Dane:

> Our age is bewailed as the age of introversion. Must that needs be evil? We, it seems, are critical. We are embarrassed with second thoughts. We cannot enjoy any thing for hankering to know whereof the pleasure consists. We are lined with eyes. We see with our feet. The time is infected with Hamlet's unhappiness, —
> "Sicklied o'er with the pale cast of thought."
> Is it so bad then? Sight is the last thing to be pitied. Would we be blind? Do we fear lest we should outsee nature and God, and drink truth dry? I look upon the discontent of the literary class as a mere announcement of the fact that they find themselves not in the state of mind of their fathers, and regret the coming state as untried; as a boy dreads the water before he has learned that he can swim.

The prevalance of questions in this passage may be taken as the mark of its dominant mood — uncertainty, in particular, the uncertainty of the son as he considers his worthiness to supplant the father. In this connection, Emerson's allusion to learning to swim is of special interest. The young Waldo was a sickly boy and a doctor prescribed curative baths in the sea, as a result of which, according to Ralph Rusk, Waldo's "fear of deep water, became a phobia." Rusk continues, "William Emerson's [his father's] insistence on carrying out the doctor's advice stirred up long-lived resentment in the boy. Some forty years later Ralph could not forget the severity of a father 'who twice or thrice put me in mortal terror by forcing me into the salt water off some wharf or bathing house, and . . . the fright with which, after some of this salt experience, I heard his voice one day, (as Adam that of the Lord God in the garden,) summoning us to a new bath, and I vainly endeavouring to hide myself." Fear, shame, and anger are thoroughly mixed in this account of Emerson's complex, and perdurable, reaction to his God-like father. The result seems to be, as with the paradigmatic Hamlet, a crippling habit of self-consciousness and self-questioning that threatens to paralyze the will. Emerson himself was manifestly *not* in the "state of mind" of his father — a firm pillar of the Unitarian establishment, minister of the prestigious First Church of Boston — when he launched his attack against that establishment in the Divinity School Address. And let us recall that the stern old war-gods (such as Henry Ware, Sr., Professor of Theology) whom Emerson was assailing and who reacted so badly were precisely of his father's generation. Closer to home, Emerson had to deal with the wrath of his father's sister, the fiercely orthodox Mary Moody Emerson, whom he loved and revered in spite of, indeed in many ways because of, her firm faith.

It is thus easy to see why Emerson's first public trial of his new state, his bold attempt to launch himself into the deep seas of Transcendental theology, should have been fraught with so much anxiety and attended, or followed, by a crushing access of self-doubt. "Literary Ethics" represents both the record of that reaction *and* Emerson's determination to reconstitute his native hue of resolution. To return to our passage, Emerson's response to Hamlet's momentous question is a brave and hopeful yes: "I also will essay to be." The world, as he proclaims in the address, "is his." But he must attempt to "possess it." Unlike the world-weary prince, who disgustedly consigns his sweetheart to a nunnery, Emerson conceives of *his* America, his new-found land, as an exciting invitation to exercise the manhood that he is in the process of rediscovering. As he says, "The perpetual admonition of nature to us, is, 'The world is new, untried. Do not believe the past. I give you the universe a virgin to-day.' "

Nature's exciting admonition, as tempting to Emerson as is Hester Prynne's to Arthur Dimmesdale, leads his thoughts, like Hawthorne's after him, away from the chilling, constricting elders and their opinions and toward the American wilderness and the promise of both new life and new literature. In the fine passage that follows — one that epitomizes as well as anything else in Emerson's writings the thrilling expansions characteristic of his optative mood — Emerson at once exhorts the young in his audience and momentarily realizes his vision for himself:

> But go into the forest, you shall find all new and undescribed. The honking of the wild geese flying by night; the thin note of the companionable titmouse, in the winter day; the fall of swarms of flies, in autumn, from combats high in the air, pattering down on the leaves like rain; the angry hiss of the wood-birds; the pine throwing out its pollen for the benefit of the next century; the turpentine exuding from the tree; — and, indeed, any vegetation; any animation; any and all, are alike unattempted. The man who stands on the seashore, or who rambles in the woods, seems to be the first man that ever stood on the shore, or entered a grove, his sensations and his world are so novel and strange. Whilst I read the poets, I think that nothing new can be said about morning and evening. But when I see the daybreak, I am not reminded of these Homeric, or Shakesperian, or Miltonic, or Chaucerian pictures. No; but I feel perhaps the pain of an alien world; a world not yet subdued by the thought; or, I am cheered by the moist, warm, glittering, budding, melodious hour, that takes down the narrow walls of my soul, and extends its life and pulsation to the very horizon. *That* is morning, to cease for a bright hour to be a prisoner of this sickly body, and to become as large as nature.

What is remarkable about this passage, especially near its conclusion, is the delicate balance Emerson strikes between his hopes and his fears. Responsive to both by turns, Emerson tries to give accurate expression to that alternation of mood that inspired his talk even as he achieves a momentary victory over it. Meanwhile, by means of a kind of literary prestidigitation, Emerson has in fact managed to attempt the presumably unattempted — to describe that world which he claims to be undescribed. He has *essayed* in both senses of the word. Perhaps with a certain pleasant shock, we recognize in the "moist, warm, glittering, budding, melodious hour" that breaks down the defensive walls of his soul and swells his beating heart "to the very horizon," precisely that virgin universe which Emerson was invited to try. As the passage ends, Emerson takes the measure of his world, ecstatically strains time and space to his enlarged soul, and thereby demonstrates that the American scholar, even at mid-life, can still be, as he is described in the last line of the address, the "beloved of earth and heaven."

Contributors

JUSTIN KAPLAN
  Cambridge, Massachusetts
EDWARD MENDELSON
  Department of English
  Yale University
JOHN CLIVE
  Department of History
  Harvard University
JAMES CLIFFORD
  Department of History
  Harvard University
VIRGINIA SPENCER DAVIDSON
  Department of English
  Harvard University
WILLIAM C. DOWLING
  Department of English
  University of New Mexico
KENNETH MARC HARRIS
  Department of Medical Writing
  St. George's University
JEAN STROUSE
  Radcliffe Institute
  Harvard University
MICHAEL T. GILMORE
  Department of English
  Brandeis University
ANDREW DELBANCO
  Department of English
  Harvard University
JOEL PORTE
  Department of English
  Harvard University